The Need for Words

The Need for Words
Voice and the Text

PATSY RODENBURG
with a Foreword
by Antony Sher

Methuen Drama

First published in Great Britain in 1993
by Methuen Drama
an imprint of Reed Consumer Books Ltd
Michelin House, 81 Fulham Road, London SW3 6RB
and Auckland, Melbourne, Singapore and Toronto

A CIP catalogue record for this book
is available from the British Library
ISBN 0 413 67500 9

Typeset by CentraCet, Cambridge
Printed in England by Clays Ltd, St Ives plc

To the memory of Ron Eyre,
who always spoke with infinite ease
and breathtaking passion.
And to my mother and father.
Much love.

Contents

6 Working Further with Texts 153

Foreword

I first worked with Patsy Rodenburg in 1985, when I was in *Richard III* at the Barbican, and often felt tempted to replace Richard's famous last line with the cry of 'I'm hoarse, I'm hoarse!'

Patsy was then the Royal Shakespeare Company's vocal coach – at the London end – and began to investigate the case of my disappearing voice.

I was playing Richard on crutches, a position which pulled me forward, yet was strongly-supported; good for releasing the breath and the voice from their centre, the abdomen. But once crowned, Richard was carried around in his throne, and abandoned the crutches. Patsy tracked down my problem to a section of the Queen Elizabeth scene. I wanted Richard to be at his most Hitlerian here, and had him struggling out of the throne to threaten 'death, desolation, ruin and decay!' In sustaining Richard's crippled position without the crutches, I was throwing back my head, and putting extra strain on my throat as I shouted.

Ever since then Patsy has advised me as coach, voice doctor, and friend.

Most recently, she did my preliminary training for *Tamburlaine*, before I moved up to Stratford and worked with another great voice teacher, Cis Berry, who has been a guru to me and, I believe, to Patsy.

What makes a great teacher? The qualities are similar to what I hope for in a director – enormous positive force, and enormous imagination – and indeed, when working on a classic role, the great voice coach can offer as many insights as the director.

A warm, steady and witty character, Patsy radiates optimism. Nothing is impossible. She refuses to acknowledge your weaknesses, or at any rate converts them into strengths. And her imagination is boundless. In the pages of this book, she constantly makes me see familiar things anew. How we use and misuse words, in swearing, in advertising, and in that daily orgy of British self-disgust, the tabloids. How young people have come to fear words, how we communicate in code, and how speaking can be a form of imprisonment, or freedom. She relates our way of talking to our politics, our prejudices and taboos, to everything in our lives.

Reading this book, I am constantly reminded how much Patsy has inspired me over the years. When preparing to play Arturo Ui, I was intimidated by the size of the Olivier Theatre, and Patsy helped by using a simple phrase, 'Breathe the space'. As human beings, we adapt to all sorts of different spaces: small or vast rooms, crowded streets, mountain tops. So whether you're playing the Cottesloe or the Olivier, the Pit or the Barbican, the job is approached by surveying the space, and then starting to breathe.

Earlier this year, Patsy and I both participated in a cultural visit from the National Theatre's Studio to Lithuania. Here, I was fascinated to witness her explaining the iambic pentameter to actors who had little experience of Shakespeare. 'It's like when there's a party in a house three doors down,' she said. 'All you can hear is the beat, *boom – boom – boom*. If you were at the party, you might be listening to the lyrics and rhythms of the songs, but it'd still be that beat you'd dance to!'

When Patsy and I began work on *Tamburlaine*, I mentioned that I was worried about the beat in Marlowe's mighty lines; the iambic is so irregular, it can become monotonous. Patsy spurned this negative approach. The iambic is like a heartbeat, she said (she'd heard American Indians use it instinctively for storytelling), and you could either leave it alone, pulsing away, or emphasize it, or play against it, or break it completely. All these options eventually proved useful in the giant role of Tamburlaine.

She was equally inspiring about one of the most difficult aspects of the role: Marlowe makes his shepherd talk like an orator. Having worked with tribal and so-called peasant communities, Patsy told me about their powerful vocal traditions. She described a Portuguese farmer speaking as though he was eating: biting and chewing on the words, with saliva flying.

And she encouraged me to consider what kind of brain produces the detailed images swarming through Marlowe's text. She quoted John Clare on madness – 'Imagine if you could see every flower!' – and arranged for us to have dinner with Murray Cox, Consultant Psychotherapist at Broadmoor, who talked to me about the imaginative language of the criminally insane.

At the same time we worked on contacting my *own* voice. A drama school training can sometimes distance you from it. We did exercises to check that I was using my natural pitch, and not one that was falsely low, learned alongside naïve concepts about masculinity, and about being an *Actor Laddy*. And she made me do Tamburlaine speeches in my original South African accent (which worked rather well for the gutsiness of the part).

Last month, Patsy and I had a happy reunion. She came up to Stratford, and finally saw *Tamburlaine*. Afterwards, over dinner at the Dirty Duck, she mentioned that she was studying Tae Kwando, a particularly lethal martial art. I was intrigued. Why was such a loving soul practising how to smash human limbs? She explained that her teaching work takes her from villages in India to the ghettos of New York, and she sometimes finds herself in potentially dangerous situations.

It made me smile. Of course, of course! Patsy is a new

breed of voice coach, light years away from the Elocution teachers of yore; grand, plummy-voiced ladies, who reigned from the depths of their armchairs. Patsy is more like a pioneer, or missionary, braving real and urban jungles to teach what we can all do with those two basic human tools, breath and speech, or, as she puts it beautifully in this book, 'That mouthful of air which forms words.'

Antony Sher
Stratford-upon-Avon
December 1992

Introduction

This book is a sequel to *The Right to Speak*.

It continues the journey I started in that earlier book by linking voice work with more extended work on language and texts. Both books together, I hope, will give the reader a complete sense of how voice, speech and text work can liberate and transform both our use of language and our sense of ourselves.

Essentially I want to explore how to connect your voice to words so that you can speak any kind of text with ease and confidence. Understanding a speaker is not just a question of hearing him or her but of being compelled to *listen* to what he or she is saying. Any good public speaker – an actor, for instance – must captivate us with a need for words. Only then will we become that animated speaker's captive audience.

The voice is a powerful instrument. When it releases the power inherent in individual words and texts we come into our own as communicators. The fact that different cultural problems and barriers block our need for words will, I hope, become instantly clear in the first part of what follows. How to work on a text and what cues it contains for the voice is the second issue this book explores.

My entire working life involves getting actors and others to speak the voice that is within them, to transform an author's script or text by means of a voice that chimes with each individual's own personality. We are all eloquent, or dream of being eloquent. We all need words and on those occasions when we need them most we best express our meaning. Language fully expressed makes us feel joyous, liberated and strong. However, so many of the people I teach confess to a deep seated inadequacy when it comes to using words. They distrust language and severely doubt their capacity to use it distinctively. The more I have taught voice the more I have come to learn about how someone must know and trust words. I have also learned some of the reasons why we fear the very words that can free us, and the bold ways we can make words work on our behalf.

I hope this book will provide some simple stepping stones that will pave anyone's way towards a more considered and animated use of spoken language. As best I can, I have tried to be simple and clear about many complex issues and areas of communication. I am writing for the general reader and not for specialists. I hope that this simplicity will encourage you to seize words and use them with a new-found passion. The right to speak coupled with a need for words is what speaking aloud is all about.

In writing this book I have a number of people to thank for both their friendship and influence. Special thanks to Michael Earley for all his advice, help and support during the writing of this volume. My thanks and deep gratitude to all those who have taught me what it means to need words in life and especially in the theatre: Mike Alfreds, Annabel Arden, Steven Berkoff, Alan Bennett, Murray Cox, Cicely Berry, Aileen Breakie, Annie Castledine, Ghita Cohen, Judi Dench, Declan Donnellan, Sharon Duckworth, Rose English, Richard Eyre, William Gaskill, Terry Hands, Jenny Harris, Nigel Hawthorne, Nicholas Hytner, Winifred Lambie, Brigid Lamour, Genista McIntosh, Ian McKellen, Nancy Meckler, Sam Mendes, Winifred Moody, Adrian Noble, Trevor Nunn, Michael Pennington, Steven Pimlott, Meera Popkin, John Roberts, John Rodenburg, Tony Sher, Deborah Warner,

Nicholas Wright and all the students and actors I have worked with at The Guildhall School of Music and Drama, The Royal National Theatre and The Royal Shakespeare Company. Finally, thanks to Methuen and to Reed Books for taking on *The Need for Words* and *The Right to Speak* with such enthusiasm.

Patsy Rodenburg
London
December 1992

Part One
THE NEED FOR WORDS

Out of us all
That make rhymes,
Will you choose
Sometimes –
As the winds use
A crack in a wall
Or a drain,
Their joy or their pain
To whistle through –
Choose me,
You English words?

Dylan Thomas
Words

1 Connecting with Words

The voice can release a word and a word can release the voice. A voice can stand on its own but when it connects with speech and language, when voice, word and text marry and mutually release one another, then something miraculous happens – the need for words

A cry of joy or an uninhibited sob can jolt us to the core, but words that express either of these passions in complex detail move us even more strongly, because they connect emotion with an intention. Pure sounds do have an integrity all their own. But words can make sense of raw passions. 'Language most shows a man: *Speak that I may see thee*,' wrote Ben Jonson.

When we need a word – really connect with it and release it in a brave, physical sense – the experience is not just an act of intellect but a feeling act felt throughout our entire being. Henry David Thoreau wrote that 'Expression is an act of the whole man; our speech may be vascular. The intellect is powerless to express thought without the aid of the heart and liver and every member.' Words that respond to need flow through us, practially becoming part of our circulatory system, touching every part of us. Sound fuses with sense. Each supports and partners the other in a shared, interconnecting network of expression.

Through this connection of one part to the other the voice comes into its own as a magnificent organ of communication. It expresses who we are and what we want. Most of all it articulates our most vital needs as a human being.

The Speaking Act

Needing words and connecting with them should involve our intellects, our emotions and our very souls. The courage we gain by accepting our natural right to speak and opening our voices must instantly be channelled into speaking words and learning to need words each time we open our mouths. Voice and the text must marry and bond.

The right to speak coupled with the need for words taps into all parts of our mind, body and spirit, is signalled in our breath, bubbles up through our voice until finally, with a sense of relief and release, the words escape us by means of articulation. Words then bob off into space as extensions of us.

What I've just described – the speaking act – is an extra-ordinary natural one that we all take for granted. You or I rarely notice a need as we speak because it is second nature. It is a physical reflex action we normally do without prompting, rarely noticing any of the connections taking place between ourselves and our words.

Yet the process of speaking naturally through needing words is one that I think each of us can sharpen and use to much greater effect than we do. We can all strike the keys of a piano and some of us can even play a tune. But learning to play superbly and movingly takes choice, practice and desire. A great musician makes a connection with his or her score. Likewise the way we use words can and should reflect what and who we are. It should also connect with the clear process of thought. Finally, it should signal variety and a facility with words. All of these connections with words are aspects of voice and speech that each one of us can master.

Distrust of Words

Most of us, I think, no longer trust in words. We have forgotten and, in some instances, have lost forever language's ancient mesmerising power. So much of our speaking energy seems wasted. So much of what we say and how we say it sounds disconnected.

Somewhere along the line we stopped being an oral society. We threw up civilising barriers between ourselves and words. The steady transmission of our family tongue and cultural identifications ceased to be by word of mouth. Storytelling, discussion, debate or just the simple enjoyment of words and word games ceased to be part of our daily lives. Oh, yes, all this is still important to us but perhaps not as vital as it was in the past.

Since George Orwell's *1984* we have grown accustomed to thinking that government and media of every sort have done a great deal to corrupt the need for accurate and honest words in our lives. We've lost the freedom to speak, some would say. We are at the mercy of 'Big Brother'. We are besieged with acres and acres of verbiage but little substance.

By its very nature political language is long on proposals but vague about solutions. It measures itself by the metre and says very little. At one time the criteria for great statesmanship included the overwhelming ability to make acts and judgements through speech. There are too few Gettysburg Addresses written for today's political voices. Mostly we hear our politicians aggressively offering curt denials about misdeeds rather than constructive programmes framed in words. Rather than build, their words tear down. We live in an age of 'sound bites' where even our leading politicians can only speak in disconnected fragments and simplistic homilies. The 'great speech' is no longer in them. It no longer rings in our ears. How many of us can say that we can name one great public orator?

Advertising has made us hostages of quick-fix phrases. The media can only speak to us in bold headlines. I find the influence of the media so all-pervasive and complex that I think it has done much to usurp our need for words and sundered our right to speak. In so many ways it has eroded our ability to withstand language for any stretch of time. We rarely have the patience any longer to follow a complex argument. Yet when we hear a carefully honed and well-articulated speech we are instantly galvanised and transfixed. We all recognise an acute need for words when we hear it. We are all intelligent enough to distinguish between a sincere and an insincere use of language. We all hear the ring of truth when it is spoken.

I believe we love hearing good speaking in the same way that we love listening to good music. As with a well-played sonata a well-read poem can move us in ways we cannot easily explain. Words, like notes, strike a resonant chord. In moments like this we find ourselves willing to trust in words completely.

Resistance to Words

I've always wondered why we seem so dislocated from the very language we speak. Why is it so hard for us to make sense? So hard to get a point across easily? So difficult to find the right word? In an age of hi-tech communication systems and fibre optics networks that can carry our voices round the globe in seconds, our verbal communication between one another and in small groups seems to be about as low-tech as you can get. We seem to use fewer words and make less sense than ever before. We simply don't seem to need words enough. Are we, on the whole, resistant to words?

We no longer seem to collect words, own them or relish them in the way we once did. I rather doubt, for instance, that the average teen to forty-year-old can quote from memory sustained lines of poetry or identify spoken passages from great texts of literature. The treasury of spoken words, once living and thriving as oral English literature, now seems like precious artifacts locked away in dusty tomes. Yet all of it is there waiting to be rediscovered by the speaking voice if the dormant need and eloquence can be re-awakened and connected. As I mean to show later, our very education has been just one of many cultural barriers which, ironically, ought to be spreading words and seeding them for our fruitful use.

In the Beginning Was the Word

'In the beginning was the Word.' That is how the Gospel according to St John begins, and it's a good place for us to start, too. Words, after all, make and shape us. Words are powerful when used with purpose and conviction.

Part of what I want to do in this book is to return the power of the word to the centre of our speaking life; to make it both the beginning and the end of our work on a text. I want to open the voice to an unembarrassed need for words and free words by means of exercises so that you can use your voice to explore all sorts of texts: from a simple story or poem to a major oral presentation to the great classical verse speeches we always think elude and defeat us. I hope what I have to say will have wide application to all sorts of speaking acts.

The spoken word once had a primacy and an immediacy in our lives which it has somehow lost. Oral literature predates written texts. Most oral cultures believe that if you speak, chant or sing powerful, connected words then you bring a potent force into the world. 'The Ancient Druids believed that the spoken word was the breath of life and that writing was a form of death' (A. S. Byatt, *Possession*). If you call for rain or tempest (as Prospero does in *The Tempest*) then the thing itself will come into existence. Words are a kind of sympathetic magic. They are evocative as well as provocative. For this precise reason the ancient Greeks and Romans recognised that speaking was a sacred and dangerous act. Hence the fearsome power of curses. In his *Epistles* Horace writes that 'Once a word has been allowed to escape, it cannot be recalled.' We have all said words we wish we could take back. Rituals and prayers are still remnants of the word's sacred function as a direct influence over events, a direct communication with something beyond us.

The Power of Words

You can still find vestiges of this oral potency – the power of words – throughout Africa, India, Aboriginal Australia and the Far East, in small pockets of Europe and in North America among Native American cultures. Enter a Portuguese church and the congregation speaks and knows the power of a simple prayer. When you listen to a Native American storyteller the vibrant choice of words makes the story live. Words are transformed into animated figures. Oral narrative has a vibrancy which text-bound literature can only approximate. Even if written literature should ever perish, stories will live on by means of the voice.

A Navaho storyteller recently explained to me that 'The sanctity of words is an essential element of the Navaho world view. We believe that the wind comes in at the top of your head. When your hair begins to grow and every time you speak it is the wind that speaks.' This seems to me to be a stunning way to describe the speaking act. Speaking, in other words, is tied into the totality of being in the physical world. It represents the recycling of energy from one source into another just as breath transforms into a word.

As I will say over and over again in this book, I do believe that sound must make sense. This is not a book about just finding meaning in words but about transmitting the sound of words in ways so appropriate that their sense is unmistakable to a listener. You must feel free to express your need for a word before you can allow it to make sense. To do that you have to capture its sound.

I am not a literary critic but a voice coach. My job is not to point you towards the value of one meaning over another but to get you speaking so confidently that you can make whatever sense you intend. Ultimately my job is to connect you to your voice and then to the power of the word as you speak it. In time your need for words ought to become acute. Gradually even the simplest exchange on the street can be filled with a compelling need to speak.

The Importance of Oracy

Oracy is the ability to be fluent with words. It's a word I like because I think of it in connection with not only fluency but literacy. It also touches on the oracular power of words; their prophetic properties. Oracy is not some pedantic nineteenth-century notion about proper oratory but about words used as passionate persuasion. Ideas transmitted by word-of-mouth. It's a good and useful word that invokes all of the pleasures of speaking that are quickly disappearing from our lives.

To put it quite bluntly, we have stopped talking to one another. We have ceased being an oral culture. Families sit round a lighted box called television 'watching' rather than 'discussing' events. Our stories come to us in pictures. If we don't see it we won't believe it. The message in words is often rigidly controlled and clipped. I suppose you could say that we have a greater need for pictures than for words.

All too easily we shift our attention from one programme to another without rhyme or reason. We channel hop to distraction. Students in the classroom learn passively, without much genuine verbal interaction or challenge. Literacy skills – reading and writing – are more highly regarded than talents for oracy – the ability to express oneself fluently and passionately in speech. What might our society be like if it suddenly became captivated by a new oracy? The ideal, of course, would be the marriage of literacy with oracy. How powerful our expressive needs would become!

We mature nowadays with a curious suspicion and dislike of those who have a profuse 'gift of the gab'. Expressions like 'verbose', 'loquacious', 'long-winded' and 'wordy' all have negative connotations. To call someone a 'word-monger' sounds like a criminal accusation. 'Oracy' is a word people even find unsettling. We are even beginning to suspect fluency (that ready command of words which I think we all secretly desire to have) and instantly accept the bewildered mutterings of speakers who ask to lead us. Apart from some actors we have very few role models to look to as public voices. The decline in great speech-making speaks of a deeper deterioration in public life we ought to guard against.

Yet it seems to me we are all eloquent. All of us naturally want the authority that good speaking and a command of a spoken text can bring us. This is not an academic need but simply a human one: a connection through words. We all want to connect a need to speak with a need for words. On the most basic level we all simply want someone to listen to us, to hear what we have to say. We also want to put our thoughts in the best way possible in order to clarify something that either troubles or thrills us.

Often this basic need for words is only satisfied privately with an intimate friend, perhaps with a therapist or even in organised sessions of speaking, as when we go to a public meeting to speak our mind on an issue. We go to sports matches and rock concerts to shout our heads off. This is a form of public therapy, too.

Yet speaking well, speaking openly and speaking fearlessly any time or place should come to us naturally. Children, for instance, love to play with words. For them oracy is a natural, unfettered habit. They readily mimic what they hear and treat language as a vast adventure playground. They even pick up foreign languages and accents more quickly than adults. Children are neither rigid, too selective nor prejudiced when they grasp at words. They seize them with gusto. We adults are always surprised and delighted by a child's frankness. The sensual quality of words, apart from meaning, can keep a child happy for days. I remember my friend Ian and myself as seven-year-olds laughing for a week at the word 'bosom'. It was not a naughty word, just a fun word to say. For a whole week we echoed that word.

We all laugh at the natural wit and oracy of children. They have the undiluted freedom to make marvellous connections with words. Some years ago on British television there was a show that asked children to describe certain phrases and words. A panel of adults tried to decipher the subject of the child's description. The audience rocked with amusement at these wonderfully surreal inventions, slyly mocking the child's imaginative word inventions. As D. J. Enright's poem 'Blue Umbrellas' shows, our child-like capacity to enjoy the uninhibited extravagance of words surrenders when we go to school and have it drilled out of us:

'The thing that makes a blue umbrella with its tail –
How do you call it?' you ask. Poorly and pale
Comes my answer. For all I can call it is peacock.

Now that you go to school, you will learn how we call all sorts
    of things;
How we mar great works by our mean recital.
You will learn, for instance, that Head Monster is not the
    gentleman's accepted title;
The blue-tailed eccentrics will be merely peacocks; the dead
    bird will no longer doze
Off till tomorrow's lark, for the letter has killed him.
The dictionary is opening, the gay umbrellas close.

    Oh our mistaken teachers! –
It was not a proper respect for words that we need,
But a decent regard for things, those older creatures and more
    real.
Later you may even resort to writing verse
To prove the dishonesty of names and their black greed –
To confess your ignorance, to expiate your crime, seeking one
    spell to lift another curse.
Or you may, more commodiously, spy on your children, busy
    discoverers,
Without the dubious benefit of rhyme.

The Deeper Need for Words

Some therapists and linguists take the need for words much further than I do, saying that without contact-points to a language of our own we are in danger of being cast adrift in the world. We all have a deeper need for words. Disconnection from words is unhealthy. Silence can shatter us. Some of us need to talk our way back to health. The way is through words.

Muteness, being bereft of speech, is a void. Talking is therapeutic when the words are needed and active. Without words we cannot make the world concrete for either ourselves or others. We can get lost when we roam too long within the folds of silence. Our feelings have no means of being charted, our ideas stay stunted and unclear, our personalities remain confused and inexplicit. Words make the world coherent. Someone once wrote that 'Syllables govern the world.' Words battle against the unexplainable, giving all things, as Shakespeare says in *A Midsummer Night's Dream*, 'a local habitation and a name'.

Speaking in a connected way can clarify, transform and satisfy us. It can also give us peace of mind. When we have finally spoken out our frustration, confusion and pain we can relax. Keeping words bottled up inside us can only pressure us. They need release. They must escape.

Lost Voices

More and more today we are in danger of losing our voice for the simple reason that we are in danger of losing our connection to oracy. Perhaps we need to conserve the traditions of oracy rather like we would a precious rain forest. Both transform the air we breathe into a capacity for words.

From my own experience I have found that contemporary speaking voices are much lighter and more undeveloped than say ten years ago. Fewer possess a self-assurance that you can hear. More voices lack the confidence to speak. We simply do not declare our intentions with words. Many of us tense up when asked to speak. We certainly tend to use our speaking instruments less and less. Few voices, for instance, can fill a space without being electronically boosted by microphones. This problem is almost immediately apparent when we hear political candidates straining to speak to us. A lost voice cannot serve the needs of a text. It cannot meet its demands. It turns off a listener's need to hear.

Much of the work I do now with Britain's Royal National Theatre and have done in the past with the Royal Shakespeare Company has been about reclaiming vocal might so that it can serve a text appropriately from a whisper to a shout. As an instrument the voice can be moulded and retuned to meet the needs of any speaking situation, any text. In most instances, I have come to believe, we can make new voices out of underpowered ones, turn bland ones into expressive ones, weak ones into strong.

Not Empty Rhetoric

We live, of course, in the modern age and cannot turn back the clock to some ancient time when speaking preceded writing, when speaking was valued over writing. But what we can do is revive, I think, a delight in certain skills of rhetoric – the arts of effective and persuasive speaking – which enabled us, for thousands of years, to show a healthy respect for the spoken word. We can reclaim a passion for words by learning to use them with more craft and skill.

Rhetoric is one of those technical words which people now shun. All too frequently it suggests impressions of false and vain eloquence. Actors who go over the top in terms of flowery speech or counterfeit passion are said to be 'rhetorical'. And, indeed, rhetoric without a commanding need for words behind it is both empty and artificial.

But classical rhetoric, like good acting technique, had

values we can resurrect and explore on a simple and satisfying level. Think of it as a series of tools that help you to feel your way towards a fuller expression of words. In Part Two (pp. 000) I'll go into this further. Rhetoric when linked with an individual's inner truth and need becomes a potent force. Whatever notions of rhetoric may surface in this book will be used to that end. Each of us has within us a natural rhetoric that manifests itself when we need to communicate. Call it our native eloquence.

Native Eloquence

I believe that all of us can speak with the native eloquence of poets and frequently do when the powerful need arises. Once we commit ourselves to simply knowing and needing a word a good part of the speaking task is already accomplished. Speaking, in my mind, is not and never should be about refining accents or forcing our voice or speech into artificial moulds. It is about gaining a passionate commitment to words through a well-primed, free voice. It is letting our own eloquence speak for itself.

Most of us let our eloquence lie dormant because the need to speak is rarely awakened within us. In precious moments of need eloquence flows from us. It is just not a habit we cultivate on a daily basis because most of us are not professional speakers and have little need to use words with authority or to use them publicly. We cannot all be like working actors who must have a ready recourse to words always close at hand. The habit of eloquence, though, is something that even professional actors do not keep up in quite the way they should.

Every one of us can use everyday words with greater care and conviction. Each day words either get us into trouble through lack of careful use or else save the day by means of judicious practice. Most of our days are spent communicating. We are creatures of words and, to some degree, words rule our lives. Too many of us prefer to be either indistinct or imprecise with the very language that could define us and make us individual. We are frightened by the challenge that great words pose.

But why, I often wonder?

We can all, I think, learn to speak texts the way great actors do. Each of us ought to be able to make a connection with Shakespeare's plays, for instance, all on our own and without difficulty. Far too often we feel either distraught or defeated when we come up against a great classical text, a piece of verse or even a humble speech. We are word-shy. We habitually believe that our own use of words is disconnected and lacks authority. I maintain this simply needn't be the case.

So many barriers have arisen between us and the spoken word to deny us both the need for and access to words; needs and access which I believe are essential parts of life. These barriers are blocks which we must confront and get past if we want to grapple successfully with the words in their spoken contexts. Even before we get to any texts themselves and exercise them through our voice, we have to sort out why we find it so hard to speak the very words that should naturally excite and liberate us. Words do have a daunting power that can sometimes shock us.

Words Are Physical

Words can touch and shake us physically when uttered with complete authenticity and with utter conviction. We all know the experience of being shaken deeply by words.

When Hamlet confronts his mother, Queen Gertrude, in the privacy of her room with insidious accusations she says in a moment of desperate anguish: 'O, speak to me no more!/ Those words like daggers enter in mine ear.' Words targeted can have this kind of unleashed fury. We have all felt the sting of verbal abuse and have used words of contempt ourselves. Sometimes words can be even harsher than physical abuse.

A critical aspect of engendering a need for words is realising the powerful effects our words can have on others. Words are manipulative and unsettling. They are also soothing and healing. They play the voice in different registers and colours, reaching out to the listener in different ways. The voice can be passive but also hostile and aggressive. The words of a song can crawl under our skin. The sound of a furious chant can be fearsome. Once we recognise that words do touch us, do get under the skin, do provoke fear, they begin to command from us a new respect.

A Three-Dimensional Process

I often portray the process of speaking as a three-dimensional one because that is how I experience it when I work with someone on his or her voice and the connection with language. We think of words as hieroglyphic markings stuck to a page and not as things of substance, weight, body or contour. As we make words in our mouth we actually sculpt them into shape.

If we can think of speaking words as a physical act rather than an intellectual one, we suddenly begin to approach the process of finding a new voice and an outlet for need within a text. In any speaking task sound must connect and fuse together with sense to communicate meaning. Frequently you find that you must throw all of yourself into the speaking act. When I work on a particularly strenuous text with an actor, it really is like training him or her to run a marathon. The whole body is used in the process, not just the mind and mouth. We hurl ourselves about in search of the right way to voice a word. In fact, we speak as much through and in tandem with our body as we do with our voice. The physical connections are vital to think about.

In doing voice and text work we frequently speak of

'grappling' with a word, or 'wrapping' our tongue and mouth round it, of 'feeling its weight', of 'mouthing' sounds, of 'savouring' words as you would a feast. We also 'project' words 'send them out into space' as though they were flights of arcing arrows 'targeting' a listener. All of these metaphors are attempts to approximate the physical act of speaking words.

I should declare right from the start that this physical aspect is part of my method as a teacher. I am not one for simple elocution lessons. In order to need words I feel you must be able to knead them into shape the way you would mould clay into sculpture. We can use words and their sounds like a series of weights and counterweights: harsh sounds mixed with light sounds; heavy words toned down by delicate ones. The voice and speech muscles must be primed to take on the task of the imagination. Dramatic speaking or public oratory can be furious activities and we must accept the fact that they take an expenditure of energy. But it is an energy that expands into greater circles or waves of communication.

I do think that any speaker who tries to improve the way he or she speaks ought to consider the process as a form of physical exertion that will ultimately bring release. Speaking, after all, is tiring, as any actor or public lecturer will tell you. As we proceed to text work later in this volume this is precisely how we'll be working with words – as a form of physical release that clears the brain of the pressing weight of what must be said. Confessional speaking is also like a purging. We empty ourselves of burden in order to feel better. The sounds we make can and should be cathartic. As you can imagine, I find speaking to be a means to health. Like laughter or sobbing, speaking is one of the best means of releasing that I know.

2 The Breakdown of Words

As our attachment and familiarity with language lessens and grows more remote, we need to identify how our connection with words broke down and where to identify problems.

The 'breakdown of communication' is a modern cliché we know by heart. The surrender of oracy and distrust of words are crucial factors which have engendered the phrase. It is always easy to blame ourselves individually for our reticent need for words and forget there may be other crucial factors at work. What role, for instance, do our institutions play in the breakdown of words? Is it possible that our need for words has been educated out of us?

The Education Issue

Public debates about education in Britain and North America are finally beginning to address the issue of the spoken word and how it is taught.

More and more there is a growing realisation that our education, ironically, has cut us off from the fount of language. Our whole culture has been designed to inhibit us from speaking by laying barriers in the path of our need for words. In a 'post-modernist' age of 'deconstruction', an age in which all language is subject to doubt and is cut off from definitive meaning, in which narrative and stories are playfully dismantled or overthrown in favour of fragments, good oral skills have been downgraded and muted. After all, if what we say can always be open to doubt and subverted, if nothing has a genuine throughline, then why speak at all? I've noticed, from experience, that my students today use language with far less confidence then the students I taught a decade ago. Through no fault of their own they seem functionally disconnected from language. More than ever before words seem to be under suspicion, confidence with words is subject to doubt and even derision. Hesitation is a common feature of the voice.

When I think back to my school-days (which weren't all that long ago!), I have vivid recollections of days filled with speaking. Perhaps some of those activities were old-fashioned and rather rigid, more of the order of oral recitations and drills in group speaking. Nonetheless we were regularly encouraged in school to speak, chant, sing and read aloud. We gave choral presentations to assemblies and poetry readings for invited audiences, and we performed scenes in classes. Arithmetic tables were chanted. At least twice a week we all had to memorise a poem, a verse from the Bible, a speech from Shakespeare. I was left with the vivid recollection that words openly spoken were part of education's function. I know that my interest in both theatre and the voice started there. Many of my contemporaries speak of having undergone the same experience. Speaking then played a part in formal education. Does it now? Should it again?

On a solely pragmatic level, my voice and speech muscles were being used and exercised regularly inside school and not just outside in the playground. My vocal instrument was being mechanically stretched in concert with words even though I suffered a speech impediment. My confidence to speak was always expanding. I think, too, that the ability to stand my ground with words must have been formed by these experiences. Words were neither embarrassing nor unfamiliar. Education in speaking was a serious part of education generally.

But on another and more crucial level I was constantly *learning* through speaking. Words and images were accelerating me into the orbit of knowledge. Obviously I was coming into a more vital contact with literature, speaking the kinds of words that best framed feelings because they were creatively wrought. In learning how to orally present myself or a text I learned how to shape ideas that could compel a listener. Conversation and debate were a by-product. When speaking aloud you simply must make sense. The word must reach the listener if it is to have any effect at all.

What concerns me more and more is that this voice education – a sort of training in personal presentment – seems to have rapidly disappeared from the curricula of most national education systems. Ironically, when English is taught 'as a foreign language' you still find remnants of these skills at work: recitation, repetition, stressing and forming words into the shape of language. To know how a language ought to sound – to know a word and begin to master it – you have to hear it and repeat it, inflect it and play with it. You have to make mistakes with it out loud, find a use for it in all sorts of ways. But for most school children speaking English aloud is no longer essential. Our lack of knowledge about words is reaching a critical stage.

A recent survey amongst my first-year students at the Guildhall School showed that only 3 out of 26 had oral reading and vocal skills taught to them at their school on anything like a regular basis. And all these students had been taught in private, not state schools. This bleak average seems even lower in America where proportionately fewer of the hundreds of university students I have taught were ever asked to read aloud or recite from memory in the classroom. This fact may explain why I always experience there a greater disconnection from words.

My Guildhall students and those I have taught in Texas are all obviously interested in theatre and speaking. They are never timid about standing up and talking in public. They like it and thrive on it. But they arrive in my classes vocally impaired and with a limited speaking capacity which takes all of three years to strengthen. Some of the things most sorely missing are a trust in language, an appetite and a need for words. The will to speak is always there but the ability to speak is still at the fledgling stage. It always takes some time before the need for words coupled with the voice connects.

Who's to Blame?

Where do I place the blame for the breakdown of words? It's hard to say.

I once put this very question to a senior education official who observed that most teachers spend an uncommon proportion of their time trying to keep students quiet so that the lesson can proceed uninterrupted. Teachers tell the students not to shout, but tell them by *shouting at them*. Furthermore, this official reported, teachers are taught to teach without being given any preparation themselves in oral skills, communication or voice classes. Through financial cut-backs and less practical training the teaching of speech and voice has deteriorated rapidly. In modern education parlance 'communication' nowadays means something audio-visual (i.e. TV). In parts of America, I am told, a move is underway to do even more of the instruction solely by means of TV rather than through direct interaction with a teacher. Teaching oral skills is a low priority on the modern teaching curriculum.

So if teachers are not being trained to speak how can a student be expected to learn the process?

If we examine the repercussions of having teachers who are unaware of the importance of their own need to speak then some very depressing scenarios arise. On the one hand embattled teachers are being asked to speak under stress to larger groups of students for hours on end all week long. Their rasping voices suffer pain and yet they believe this is a *natural* occupational hazard. Most teachers I know think of their own voice problems in this way. This worries me because I have talked to lots of teachers about the problem, which has become a serious affliction among teachers. When the voice suffers stress it surrenders or seizes up. Lost and tired voices are the result and with teachers this is a particularly telling syndrome. The result is blocked communication between teacher and pupil.

But the repercussions go even deeper. If an untrained voice is asked to produce sound regularly, some will naturally find the way to do it properly while the larger majority will do it painfully. Children are therefore receiving lessons presented to them through a vocal push which renders material bland and uninteresting. The image I get is of a teacher or lecturer droning on and on without animation and life. An overworked voice cannot speak with excitement. Shades of enthusiasm are bound to get lost. And students thrive on enthusiasm. Words can be heard, factually, but expressive knowledge is lost in the communication. If a voice grates on our ear we shut down. A dull lecture, no matter what brilliance it imparts, either sends us to sleep or turns us away. The excitement of energetic narration pulls us in and makes us alive to the communication.

Part of the process of learning, I both think and have found, comes from hearing words and trusting in the voice that speaks them. In essence the teacher–pupil relationship is really a two-way conversation. Each voice needs the other's ear. Knowledge is circulated through the open channel. Each is trying desperately to express words to the other. If a teacher denies the importance of voice in the classroom, sees the sound of the voice as a distracting nuisance and refuses to make it part of the classroom environment, I fear that our oral skills will continue to decline even further. A vital part of education dies with the dying voice.

I feel defensive when I hear young students and budding actors attacked for a lack of oral prowess, especially when you consider the fact that their whole education has discounted the joy of speaking and the need for words. How many children hear good literature read to them at home, much less at school? How many parents pass on a command and love of words to their children? Most children's books are strong on illustrations but sparse on words or narrative. No wonder so many more young adults than ever before are seeking out voice work. Their voices have been deprived of some essential schooling. Like professionals, the average person is now trying to make up for the neglect his or her voice has suffered.

It continually fascinates me that top business managers and other professionals go on courses at considerable expense in order to learn basic oral skills – the same skills that are taught to a first-year drama student. Why were these options not available as part of a general education curriculum?

I don't think I am painting an unnecessarily black portrait of the state of voice and words in today's schools. As an educator myself I place a high priority on both voice and speech training but also on the imaginative investigation of speaking texts aloud. Like any sort of necessary research and development, we must invest in teaching an imaginative response and responsibility to the word. Without these skills on our curricula we risk fostering yet another generation of silence.

The Written Word v. the Spoken Word

I think it is fair to say that in our schools the written word has triumphed over the spoken word. Literacy has had a far greater impact than oracy.

Until fairly recently an oral examination was as important a part of matriculation as a written test. Being made to speak about your subject was a vital rite of passage. Meaning had to be defended by means of discussion and debate.

A student today can now move brilliantly through school, college or university without ever having to utter a word. We attend lectures but we don't participate in them. In many cases the words spoken, regurgitated, simply have to be those set on the prescribed curriculum or spoken by a lecturer. Oracy has become a passive exercise, an unexercised skill. We read, listen, take notes, but we are rarely encouraged to answer back, speak our mind or voice an opinion.

Over the last fifteen years, for example, I have noticed my own students grow quieter and quieter, less willing to challenge and more willing to submit; precisely at a moment in history when voices need to be raised against the new perils that assault us each day. And yet voices are retreating into silence. The response to famine or war, for instance, seems to be: 'What can you say? What weight does my voice carry?' I suppose this is one of the reasons I never allow note-taking in my classes. I want students to engage me and question me, to provoke me with words. For I do believe that once you have been made to address a topic yourself, analysed it through discussion and not just writing, you come to a greater awareness and ownership of necessary ideas.

As so many pressures in society conspire to cut us off from spoken language, education must lead the battle against any force that would silence us.

Speaking Your Way into Writing and Reading

One of the great benefits of needing to hear words aloud is that speaking encourages both good writing and good reading habits.

Great speaking needs great writing. Once we have learned to connect to words our appetite for reading becomes voracious. We suddenly become keen to explore words in all sorts of contexts. Through speaking it we come to know the written and read word. I would suggest that one of the joys of reading the prose of, say, Charles Dickens is hearing the tales and characters come to life through a speaking voice. Sound enhances sense.

In the text section in Part Two, I have included a number of selections to work with out loud. The great joy of speaking these selections comes from the fact that they are written for the voice; scored, if you like, for the voice as though it were a musical instrument. The 'read aloud' test can often tell how good and expressive a piece of writing is. All of these selections illustrate my notion that the best writing leads to the best kind of speaking. Shakespeare the writer, for example, feeds the needs of the voice because he wrote for speaking actors and for a public theatre of listeners. He made plays to be heard.

When government and educationalists panic about the decline of literacy in schools they often fail to trace the cause to the speaking connection. Government is more concerned with cosmetic education that leaves a student with minimum practical skills to enable him or her to become productive members of the work force. I wonder what good is the skill of basic reading and writing unless it can release thoughts through the voice? Once you have learned to sight-read a passage from literature, for instance, you have learned to master not just speaking but writing and reading as well. You have started to know words in their context. The simple confluence of all three processes makes a necessity of each individual skill. Education should be the conjunction of all three: reading, writing and *speaking*. Again we return to the connection with words through speech.

Discussion and Debate

After writing and reading, other crucial skills that seem impaired are discussion and debate.

How often do we feel that our brain is really being stretched and challenged through a contact with words? How often are we stimulated by a really good discussion (about subjects other than personal ones) or by lively debate? I can remember dozens of instances when a really good discussion or debate has been capsized or kidnapped by a sudden change of topic that blocks the path back to the main thought.

Along with other barriers I've been mentioning in this education section, I think we shy away from sharing stimulating thoughts and ideas. It is as though speaking in depth about any topic is rude. We are blocked from being innovative with words, barred from passion. Being direct seems like a taboo. I would suggest that most of us yearn to have a few of the cobwebs in our brain blown away by a really fresh breath of deep conversation.

Education and its distressing lack of opportunities for general and unthreatening debate has left our society bereft of speakers who can speak keenly about a range of topics. Youth is repeatedly attacked for its incoherence and loss of values. Many educationalists argue that regular sessions in school of discussion, debate and philosophical exploration would gradually heighten coherence and a greater sense of discrimination. These speaking tools would also heighten our need for words. However, these modes of verbal interaction are only encouraged in privileged schools where thinking and talking have a tradition.

One issue I am particularly passionate about is debate. I use that word a lot in this book. Debate is a key means of allowing new words to circulate through our system. Debate is probing and questing. We relentlessly pursue an issue and not just sniff round it. We confront another speaker with the urgency of our needs and sometimes compromise when challenged by a need that is even more vital than our own. Our ability or inability to debate is formed by the openness or lack of it in our lives. If it is not encouraged by parents, teachers, political leaders or even employers the yearning for discussion and openness to opinions other than our own withers. Influences are vital here. Debates and discussion are easy to snuff out.

I will always remember a teacher I had when I was seven years old. She taught us, of all things, philosophy, and her bracing enthusiasm and passion were something quite out of the ordinary. She was a genuine 'Miss Jean Brodie'. Surely she was a visionary. With her we ranged imaginatively over fields of subjects. She met us on our level and took us up to hers.

I brought her a yellow flower once. She asked me why I liked the flower.

'Because it's yellow like the sun,' I said.

'How do you know it's yellow?' she asked.

'Because the sun gives it something,' I replied.

'How would you describe that something?' was her retort.

On she went in this fashion, steering the conversation from the simple to the complex, from the general to the particular, re-inventing with me the Socratic method: seeking the truth by means of questions and answers. What we had were dialogues, not monologues. Give and take debate, thinking growing to a conclusion. I was allowed to discover and make my way, however rudimentary, through thought by means of words. I never felt intimidated or out of my depth. Her questions were more like a quest, a pathway opening through ideas.

I will always be grateful to Miss Otway for taking me that way and not leaving me confined. What she handed me was a map of understanding. And over the years I've learned that once you've cut a path through the thicket of ideas you can never get lost.

When I think back to the people I have lost and most painfully miss, I instantly think of the ones I could talk to on equal terms. The ones with whom I could exchange ideas without threat. The ones who listened. People who were fearless with words and sensitive to the words of others at the same time. That alone has been an inspired education in the need and respect for words.

If a parent encourages debate we are lucky. If our urge to debate is either mocked or meets a barrier of silence or dismissal the rules of debate are infringed. A quite brilliant friend of mine who loves to discuss everything can, for almost no reason, be provoked to anger and resentment in the midst of debate. He oversteps the bounds and becomes rampant

with rage when the debate does not follow his lead. Then he
solved the problem. He realised he is the son of an angry
father. Whenever discussions took place at home they would
always end in anger. So my friend learned that all discussions,
all debates, should end in anger and not accommodation.

Training Young Actors

Here I want to turn to something I know a good deal about:
the way young actors are trained and not trained in the use of
words. If actors are, as Hamlet says, 'the abstract and brief
chronicles of the times', they provide us with a good litmus
test of the state of speech.

Young actors bear a terrible burden today. They are always
the ones singled out by critics as having the sloppiest speech
and voices, particularly when the text is by Shakespeare.
There is some justification in this criticism above and beyond
a lack of experience. Yet the blame should not be placed on
the actors alone.

From my own experience I don't think the various forms of
actor training, either in Britain or North America, pay nearly
enough attention to the connection between voice and text
work. Both areas are sorely neglected and never appreciated
to the full. This may, in fact, be the weakest link in the
training process.

I have actually heard directors and read critics who berate
contemporary actors for being less intelligent than their elder
colleagues. *Less intelligent?* Less sensitive to needing and
caring enough about words, perhaps. When oracy is underrated, when education fails our speaking needs, the care we
give to words, even in everyday speech, is certainly liable to
be imprecise and unclear, even tentative and uncertain.
Naturally this underdevelopment is betrayed most clearly
when an actor comes to speak a classical text in a large
auditorium.

And yet the younger generation is one which responds

superbly to rock and rap singers, switched-on comedians and all the excessive jamming that constitutes 'youth culture'. I wonder, though, if this isn't just a noise ghetto where the voice is forced to imitate fragmentary static and not take risks on its own. Many training actors will often seem to be lip synching their way through dialogue, aping the way they have heard another favourite actor perform it. Rather than act with a singular passion all their own, they mimic.

The biggest hurdle a young speaker faces is the belief that extravagant, brave and passionate speaking can be truthful, that the ownership of language can be original and distinctive and not simply a derivative echo. Along with a distrust of words there is a distrust of extravagant passion. Younger speakers like to take small, tentative vocal steps rather than boldly make huge leaps across the pages of a text. Somewhere along the line younger actors get it into their heads that being small is more truthful than being large. I suppose that television and film performances teach them this. They shy away from bold gestures and away, especially, from big words. They cultivate the stunted voice rather than the expressive one needed to traverse a rich, changeable text. The tentative voice is one that most actors start with and the one they are always in danger of remaining stuck with. With each passing generation there is always the hazard that we will be left with a dearth of superb classical actors.

Until you practise speaking through a variety of texts and explore all the ranges of a text orally – sounding all parts of the word through your voice – the sound score will never be released. I have sat through so many rehearsals where actors simply mumble their way through a text, 'saving' their voice for performance. The result is the incoherence for which they are frequently blamed by critics. Almost from the beginning of rehearsals voice and word must begin connecting. The connection cannot be something you find at a late stage.

Actor training in the West is generally based on finding truth in intimate spaces, being private rather than public, pitching the voice at a low, conversational level. Actors are not trained on large stages or in outdoor spaces. Most might flounder if challenged to perform in Shakespeare's original Globe Theatre. They rarely speak to even a hundred people at a time, much less thousands. They spend a lot of time making small vocal gestures in little rooms. The truth of sharing a classical text outwardly with the passion and energy required by the words is typically never tested. On this level I think our training fails young actors. We do a marvellous job of preparing the actor for the eye of the camera but not enough for the demands of, say, the Royal National Theatre's Olivier stage.

Up to twenty years ago a young actor would typically progress from training into the regional repertory system and then spend years of apprenticeship speaking a variety of classical and modern texts, using his or her voice daily to fill large auditoriums. The voice would circulate through the dramatic repertoire. Facility with words became bolder and surer with each role. Rehearsals were short and interpretation of text inconsistent, but at least the voice was firing on all cylinders and had to be focused and flexible. At every point the voice was growing to suit the word and the action of the role. Connecting to language happened more instantaneously through repeated performing. The actor was tackling a robust text on a regular basis, grappling with language in front of listeners daily, taking the measure of a word or phrase at every juncture in front of a public. But no longer.

Decent voice and text work is always kept to a minimum because of stricter rehearsal schedules and is consequently always in peril. The voice gets rusty through lack of challenge, the lightning-quick need for words becomes sluggish or blunted.

The way we educate performers is undergoing constant change in an effort to produce actors who can shift their voices and speech to suit any part. I do think we should welcome any treatment of a method that will liberate the actor from the kind of minimalism that stunts a performance. But for many actors the connection to words becomes a harder and longer process. It does not happen easily, as I can certainly testify.

Guarding Against Quick Fixes

In our ever growing attempts to find quick fixes for most problems and instant gratification through swift results we tend to ignore the demands of the voice and its needs when it comes to text work.

We must allow ourselves a period of growth where the voice and the word are concerned. It takes time to train a voice and to stretch it. It also takes time and maturity to become sensitive to language and the gravity of words. The quick fix we usually employ with the latter is to busk our way through a passage of text in a uniform, general way. It's a bit like speed reading. A word is touched on swiftly but never has the opportunity to form as an image in the listener's mind. Each word, from start to finish, sounds exactly the same and has uniform value. In speed speaking words get blurred.

Natural speaking, on the other hand, is slower and more measured. The voice is carefully prepared for the challenge. The words have both individual and connected integrity. There is a world of difference between needing to get through a speech quickly and needing the words to take you through the journey of the text.

Proper voice and text work, done over a period of time, allows for space to grow between the words. Pauses and silences give words the room they need to reverberate. And in that reverberation meaning resides. But only when you invest trust in words will you gain the confidence to speak this way. The modern speaker has been taught to abhor a vacuum and to fill in all the blanks. Yet great speaking takes its time and obeys every pause. Often a great speaker will tease and taste a word before even completing it. The great speaker knows that arguments build slowly, that surprise catches a listener off-guard, that you must make the listener need each word in the chain of a thought. Speaking is connection through contact with voice and word.

The Shakespeare Debate

As I write this book a frantic debate has erupted in British education circles about how Shakespeare should be taught in schools. I suppose it is one of those debates that never ends but will simply go on and on as a clash of views. A healthy clash, I hope.

On one side of the argument there is the belief that Shakespeare is too difficult for many pupils and that teaching his texts to students who are too young can put pupils off the experience. From the other side of the debate comes a passionate plea from government (and even from a member of the British royal family) to keep the tradition and heritage of the English language alive primarily through a writer like William Shakespeare. So plays like *Romeo and Juliet*, *Julius Caesar* and *A Midsummer Night's Dream* are intended to be fixed notches on the English curriculum in the years to come. What pressure to put these wonderful plays under!

I can certainly affirm that many students have been put off Shakespeare through a tedious examination of the text and an ultra-literary approach that stresses reading over speaking: a sight-specific process in which the mouth is never called upon to grapple with the words. What I dread will happen is a cosmetic approach to teaching Shakespeare as a 'Great Writer' of ideas whose greater power as a word poet, whose playfulness and power are ingrained in the text and are released through the voice, will somehow get lost in the process.

There is no way you can possibly begin to enjoy Shakespeare without speaking him aloud. His words are written to be spoken. The physical aspects of the language (a thrill that only comes from speaking it), the rhythm, line length and rhyme all have a sensual appeal that speaking activates. And this exuberant physicality can be enjoyed by speakers of all ages. I spend most of my time teaching Shakespeare to professional actors. But I have also taken children and adults through the text in much the same way and have seen delight and thrill enter their voices as they 'speak Shakespeare' for the first time. He wrote for king and commoner alike. Children always seem to have a natural capacity for Shakespeare's language. When you allow yourself to speak it you find immediacy, sensuality, playfulness, rebellion and numerous riddles and games. The words are an adventure for the speaker.

My instant reaction to legislating that children learn Shakespeare (and how they learn him) is to ask the following question: Do we have teachers who are sufficiently trained to encourage free, uninhibited speaking of the text and do they have the skills, overall, to get children to speak? Any serious teacher wants to teach Shakespeare well and their training ought to support them in the process. Too many of us who are teachers love Shakespeare so much that we become impatient and even furious when we hear the texts spoken in any way other than our set notions of how it ought to be spoken.

Who's to say how we should speak Shakespeare?

Recent productions of his plays performed in a thick Yorkshire accent were enjoyed by critics and audiences alike. But does speaking of this sort appeal to the purist?

I like to think that Shakespeare's original audiences – who went to 'hear' rather than to 'see' one of his plays – treated it as a language concert in the way we think of rock or jazz concerts. His audiences went to hear debate, clever turns of phrase, solo speaking, riffs of all types on the spoken word. It is always surprising that, as with a good song, a good Shakespearean speech instantly strikes a beat, a melody; instantly stirs the emotions. Before any time has passed we are quickly swept away by the Shakespearean tune. Now this doesn't take education but just attentiveness.

More and more today the approach taken to acting Shakespeare is a 'how to' method. Young actors, for instance, are drilled in iambic pentameter verse in all sorts of strange ways. But there is no simple 'how to' method of tapping into an individual's capacity or emotional life, from which the need to speak Shakespeare's words must ultimately spring. We may be able to educate someone about the facts concerning Shakespeare's language, formal structures and dramaturgy, but only speaking his words will uncover the rhythm and soul of the text.

You keep Shakespeare alive in the mind and heart by speaking him. Once you've discovered the facts about the text you can and should dive deeply into the sound to discover even more resonances. Once you are in among and surrounded by the words you swim with Shakespeare's shifting current, riding the crest of the turbulent waves he gives you or floating with ease down the gentle stream of his verse. Once you've made the plunge the coordination of breathing and muscle control help you navigate the rest. Again, the image of physical grappling comes up when we talk about speaking Shakespeare aloud.

After this if you want to work further on the text there are so many intriguing issues to consider: the structure of the verse, caesura and line endings, classical rhetorical devices, peculiar uses of jargon, complex image patterns, issues drawn from politics, philosophy and religion, and so much more. You will want to fine-tune your approach because the need will be there to encourage it. As your strength and confidence as a swimmer through Shakespeare's language grows stronger and stronger you will naturally learn new strokes and go for longer and greater distances. As you do so the words will keep you afloat and you will soon learn just how much you need them for ballast and balance.

As you should have noticed by now, Shakespeare is a key

writer in this book. We'll be returning to him again along the way. I want to end here, though, by saying that I think the approach to Shakespeare through the shoals of literature very often proves debilitating. When we approach his texts without a single preconceived literary notion, approach him through speaking the words as best we know how, a world of verbal delight always seizes the speaker. Teaching Shakespeare must begin with speaking Shakespeare aloud. That's when Shakespeare is at his best.

3 Cultural and Physical Barriers

When we speak words, in whatever context we use them, we instantly come up against all kinds of barriers, cultural, mental and physical. There are even technical barriers learned from school that are attached to certain words. Words like 'poetry', for example, immediately throw up barriers.

You may not instantly notice them but barriers are often there. They are the same sort of blocking mechanisms to words that habits are to the speaking voice.*

Tension and a resistance to words are clear and primary barriers to speaking. A simple hesitation to speak aloud can be a minor barrier. Becoming tongue-tied when you do is another minor block. An inability to speak at all can be a major barrier and speaks of a greater problem. In such cases the role of speech therapists is crucial. A voice expert is simply not enough. Stroke victims, for instance, frequently suffer from aphasia: the loss of ability to speak or understand speech. They need to be brought gradually to speech through careful therapy. Dyslexia, a language disorder that affects the ability to read and understand words, is a highly controversial affliction that language experts and physicians continue to argue about. How does it start and how is it healed? Many dyslexic readers, however, are wonderful speakers and actors. Dyslexia should never stop us from speaking. There are a number of other speech disorders and language pathologies

* See *The Right to Speak* for a discussion of the habits that inhibit the speaking voice.

that can get in the way of words, though they are outside the scope of this book. I am more interested in addressing the kinds of barrier that you can identify and do something about almost immediately.

We cannot begin to enjoy a real need for words until we get past word barriers and vocal traps. I think the primary consequence of any of these barriers is that we have been left with stunted voices or ones lacking in confidence when we approach words.

The Age of Cacophony and Image Saturation

Every day we come up against the noise barrier. We live in an age of cacophony, of dissonance and discord. Constant noise bombards us from every side. We are easily distracted as sudden noises interrupt our speech, particularly those of us who live in urban settings. Cities are a special noise trap. Our ears have been dulled as a result of too much sound exploding round us. In order to hear best we must experience silence. And yet we have to listen relentlessly to piped-in music, aircraft overhead, drilling and traffic as we walk the streets. Only the loudest sounds get through our aural defences. The advent of the Walkman means we have to literally plug ourselves into a sound channel or let a cassette be our guide. Our ears have become desensitised, unable to distinguish natural sound from the jangle of electronic mixing. The simple joy of words comes as something of an anti-climax. Finding the pleasure in spoken words often means competing with an overwhelming soundscape blocking our path.

As we have ceased to speak and be aurally stimulated (except, perhaps, by music) we have surrendered more and more to visual saturation. When we speak of 'communication' nowadays we invariably mean something visual: television and video, films, endless streams of advertising clutter our sight-line. How often do we talk back to the television, stop and argue with an advertising hoarding? We accept it and often let it pass without comment.

I remember witnessing the introduction of TV into a small village in Portugal in the late 1970s. The first set appeared in a workers' café, a local gathering place where gossip was exchanged and stories told. It was an exciting place to visit because it was so alive with talk, especially in the summer when words would drift far into the night. It was also a place where every level of society and age mixed. Children would listen to elders and become part of an ongoing story which was that village and those people. Then the television set arrived. Gradually the place fell silent. Watching replaced talking. Then mainly watching. Rather than remaining a tightly knit group of speakers, speaking for themselves, the people in the village surrendered to the patterned speakers beamed in from Lisbon.

A colleague who attended a theatre festival in Caracas, Venezuela, noticed that all the small houses in the *barrios* on the hills that surrounded the city were studded with television antennas. He remarked on this to a local official who cheerfully replied that TV was still the best control and narcotic for vocal dissent. Particularly daily soap operas!

We all know the power of television. What we have not yet sufficiently discovered is the way it has stopped our need to use words.

Loss of Enjoyment

I think that too many of us hit a barrier when it comes to enjoying words.

We have lost the ability to engage with language as a kind of healthy recreation. One of the great joys of speaking lies in bantering with words. Words rarely make us giddy with delight the way they do a child. We risk seeming foolish, indulgent, theatrical or untruthful if we enjoy a word's sensuous or silly appeal. We rarely venture into any extravagant experimentation when it comes to words. Jokes, puns, aphorisms and witticisms are terrific examples of words on holiday. If we always think of language as a sober business I do think we lose an essential thrill about speaking from which none of us recover. Many of our duller speaking habits are engendered by a seriousness of purpose. Words can and should be a sort of refreshment that revives our appetite for speaking. We need to hunger more for words.

When you begin to enjoy words you suddenly discover how to tease with language, how to seduce with it and how to time its delivery for your own purpose. One of the great pleasures about the current renaissance in stand-up comedy is the licence it has encouraged among young speakers to drop a too-rigid barrier about what it is acceptable to say. Good comic speaking, like good juggling or magic, forces you to keep the words in motion and make each new invention a sudden surprise. Embedded in each joke or humorous situation is a eureka factor in which a key word or phrase bursts to the surface and we find ourselves richer for it. A classc case in point from Oscar Wilde's *The Importance of Being Earnest*:

> JACK: I have lost both my parents.
> LADY BRACKNELL: To lose one parent, Mr Worthing, may be regarded as a misfortune. To lose both looks like carelessness.

Regaining and refining an enjoyment of words becomes an asset rather than a liability. Oral societies know that shading the dark with the light gives speaking a richer hue of colours from which to choose. One aspect of enjoyment is that it gives a dead delivery of words instant sparkle, a facet that good speaking cannot do without.

Wit and Wordplay

In the play of words there is no finer achievement than to be witty with it. Wit and wordplay demonstrate the mind's agility to mint boldly inventive phrases on the spot. The use of words becomes like sleight of hand.

Our speech and language ought to seem entirely effortless each time we voice an expression. But I imagine all of us have met only a few people in our lives who have the genuine skill to do magical things with words. Stumbling and hesitating our way through a witty passage of text destroys the essence of wordplay and repartee. Using language in this way must be confident and quick (i.e. not 'nitwitted' or 'witless' but 'quick witted' and 'sure witted'). Unfortunately it is hard to train and plan for moments like this. I do think there are people who are naturally witty.

But practice in wit and wordplay does force us to see the beauty of language in small, neatly wrapped parcels (i.e. aphorisms and brief utterances) as in Alexander Pope's couplet:

> True wit is nature to advantage dressed,
> What oft was thought but ne'er so well expressed.

The rhyme and reason of wit and wordplay teach us that a few words can say more than paragraphs. Someone who is witty addresses the truth with keen perceptions. Judgement mingles with a sense of the ludicrous. Neatly succinct wit and wordplay flash and sparkle. They are the linguistic equivalent of fireworks. Wit and wordplay can also wound by striking the right nerve.

Someone with wit is a dangerous figure in society because he or she can expose, with intelligence and devastating clarity, the ridiculous pomposity of the 'curiosity of nations' and 'plague of custom'. The various fools in Shakespeare and rakes in eighteenth-century literature perform this function. They are anarchic yet protected creatures, despised but also feared, satirists and also truth-speakers. And they usually get away with what they say. They are refreshingly cheeky.

Wordplay is a fun means of sparring with and enjoying

language for its own sake. In some ways the ability to play with someone through words binds us to them. Well-matched couples, for instance, always display this facility naturally. As soon as we hear Kate and Petruccio (in *Taming of the Shrew*), Rosalind and Berowne (in *Love's Labour's Lost*) and Beatrice and Benedick (in *Much Ado About Nothing*) play with words together we know they are destined for one another. They may sound vicious and go at one another mercilessly, but the wit of each is a great equaliser. The words naturally harmonise:

> PETRUCCIO: Come, come, you wasp, i'faith you are too angry.
> KATHERINE: If I be waspish, best beware my sting.
> PETRUCCIO: My remedy is then to pluck it out.
> KATHERINE: Ay, if the fool could find it where it lies.
> PETRUCCIO: Who knows not where a wasp does wear his
> sting? In his tail.
> KATHERINE: In his tongue.
> PETRUCCIO: Whose tongue?
> KATHERINE: Yours, if you talk of tales, and so farewell.
> PETRUCCIO: What, with my tongue in your tail? Nay, come
> again,
> Good Kate, I am a gentleman.
> KATHERINE: That I'll try.
>
> *She strikes him.*

Witty speakers partner each other, giving tit for tat in an elegant dance of words. If you do enjoy playing with words then there is always something extremely dismal about people who cannot join in the fun or keep up. Most children play in this way but forget the native skill when they get older and more soberly adult. Wit and wordplay protect us from being too serious. They allow us the freedom to free-associate with words. In fact, wordplay like Petruccio and Kate's is like flirting with language. Language used in this way is always sexy along with being fun. You invite another speaker into your world and together you create a fantasy one made up entirely from words.

Wit and wordplay also serve a very serious purpose both emotionally and intellectually. The best writers use these devices to get our attention and make us stop and think. Later in the text section there are examples from Shakespeare, Congreve, Wilde and Shaw where these humorous devices have an earnest side to shadow the comic one. They make arguments clear. We make a mistake nowadays when we think of wit and wordplay as frivolous inventions. They never are. When used too fiercely, wit and wordplay put you outside society, a place where most of us choose not to be. Today the word players are few and far between because I think we fear standing out through our language. Wit is risk. Many people mistake sarcasm for true wit. We think it means a put-down. We use jokes to fill time and space, not connecting them to the arguments at hand. Nothing is worse than wit or wordplay that is laboured and hollow. Many speakers use it as a pose and it sounds unnatural. Real wit and wordplay, however, comes from a genuine need to exploit pomposity and emptiness. It is necessary anarchy. So spontaneous that it frequently erupts when we least expect it. It is also a great means of defence. Powerful people are frightened of wits. Many children survive bullying at school by developing language muscles that result in razor-sharp wit. Gays and blacks have learned to attack by means of lacerating wit when society attacks them. The newest waves of comedy always seek to establish themselves by refunctioning the traditions of wit and wordplay.

Irony and Satire

Allied to wit and wordplay are irony and satire. All four appreciate the need for words, though the latter uses language with far more edge and cunning.

Irony (literally meaning 'a dissembling') is a mode of speech that creates a conflict in the listener's ear by disguising the real message of what is being said behind humour. But that conflict conveys a meaning with greater force by means of opposition. Irony works by indirection and often needs to be deciphered through careful listening for a subtle twisting of tone or stress (e.g. 'The best way to *keep* one's word is not to *give* it'). If we don't appreciate listening for the key conflict in the sentence, the effects of the opposing words of an ironic statement do not penetrate the barriers. It is amazing how many people lack irony and haven't the ability to use it or recognise it being used against them.

Irony can be a safe blind to hide our intentions or to reveal them gradually. 'But Brutus is an honourable man,' says Mark Antony a number of times in *Julius Caesar*. Each time he says the phrase it moves away from innocence and becomes ironically darker and more accusatory. Gradually it dawns on us that he means that Brutus is a *dis*honourable man. Through the magic of irony and dramatic intention the phrase shifts to its opposite (and negative) meaning. Irony is one of those skilful rhetorical devices which is at its best when linked to spoken speech. Sarcasm is mean and spiteful. Irony is so much more deadly because its meaning sneaks up on us, as in: 'Puritanism – the haunting fear that someone, somewhere, may be happy'.

Satire is on an equal plane of elegance. It uses irony to make itself felt, usually by creating an outrageous proposition that sounds wholly credible until we suddenly realise we are trapped in satire's grip. We always forget that one of the jobs of satire is to tear down an old order to build a new society, that words used humorously can cleanse the world of its untidiness and bad taste by restoring our jaded vision to balance and harmony. Great satire, like that of Jonathan Swift, can put words to ferocious, almost surrealistic use so that the comic and the horrific mingle to create the grotesque. Satire is one of the most powerful ways by which literature seeks to right the wrongs of the world.

Both irony and satire demand exceedingly good language skills and a listener tuned in to the games these devices play.

Both turn the world upside down or right side up, depending on your perspective. Provided we are willing to enter their dynamic world, both irony and satire can change our point of view by angering or enlightening us. Our blunted use of language often means that we cannot scale the heights of either irony or satire because we too easily settle for cheap sarcasm and innuendoes that wall off the listener to any further communication. Irony and satire should tease a response out of a listener, not shut him up. They are devices which provoke and not obstruct.

The Tyranny of the Intellectual

In essence I believe the need for words is something beyond the intellectual. It is a physical, emotional and sensual engagement fed and flavoured by the intellect.

Surprisingly, most of us fear being too simple, clear and direct. Intellectual notions of discourse are a barrier to an easy access to words. So many of us are quick to qualify whatever we say and overburden our communication with clarification. When most actors approach work on a text their immediate instinct, learned from school, is to confront and understand the text intellectually. They are guided by interpretation rather than first by vocal evidence. We never seem to make the immediate connection that there are other forces powering a word. Too much time at rehearsals is spent sitting round a table discussing the text rather than physically grappling with it. The mind is forever censoring the intuition. The head is overruling not only the heart of the text but also its pulse and feeling.

I am not saying that an intellectual exploration of a text is not necessary. Of course it is. But it seems to me that it is just one part of the equation and not just the only way of entering a spoken text.

The barrier of the intellectual means, of course, that we would prefer to entrust our understanding of words to academics rather than to instinct. This is especially true of great texts. So many people I work with say that they cannot speak Shakespeare. They claim they are not educated enough, worthy enough or 'intelligent' enough. Yet it has always amazed me that you can hand Shakespeare to non-English speakers in, say, India, to Native Americans who have no connection to Elizabethan culture, to prisoners and mental patients cut off from the experience of plays, and everyone will make sense of the words. Each speaker will always find something to connect to in the words. Maybe just a sound will release the connection. But connection does come if the urge to speak is there.

Children are exactly the same. When given an oral text to speak there are no barriers. They will very often release a power in the words that the more 'mature' adult (handicapped by intellect) will miss entirely. Children will immediately seize on the play of words and whatever is in the word that can be sounded. But that, I maintain, is the best route into speaking Shakespeare: through the sounds of the words.

Once you break through the barrier of the intellectual you allow yourself to explore the evocative sensations of words. You discover that words 'move' just as much as they 'mean'.

The Rule of Grammar

Most of us suffer from the fact that language seems controlled and confined by rules of grammar. We think of grammar as a group of rigid principles that most of us learned in our school days (or had drilled into us) and then gradually forgot. Something that should aid us in the formation of words actually keeps us from them.

A good many of us probably found grammar a hopeless task in school; all those sentences diagrammed like a maze of motorways we had to navigate our way through. We still become frozen with fear at the thought of syntax, subjects, objects, predicates, verbs, and split infinitives.

On so many levels these rules are all necessary for clear communication ... in writing. But our subject here is speaking, where the rules are less clear and far less rigid. Linguists, in fact, are always in hot debate over what constitutes correctness in speaking. If we are learning to speak Standard English (as most foreigners who learn English are forced to do) then rules of phonetics and pronunciation invariably need to apply in order to give the communication an acceptable coherence. But any set of rules can be too rigidly applied and seem like tyranny. Perhaps our native accent is not the accent of the prevailing powers. Should we surrender it? Maybe our pronunciation of words is unfashionable or our formal grammar flawed. Does that mean we shouldn't speak, or feel like failures? Some of the best speakers in the world disobey all the rules, have accents that are anything but standard and yet their connection to words and to listeners is not the least bit impaired. If words are needed they will make themselves heard no matter what their form.

Breaking the Rules

Right at the start I want to declare myself to be against any form of rule that infringes any speaker's right to speak or need words. And sometimes we have to break or bend the rules to make our speaking sound natural.

We must, of course, have rules to aid us in universal communication. But think of them as useful guidelines and not narrow interpretations. I am certainly not against using correct grammar, but I am against its imposition if it leads to tension and stiffness in speaking. You can listen to someone with flawless speech and diction who speaks in complete, perfect sentences. Yet if they sound bland and uninspired, if they are not connecting words to voice, then the sense of what is said is compromised severely. All the perfection in the world will not save a dull sound. I would much rather listen to a passionate speaker who can move me by his appeal, even if it comes forth in flawed sentences.

What makes the speaking of English so wonderful nowadays is its sheer dynamism and variety. In fact the great oral tradition is probably kept most alive on the street. If you spend a day wandering round London you will hear the rhythm of it shifting wildly in all directions as so-called 'standard' variants merge with East End Cockney, Irish, Australian, American, Bengali, Rasta talk, African variants and dozens of other distinct native sounds. The same would happen, I imagine, if you walked through, say, downtown New York, Toronto, Los Angeles or Sydney. Who can put a value on one version of English above another? And why should we?

Think also about the vitality of language on the street and in unofficial places: words that have not been sanitised – like slang – forms of spoken English that retain an exotic connection to creativity – like various forms of pidgin or creole. Primary and adopted languages clash and connect. Language and words really ought to be left to flourish outside the state of rules.

We should realise that as our passions rise and we become emotionally heightened, rules may need to be broken. Our native accent is stirred to make the sound that suits us best. When we are speaking most naturally and most comfortably, we return to that accent for ease and familiarity. And in that accent we are often most eloquent.

Interestingly, a great deal of the best modern dramatic dialogue in stage plays would fail most grammar checks. Writers are always breaking rules. The speaking need does not always follow a logical order. Nor is it always coherent. More often than not it is spontaneous. Need instantly creates it own set of rules and conditions. The cry from the heart may not neatly match the laws of syntax and word order. Shakespeare and every other great oral writer of poetry and plays writes just as much, and in some cases more, for the speaking voice rather than for a reader's eye.

The voice must always be alert to why language might go off track and what that signals about a character's emotional state. Stage language is not always cool and precise. It is frequently hot. In fact, I contend that you cannot possibly understand a great oral text fully until you speak it aloud and discover its snags and confusion. That instantly tells you something about a character's critical state of mind. Silent reading dulls one of a speaking text's necessary functions: to make sense best as it is being spoken. As we will see in the later part of this book, great writers often break formal rules in order to release the spoken word. In speaking these writers, in bringing the echo of their voices back into the world, we guarantee their survival.

I shall always remember the final image from François Truffaut's film of Ray Bradbury's novel *Fahrenheit 451*. A group of dissidents in a futuristic society where all books are burnt and destroyed walk through the woods, keeping their small cache of precious literature alive by reading it aloud and recycling the texts orally through memory – a literary society returning, by necessity, to its oral roots.

Words survive because in the end we need them more than we need rules of grammar. The physical nature of a word fits the feeling and action of the moment. Shakespeare will never truly be Shakespeare without our oral (and aural) engagement with his texts.

Public Speech

What about the dire state of speaking in public?

We are too willing to let others, like television commentators and media spokespersons, do our talking for us. We abdicate our right to speak and let politicians be our voice when it comes to making important decisions about the economy and social needs. *Vox populi*, organised and vocal public opinion and dissent, has given way to vox pop, the informal and individual gripes phoned into radio chat shows. We've begun to stop speaking for ourselves or speaking up as citizens.

I have noticed that when I speak in front of groups people are hesitant to ask questions publicly. They are shy about speaking up. And yet they will linger in streams afterwards, waiting for a 'private' chat which is often an animated one. Words tumble out of them. People are so frightened of unburdening in public, of revealing a public voice, of speaking their mind except through anonymous mass demonstrations or 'letters to the editor'. Crucially, we seem to have cut down on public forums. And apart from a variety of evangelists, the art of public speaking is in serious danger of dying out.

The media, of course, now carries the message more efficiently and to a greater number. But to hear and judge a message directly, in the flesh, may be something that human beings need. Theatre is a public forum where messages are still carried in the flesh. When the word is made flesh it really does dwell among us and move us in ways that electronics will never duplicate.

The Inability to Listen

In an age of diminishing attention spans, the inability to listen beyond the compass of a few words is one of those barriers we find ourselves coming up against time after time. We have all experienced a closed ear, the listener who turns away from what we are saying.

Needing to listen and to hear are just as essential as a need for words.

If you just allow yourself to close your eyes and listen to the silence for a few minutes, what do you begin to hear? A multitude of sounds and maybe even voices. Go deeper with the listening test and you will probably hear even more shades and levels to the sounds; perhaps as many as a dozen separate ones all together.

All of us are in need of sharpening our blunted listening capacity. We have to will ourselves to listen not only to sounds but to other points of view different from our own; to take in and assess other words. We are too quick to discount other opinions, too dismissive of new or alien ideas. We only want to listen selectively, staying deaf to all the variety around us.

Non-listening and selective inattention are great barriers that many of us use to avoid speaking: 'Why don't you answer?' 'Because I wasn't listening to what you were saying.' In order to speak well and debate well we have to listen to others and take in their words and arguments. We also have to trust that someone will listen to us in turn.

In a two-way conversation active listening is as important as animated speaking. I do think that so many contemporary speech habits come from the fact that we don't care enough about listening. If we mumble, what does that say about our overall capacity to listen to someone else or judge the listener's needs? These habits have developed, too, because we don't have the listener's best interests in mind when we speak. We pass over information either too rapidly or too incoherently. We make the listener either come to us when we devoice (speak too low) or push him or her away by blasting out directives. In either instance the needs of the listener are not being served and the speaker is suffering from blocks that inhibit communication. I know I have said it earlier, but I do think that many speakers are compelled to shout, push and rant because they fear that no one is listening.

When a listener is thrashed and battered by a voice in full flight, what happens to the words? They simply get in the way. They are endangered because they become little more than flailing gestures. We begin to trust their power less and less. A physical habit undermines our connection to them. And the speaker of these words? He or she has lost control over words as much as they have lost control over our capacity to listen. In the end they lose control over us.

When a listener's needs are taken into account the voice is

suddenly forced to respond. You will never acquire a capacity and need for words unless they are appreciated. When you are speaking only to and for yourself you speak into a void.

It is always a great comfort when we sense someone is listening to us with patience, compassion and undivided attention. We then get a chance to make sense of our needs. People stop listening for all kinds of reasons. Perhaps our accent is not to their liking. Maybe we speak too slow or too fast. But I contend that someone stops listening when we stop compelling him or her to listen.

On the other side of the equation the speaker must recognise the listener's needs. This cannot be stressed enough. Actors, for instance, will not only ignore the needs of the audience but those of the other actors on-stage. Their capacity to concentrate must take the listener into account. One is not talking here only about being heard. What I really mean is gearing the speaking act to the listener's special needs, in terms of pace, rhythm, tone, modulation and silence. Speakers generally disregard these listening needs when they vocally push or shout, speaking so frantically that the listener must close down before being lashed senseless. The concentration, on the part of the listener, to understand a mumbler is so demanding that we cease trying after a few minutes. A monotonous range lulls a listener to sleep. A falling or unenergised line will disconnect us from a thought. A hesitater will annoy us. The overstresser or pedantic lecturer fills us with too much detail. You can quickly see what happens in all these cases: the erection of barriers on the part of the listener.

Tensions and Physical Habits as Barriers

One of the greatest barriers that hinders our connection with words is tension. The relentlessness of noise and swiftly passing images help create tension. But usually tension lodges itself inside us.

Many of the speakers I work with (and this includes professional actors) are in conflict with the speech act itself. They either attack words or hold back on them, squash their voice at the crucial moment or push it beyond its capacity. We don't give words enough space to breathe or to be. They need tension in order to speak.

Very few speakers I work with use words with ease and confidence. Words have become dreaded obstacles to them. Actors may approach a text with suspicion and fear, rarely with familiarity and confidence. Only a small minority are able to connect voice to words in a well-timed explosion of sound and sense. In speaking freely that is the simple act you strive for.

So often tension is a physical problem and the result of habits we have cultivated during a lifetime. There are any number of ways of releasing these kinds of tension.*

More often than not, tension in speaking comes from a lack of confidence in words themselves or in our ability to use them easily. When you are out of synch with a text and what you are saying, tension will invariably be the result. When you are in tune with language, tension miraculously disappears. It is also surprising how simply needing a word will bypass all the circuits of tension and allow us easy access to the voice. The call for help, for example.

As I repeatedly tell actors and other professional speakers, physical care and relaxation of the voice by means of exercises and workouts is a critical means of releasing tension. Since using words is such a physical activity, the muscles and joints used to form words and the breath needed to sustain extended speaking must be allowed to work with the words and not against them.

Our non-oral society has left us with many voice and speech blocks which act as barriers to any essential communication. These habits manifest themselves throughout our bodies and

---

* See *The Right to Speak* for a description of tension and exercises to reduce and remove unnecessary tension.

voices, contributing, I firmly believe, to our distrust of words. The habit of never speaking or lapsing into silence, for instance, radically diminishes the need for words. But these physical barriers can simply include such manifestations as:

- Physical tension and nervous fidgeting when called upon to speak.
- A strained and constricted vocal capacity.
- A held or slumped posture that prevents sound from escaping us.
- A breathing problem like a locked or hesitant breath; breath that comes in gasps and is never taken deep enough.

Physical holds and habits* really do show up instantly in the voice. What they do to words can be quite devastating. A tight or held jaw, for instance, can strangle a word as it is spoken. Severe nervousness can kill the urgency of what we need to say. With a held or slumped posture we can often sound generalised rather than specific when we speak; lethargic rather than animated; bemused rather than bright. As the voice becomes underpowered and undernourished from lack of breath we literally run out of steam as we speak. Our sentences flatten like a leaking tyre, our paragraphs fall rather than rise. Whatever colour and attraction the words may have, they are rendered lustreless and flat. Physical barrers can kill the words we speak or make every word we speak sound the same. The simple lack of tonal variation can make each sentence, no matter what the subject, a regimented replication of the one before. It is all too easy to take on vocal masks (e.g. sentimentality or assertiveness) when the physical act of speaking is not properly exercised.

Psychologically we may be suffering deeper barriers when we speak. Some of us, sadly, have been so firmly silenced by a trauma, event or admonishment in the past that we find it almost impossible to use words confidently and without

* I have written about these at some length in *The Right to Speak*.

hesitation. Blocks make us grope for words out of sheer terror and deny us easy access to them. If we have been led to believe that we are never being listened to, we think it is hardly worth taking the trouble to speak.

If we never get a chance to practise speaking enough, our whole vocal equipment gets rusty from lack of use, and along with it our intellect and emotions get clogged up through the loss of a vital outlet. If we rarely need to speak we learn to deny the power of words in ourselves and others. As we lose trust in ourselves and our voices, the blockage embeds itself deeper into a distrust of everything we say. Suddenly every word we speak is full of qualification. Hesitancy or quavers may enter our voices and upset our rhythm. Sentences come out sounding clipped or unfinished. The voice habitually tails off at the end of a sentence. We choose words that lack vitality and precision. Everyday speaking becomes a chore.

Coupled with this vocal shyness is vocal laziness. Most contemporary speakers, to one degree or another, allow their voices to be either overbearing or underpowered. They cannot or will not vary their voices to suit different vocal tasks. Many actors, particularly, never seem to understand that careless speech habits cannot be imposed on the great oral texts which demand so much clarity from the voice. It is the norm nowadays to be casual and off-hand about the way we speak. To some degree we should probably welcome the fact that stricter formalities have been dropped from most social interchanges. Yet to an even greater degree formal speech has been replaced by telegraphed and off-hand speech. We try, as it were, to get away with as few words as possible.

Poetry

All of us, at some time in our lives, have spoken poetry.

As the routine events of life suddenly become more urgent and vital, normal language is no longer sufficient to our needs. At such moments the quality of our language changes and we probably speak poetically. In order to express horror or joy, fear, love, hate or the incredible experience of feeling alive, poetry serves us better than prose. Fewer words and stronger images focus the thoughts. We reach for simile, employ metaphor, attempt through onomatopoeia to reproduce the sound and sense of the experience itself in order to possess it. As patients break through in therapy, as children recount a new experience, as we speak of loss of joy then we resort to poetry. Poetry needn't only reside with professional poets, be studied in university courses or heard in the theatre, or grace the pages of the well-read. It is territory we all know and traverse daily.

Many factors have conspired to alienate us from needing and speaking words poetically. The word itself has had a bad press, it breeds pretension. Yet when you travel on the London Underground nowadays one of the special joys in among the route maps and cardboard adverts tucked in panels above the windows are the poems which began appearing several years ago. There amidst a sea of sullen travellers and a dead sea of advertising there are these verbal tints that brighten a journey: 'Poetry on the Underground'. In this context nothing could seem less pretentious because the poems are like an escape to a new world of pleasure. They are playful and succinct. We look at them and then look at them again. They put words in new contexts and shape, giving the eye and mind a sudden refreshment.

I remember as a child crying when I spoke Coleridge's line: 'Quietly shining to the quiet moon' from the poem 'Frost at Midnight'. My teacher asked me why I was crying. I didn't know. The words just made me. She laughed but I knew that I had experienced something having to do with the pattern and sound of those words transforming into a phrase that sparked a meaning far beyond the intellectual. Poetry is often nothing more than words organised to have a high, sudden impact. That's partly the reason why great poems and even great song lyrics are unforgettable in every way.

Profanity

I have often been intrigued by the fact that as we lose more
and more contact with the sorts of words that make us fluent,
many of us only find release and satisfaction in profanity. We
express it quite openly and publicly with little embarrassment.
What is even more intriguing is how swear-words have
changed their function from being oaths of truth ('I swear on
a stack of Bibles!') to oaths of abuse ('I swear I hate you
mother f – er!') We have gone from swearing to pledge our
honour to pledging our enmity.

All swear-words are great to speak. They are frank, sensual,
physical and dangerous. They satisfy an inherent need to be
specific and emotive. Perhaps we like them most of all because
they break taboos, allow us to speak in a vulgar tongue for a
change. Children, for instance, love to say them. Could
profanities also be the last remnants we have of a pure joy in
words? A kind of consolation and release from the domain of
correct speech? Profanity is, after all, blasphemy, a kind of
irreverent revolt from the straight and narrow.

But I wonder, also, if swear-words have begun to lose their
original power as signs of contempt as they litter our lives and
begin to sound banal. The trouble with swear-words is that
they often reveal an essential loss of coherence. They have
even lost the power to shock. With profanity you can never
adequately explain to the world or to a listener the root of
your frustration of pain. Swearing usually signals that the
defences of tension have sprung up to shield us from deep
confusion. It engulfs us in a whirlwind of passion where all
sense is blown away, as in this torrent of words from David
Mamet's play *Speed-the-Plow*:

> FOX: *Fuck* you . . . *Fuck* you . . . [*He hits* GOULD] Fuck you.
> Get up. [*He hits him again*]. I'll fucken' kill you right here
> in this office. All this bullshit; you *wimp*, you *coward* . . .
> now you got the job, and now you're going to *run* all over
> everything, like something broke in the *shopping* bag, you

fool – your fucken' sissy film – you squat to pee. You old *woman* . . . all of my life I've been eating your shit and taking your leavings . . . *Fuck* you, the Head of Production. Job I could of done ten *times* better'n you, the press, the *money*, all this time, and now you're going to be some fucken' *wimp*, cost me my, my, my . . . *fortune?* Not in This Life, Pal. Your Writ Has Run. You hear me . . .? [*Pause*] Bob . . .? [*Pause*] Do you hear me . . .? You want somebody to take charge? I'll take charge. Do you hear me, mister . . .? You need an excuse to cop out, I'll give you your fucken' excuse. [*Pause*]. We have a meeting. Can you fix yourself up?

Language of Gestures

One of the physical barriers we have used to replace words is the language of gestures. So many of us resort to sheer physicality – wild gesticulating or rapid hand movement – to do the power of words. We might force our words on someone with a jabbing finger, for instance. As our world becomes more and more verbally impoverished and vocally diminished, we resort to aggressive gestures: we shout, grimace, whistle, stomp, laugh, widen our eyes, put our hands across our mouths in a repertoire of physical signals that take the place of words. (But please don't confuse this with sign language which, I think, has a gestural eloquence all its own.)

Too easily, when confronted by uneasy situations, we allow ourselves to become 'tongue-tied' and word shy. We claim to be speechless or 'gob-smacked'. We physically push to be understood rather than search for appropriate words that clarify our will. We believe that tension and conflict can only be resolved through actions, not words, because, as the cliché says, they speak louder than words. It should, in fact, be quite the reverse. As Hamlet advises, we 'should suit the action to the word, the word to the action'.

Listen carefully to people who mime and physically bully their way through an argument. Generally their voices stay trapped within a limited register of notes limiting their range.

Their voices may also be trapped in the back of their throats or in their chest, relaying a sentence forwards into the mouth and out into the world. Air is gasped by the mouthful. The jaw and head will jut forwards, limiting breath and sacrificing sound. The speaker will tend to mumble and swallow words. Expression is limited. Words and sentences will neither start firmly nor finish solidly. The speaker will pull back from critical words and resort to cant. Useless and incoherently garbled phrases become fillers in the sentences along with swear-words and repetitions. Language, in fact, merely becomes a punctuation for gestures and not a thing in itself. Without rhyme or reason the speaking quickens or slows, sounding directionless and rootless. Emotions are unclear. Monotony soon enters the communication. This is a grotesque portrait of a speaker who clearly needs the gestures more than the words. This is not communication but the example of someone actually fighting their very need to communicate.

Codes and Code Breaking

Even a very informal survey of an average day's speaking will reveal that most of us speak in codes, and that most of us switch codes dozens of times throughout the day.

We speak a different code to our family – perhaps each member within the family has a special code – than we do to our boss, bank manager, teacher, the ticket collector, or the taxi driver. If we are sensitive and quick with words we can pick up a new code swiftly and use it on the spot. Some codes we can understand to some extent but cannot speak without appearing foolish by exposing our deep ignorance of code words. This happens to me when the talk turns to the economy and words like 'inflation' and 'devaluation' enter the conversation.

Some codes, like jargon, are essential to performing a task: the 'DOS' language used in forming most computer pro-grammes is a code you need to master in order to perform basic keyboard commands. Air traffic controllers bring aircraft in safely through codes; a short-order cook prepares your meal by means of shorthand phrases. The Navaho language was used by the Americans in World War II as a code to stump the enemy. Most codes like this require periods of initiation into their mysteries, the length of which can vary. In new workplaces, for example, we instantly know that we are ignorant of codes that provide a smooth functioning of systems. Within hours or days we find ourselves cracking them and making progress. A medical doctor's codes take years to learn. On top of that transfer to a new hospital may necessitate learning a whole new strand of sub-codes. Codes can be ethnocentric or multicultural, revealing either prejudice or tolerance. Slang words are code words. The ravages of AIDS have brought a whole new batch of medical code words, like 'HIV positive', into everyday usage. We live and die by code words.

There are many layers to breaking codes. Cracking through the first series of barriers can be a painful process. But in modern life we find that the more codes we have the greater our communicating power becomes. It is like mastering different languages. The more sensitive we are to the shifts in language codes, the greater our ability becomes to manipulate systems and people. A school teacher is out of touch if he or she cannot follow the new playground codes. Teachers have to be flexible in their use of codes. They must be able to move towards a student's way of speaking as well as raise the speaker's codes up towards more formal and heightened forms of codes. The best teachers have the unique ability to cross the barriers of codes and mix them with ease and facility.

Many codes are specifically devised by a group of people to keep others out. The world of gangs is full of codes. Secret societies have arcane codes and signs. All of us have had the uncomfortable experience of sitting amongst people who know each other well and are speaking a language we, in theory, understand, but in a code that escapes us.

A code can be between two people or can encompass an entire group or society. Culture is made up of codes that keep one group of people distinct from another. Religion is a kind of code. The elaborated use of any language *should* be decipherable to anyone who has access to a dictionary. But the exact same word, when loaded and coded, can mean different things to different people.

The plea we hear from those who guard the standards in any language is that we need well-written or spoken language so that any educated person can understand it. However, I do think that human beings love the barriers and superiority that codes engender and cannot stop devising them. I suppose the exertion of power would not be possible if everyone spoke the same words on the same level. Codes, as in spy novels, promote ambiguity. They are unsettling. If we only have access to a restricted number of codes then we are barred automatically from the seats of power. On the other hand, if we are not sensitive or caring enough to crack other people's codes then we may be denying ourselves the richer capacity that some codes can introduce into our lives: the codes of connoisseurship, for instance, the finer points of art, music, dance, design or a new sport.

One of the top priorities of the actor's job is to understand the character of a part through the shifting codes of language to be employed. In Shakespeare that may mean understanding why someone shifts from speaking in verse to speaking in prose, but also why so suddenly poetry is needed, or the thoughts lengthen, or new and unusual words are suddenly being spoken, or you are struck silent. The ability to crack a code breaks the silence between you and the character. You begin to have a dialogue with yourself, understand an enormous amount about character, situation and who is in power.

We know where we stand in the pecking order by the codes we use. Some of the most embarrassing moments we have each experienced are those times when we have used the wrong code to the wrong person. Perhaps being too informal with the boss or too formal with an assistant. It is always a fine balancing act getting the code right. The boss who cannot shift his or her code to accommodate employees is never popular. Equally the assistant who thrives on informality finds he doesn't get advancement. Unless we understand and can practise shifting our language codes we will stay stuck in place, never leaving it or enjoying communicating with others from outside our sphere.

The well-publicised breakdown of communication between young and old, parents and children, teachers and pupils is often only an entrenchment of codes on either side – barriers created by words. The gracious communicator – the negotiator familiar with the codes of both sides – will shift or mediate code language, searching for the balance that will harmonise.

The Media and Tabloid Thinking

I think we all have our own various responses to the role which the print and electronic media play in our lives. We are dominated by them, a fact we must come to terms with.

On the one hand, when the media do their jobs well they can enlarge our capacity for words and our appetite for debate. When they abuse our trust and saturate the airwaves with capsule summaries, irresponsible speculation, sound bites, intemperate emotionalism and the frightening assumption that we are incapable of thinking for ourselves, I think their presence in our lives is a genuine barrier.

By their very nature the media can never treat a topic 'in-depth'. They must 'skim' across surfaces, reduce attention span to three-minute parcels, treat the world's ills in a few column inches. In other words, the media shrink our capacity for enduring words. The most riveting TV and radio experiences I can remember have been those where I was engaged in some sort of emotional and intellectual journey. Where questions to an interviewee involved some form of quest.

Where the words were important and not obscured. Where the message was simple and pure.

Yet part of the media's method is to harangue us. We are artificially hyped-up by jargon and the promise of catastrophe. ('Violence fills the city with terror. Full details in the News at Ten.') I think part of the reason some of my students seem filled with excessive emotionalism is that their attachment to the media is so concentrated and dependent. They are full of headlines or what are more appropriately called 'shout lines'.

The media reduce our ability to listen and to concentrate. News junkies need their daily fill of news that within twenty-four hours is stale and has disappeared as an event.

Look at any tabloid paper and read any item. Something terrible is being done to our brains, our intelligence and our use of language.

The headline will generally give you all the information you need. The article will repeat the headline information in different ways. Ideas are never taken forward but repeated *ad nauseam*. Knowledge and facts are related to nothing beyond the headline. If another opinion is given it simply reinforces the original one. This limited and tight spiral is what I call tabloid thinking.

This type of thinking blunts and dulls our ability to think through words, to need appropriate words and to make a journey with language. Let me give you an example. My students like to sit, chat and conspire in a dark little cul-de-sac off the corridor. I like to think they are caring intelligent people who want to discuss issues and be actively involved in debating ways of solving the world's ills. I coined the phrase tabloid thinking recently while I was eavesdropping on a group of them in their warren.

As I passed they were passionately discussing the neo-Nazi movement then on the rise in Europe. They were telling horror stories taken from the day's headlines.

One hour later I passed the same group again. They were still at it, repeating the same headlines, shouting the same phrases. They thought they were discussing issues but all they were doing was parroting captioned phrases and simple anecdotes. They hadn't related any of the issues, background prejudices or beliefs of Nazism to anything outside a limited context. Ideas were not growing, conversation was not enlarging and no conclusions were reached.

When I questioned my students and suggested that they had spent over an hour chasing the same tale round and round, that they had not shifted their thinking forward, introduced new ideas or related their concern to other issues, they sadly agreed. Then one of them said something crucial – one of those statements that shows the influence of the tabloid press. She said that she was frightened of advancing an opposing view for fear of rocking the boat. Tabloid thinking mocks other points of view, abhors dissent. It delights in the simplistic and scorns the complex. Opposition is viewed as apostasy. Might overpowers right. New ideas are not bred but dreaded.

Simple personal anecdotes are crucial when they can illuminate something larger. They are terrific when they can encapsulate a point. But if they are used to stop a discussion dead or reinforce the same point again and again, then they constipate debate and discussion. Tabloid thinking is circular.

Just think about some of the most boring people you know or recall the most tedious evening you spent in the company of others. I bet you felt trapped with people telling anecdotes that went nowhere. Perhaps vaguely interesting or amusing but finally directionless and leading again and again to the same point.

Without substance or growth anecdotes are unconvincing and meaningless. I am not attacking great, urgent stories that contain a wealth of knowledge and experience but motiveless anecdotes that leave us empty and adrift.

It could be true that we cannot happily discuss issues because we are frightened of being mocked. This must link to a growing inability to listen carefully to other points. There seems to be a sense that if we disagree then we are attacking the other person. There are several radio DJs whose main appeal is their aggressive attack and mockery of any idea outside the tabloid norm. So the media reinforce the view. To debate we have to relearn not to be tabloid thinkers but to be genuinely interested in other ideas and listen as they are expressed. We also have to find a joy in learning about new views and then try to connect them to other scenarios and use our imagination to try and understand and not reject alien experiences. Real ignorance, after all, is not having empathy with others and being fearful of new ideas. Any idea or notion outside the realm of the 'normal' antagonises us. Debate is consequently in danger of being quashed. In order to be imaginative with language and ideas we must feel safe and able to explore without being attacked. Our culture's notion, at the moment, seems to be one of isolating anyone expressing new ideas. Sadly we mock them.

Solipsism

One of the barriers that takes hold as we feel more isolated and threatened by words is a rigid solipsism: we are the only ones who exist and our opinion is the only opinion.

Any debate immediately revolves round the equation: 'I think therefore it is; I like it therefore it must be right.' Solipsism is reductionist. It seems that as the world grows in complexity our opinion-making function becomes more simplistic. In debate or discussion the rule of one is in force. No experience outside our own is valid. We are battered with a series of 'I's and 'me's. There is no transforming into the world but a reduction of everything down to 'Wayne's World' in the basement. Rigid boundaries are set and never removed. And the trouble is that the age of solipsism grows younger each year.

For the solipsist words are fixed and unmovable. Ideology of the most unyielding variety is solipsistic. Imaginative curiosity is in danger of being stifled. Shakespeare, for instance, is driven by a passionate curiosity for all things in the world. As soon as he detects a whiff of solipsism in his characters we know they are ripe for enlightenment. Even when life is collapsing round them – as it does for Hamlet or King Lear – Shakespeare's characters widen the scope of their curiosity. Adversity does not make them more closed but defiantly open.

When actors approach a text I've come to notice that they will stress and even bash the personal pronouns and personal adjectives ('I', 'me', 'my', 'mine') even when the stress of the verse is off these words. Their need to assert self is liable to be so strong that they cannot or will not see humility in character; that 'you' or 'your' can be equally valid. This, of course, is Lear's problem; he must learn to tame and temper his 'I's and 'my's. When I correct this stressing flaw I will frequently get glares that say: 'How dare you take my self away.'

Well, solipsism shields us from life and even from great art. I do think that there must be a large measure of personal ego in acting. But the process is also about turning yourself into someone else. You do not hoard the words that establish a personal claim to character ('I speak therefore this is me') but use the words to connect and marry with a new persona ('She [or he] speaks through me').

Solipsism is a danger. It makes us wary of words that do not confirm what we already know, or think we know.

Advertising

Advertisers must take a healthy share of the responsibility for the mistrust we have of language. They see the need for words as a means of creating a greedy need for products. Good adverts seduce us with words. They use all sorts of verbal devices – puns, rhythm, rhyme, jingles, catch phrases – to snare our attention. Their task is to woo and then deceive us through linguistic villainy.

When some of our most powerful words are used to sell trivial things, words take a real battering. A perfume ad uses a famous line from *Julius Caesar*, 'I see that passion is catching', spoken by a Hollywood actress to promote its product. Great literature is appropriated and reduced to slogans. A stunning observation about crowds and politics is reduced to trivia. Language associated with human passion used to promote hair sprays, cars, beer or candy bars steals trust from words. As we search for truth and seek words that will help us communicate a higher need through those words we suddenly find the words have become bankrupt. Poetic language that expresses nothing but the glories of merchandise will leave us cynical to poetry. There is a world of difference between a slogan and a sonnet.

Because a good advert seduces us with wit and, to a greater extent, the promise of sensual pleasure and an eternity of youth and brilliance, it plays on our needs and anxieties. Jacobean plays use language in the same extravagant way, except that there the stakes are so much higher. Seduction has a purpose in the moral plan. It holds a mirror up to nature, showing us our vanity and faults. As we read about the transforming effects of cosmetics we somehow know it isn't true though we wish it were. The language beguiles us but we know it lies. That knowledge erodes our trust in words when they are used on a higher plane.

Power Talk or Don't Talk Back

I have a feeling that once upon a time, when words were needed and debate necessary, dialogue rather than monologue was a dominant mode. When those in power spoke to initiate debate or stimulate discussion, public leaders were like the Chorus leader of ancient Greek tragedy. This does not apply today. Listen to anyone in a position of power pontificate:

religious leaders, political leaders, educationalists, medical experts, pollsters, even cultural dignitaries. The power talker's big message is a barrier: don't talk back.

Listen to television and radio debates or interviews where important issues are being addressed: war in the Balkans, for instance. The experts are unfailing in their expertise. Anyone who assumes knowledge over the rest of us wields it with might. But listen really carefully. It sounds intelligent but do they make sense? Are words being used to further a debate or are they merely self-serving? How many new ideas are introduced into their verbal acreage? How much of what is being said sounds scripted?

What I am suggesting is that as our culture declines verbally we lose the language skills that help us to overcome the barriers of power. Those with power no longer even expect to be challenged by reasoned dissent as they speak. In fact the power speaker, like a good stand-up comedian, uses words to silence dissent and debate. Words that say don't talk back render his audience silent, manipulate and control it. As long as the language sounds compelling and meaningful, it doesn't actually have to say anything. Instead of exciting an audience with words, encouraging them to respond, the power speaker can threaten us into silence. (The underpowered speaker lulls us to sleep.) No longer are words weapons and tools, but threatening units of sound that finally make us impotent. Most of us have sat through meetings as those in power have spent hours saying nothing. In many ways fist-pounding verbal ineffectiveness adds more strength to those in power.

If you manage to say nothing as you speak, how can you be challenged? The challenger has no foot or hand hold to grip in order to enter an altercation. As we become less oral and our listening skills diminish, those who speak to us with authority now can and do speak *at* us, blanketing us with words that smother debate.

Being an optimist I believe we all know when this bluff is

happening. But do we have the confidence to confront it? Power speakers, even when they are witty and mesmerising, have something of the totalitarian about them. I recently worked on a production of Bertolt Brecht's *The Resistible Rise of Arturo Ui*. In the play a rather ridiculous creature – part Adolf Hitler and part Charlie Chaplin – rises to power on the strength of words and verbal bullying. He is one of drama's best power speakers. Brecht's message was clear: as long as we feel inadequate and remain silent the power speakers and not the meek speakers will inherit the earth no matter how ludicrous their message, no matter how big the act. They will continue to speak without meaning, they will force us to turn away and they will seize the advantage over our silence. Part of the strategy of an Arturo Ui is that he does not expect to be challenged. He does not expect back talk.

The Passion-Mongers

When you spend any time in the American South and turn on the television you are faced with a number of religious broadcasting channels fronted by a host of evangelists who can only be called one thing: passion-mongers. They are, in fact, among the most technically proficient and expert speakers you are likely to hear. In an age of political uncertainty the passion-mongers have our ear. Flip to a TV channel anywhere else in the world and you are likely to encounter the ubiquitous talk show hosts stirring secular passions. They, too, feed off our curious desire to be preached to rather than talked with.

The passion-monger throws up a barrier to debate and cool discussion by means of a flood of zeal and emotion. I am not attacking any form of religion when I say this. In fact, as a voice coach I am rather captivated by the commitment and need exhibited by these speakers. What they possess is the theatrical skill to hold an audience. What I do quibble over, however, is the message and the words even while I admire the technique. The listener to these harangues is left defence-less by these speakers in the box. We cannot answer back but passively listen. The might of religious or perceived moral belief is on their side. And their control over their audience grows and grows.

Manipulation is a key ingredient here. We feel and are aroused. But where is the substance? Words are flipped past us like card tricks. The language used, in some cases at least, is the language of charlatans: 'trust', 'belief', 'love' are key words that break down our defences and draw us into passion's powerful web. Where all this leads is usually towards the need for a donation, or to a commercial break.

Passion-mongering has always been a key element in the process of charismatic religions. We know the sway it holds over the Middle East where public loudspeakers are likely to transmit fundamentalist speeches that go on for hours at a time. The words hypnotise and transform us into true believ-ers and followers.

These prompters of passion also come in the guise of high-pressure salespeople, purveyors of lay psychology, and social engineers. A few cogent words and ideas are spun out like a web, catching us in a net of well-tempered phrases. The voice of the passion-monger uses a lot of rising inflections, gradually lifting in pitch. These two vocal tricks alone – extremely effective ones – can quicken pulses and speed-up heartbeats. They rouse the general rabble. The voice works on us physically, urging us to listen and not turn away. As the excitement mounts, the voice can suddenly make us respond, make us believe that we can heal or find hate in our heart for people of a different religion, colour or persuasion. Passion-mongering uses certain other essential tools. It closes off debate, silences discussion. It uses rhetorical and unanswera-ble questions. It quotes statistics and various Good Books. It speaks through smiles and fixes us with a stare. It is always holier than thou.

Anyone who has been in the audience of a passion-monger

will know just how weak is the barrier of resistance, how frail we are when it comes to challenging. You risk being pilloried by the converted. As the spell takes effect and the hype intensifies, we begin to mistake gross sentimentality for genuine sentiment, untruths for truth. The trump card for the passion-monger is winning our trust. With our defences down we are swayed. The passion-monger says 'come follow me' and we do. We go because the need of the speaker compels us.

But do we always remember what was said in a fit, a dream of passion? Not always. In fact, compare this kind of speaking with a sermon by John Donne or Martin Luther King. They arouse passions as well but through clearly articulated words we can still read, say and be moved by. The words logically pursue a connection. Donne's and King's view of freedom is free will and free debate, not mindless passion and reasonless devotion. The sermon is used to make wide references in the same way as a Shakespeare sonnet sets frames within frames. They offer the listener a choice. The true prophet is both an advocate and an innovator with words. We need them not because they arouse passion alone but because they fire us with passionate thought.

Sentimentality

Despite all the harsh words that exist in the world today and all the dismissive attitudes we pronounce with words, nothing we do can ever smother the language of sentimentality.

We gush with feeling at the slightest cause, provoked by advertising and media. The words we often use with each other are like a vial of artificial tears: sentimental mutterings not moored to any strong intent. The danger of sentimentality is that it is a barrier to genuine feeling. It blocks the need to speak because it is so unauthentic. We carry with us a host of caring words and phrases that coat and dull real expressions of pain, rage, joy and delight. Sentimentality also masks our violence and satisfies our sense that we should be feeling something but not too intensely. It is as though we can talk with some feeling, feign instant familiarity without looking at the true intentions and beliefs behind the word. The roundly mocked American phrase, 'Have a nice day!', are words used aimlessly and unconvincingly.

To speak convincingly we have to dare to know a word and make contact with it throughout our bodies and breath. What do I mean by 'know'? I am not talking about knowing the word from the dictionary but intuiting the word through a connection to our emotional life and sensual being. The intriguing thing about needing words is that they make rivulets and bridges between head and heart. Great texts reinforce that connection. Take a sentimental word like 'love', much used and abused. Even before we have experienced the feeling (usually sprung at too quickly in an urge to be falsely sentimental) we have to convince ourselves of the sound: LOVE – (LUV) – LOOOVVVE. The deeper resonances of the sound must take on meaning. Then the sound may be attached to an image: 'My love is like a red, red rose.' Not just any flower or any rose but a *red, red* rose. LOVE and ROSE share an intimate connection through the *red, red*. They are also very strong words too often portrayed as clichés. We begin to take the image in and it inhabits us and grows. As this movement away from sentimentality and towards connection takes place, we test the word and image in the context of an intelligent statement totally devoid of all sentiment, as in Shakespeare's Sonnet 116:

'Love is not love/Which alters when it alteration finds.'

To speak this line we are forced to confront what love isn't. It isn't fickle, conditional or changeable. It does not vary when it finds that circumstances alter. The sound of the sentence is anchored and secure. It defeats sentimentality by being grave. If you substitute a word like 'earth' for 'love' you signal the weight of the thought even more strongly. This 'love' is a strong love not given to retreat. Love need not be sentimental.

By definition a great actor is one who knows, needs and connects to every word without resorting to artificial sentiment. Let the word anchor you first and compel you in the right way. If it touches a shallow feeling that will instantly tell you something about the word's slight capacity. But if it strikes a bottomless, complex emotion the word is telling you it has a value beyond that of superficial sentiment.

I'd recommend we start looking at all words in this way.

Fillers and Clichés

Fillers are when our words do little more than obstruct meaning. These are those words, phrases, sentences, bits of conversational refrains and sounds that fill out silences but have no communication value whatsoever. They are what we say when we are trying desperately hard to think of what really to say. This used to be politely called 'small talk'. It is very small indeed.

When the active use of a word or phrase dies and enters the realm of the cliché it becomes a filler; a kind of block we use to fill a blank. Language used in this way is just on the borderline of survival. There is nothing vivid or vital about a filler. It is language held in bondage, language just serving time and waiting for something better to say. It is also language at its most boring and vapid.

Cliché literally means a 'stereotype', a word or phrase which has lost its original meaning through frequent overuse. But what fun it is to be suddenly confronted by the origin of a phrase which has become a cliché. How wonderful to discover the phrase freshly. Take 'pecking order' for instance. I was watching free-ranging chickens in a Portuguese village once. As they grubbed around for food, the pecking order soon became apparent. There was one hen, in particular, who pecked the most, even pecking the other hens. Then there was another who always lost out. The cliché was renewed for me: first and last in the pecking order.

We easily forget that fillers and clichés may originally have been bold, new words. My dear Northumberland Nanna patiently tolerated my enthusiastic discovery of *Hamlet* when I was twelve. She did not know the play and I, patronisingly, thought I would educate her by reading out the best bits.

I intoned Polonius' line, 'There's method in his madness.'

Nanna interrupted. 'I don't think this Shakespeare is that good.'

I was horrified. 'He's the greatest writer, ever!' I yelled.

'I've been saying that phrase all my life and my mother said it before me,' was her reply.

Stunned, I shouted, 'You only say it because he wrote it.'

Quick as a flash she came back at me, 'He only wrote it because we said it!'

She may have been right.

Sexual Politics

I don't think there is anyone of either sex who has not come up against the barrier of words in the context of sexual politics. More and more in the later phases of this century the sexes define and proclaim themselves through different kinds of words. Hard on the heels of feminism has come both a backlash against it and even a new 'maleism'. As you can imagine, new words to describe the old sexual battle are being coined all the time: 'male bonding', 'female tribalism'. Each sexual persona has its own identikit in terms of language; even the middle ground where the sexes blur and cross-over has its own curious transcription. For the field of words these are enticing predicaments.

Women have traditionally been the listeners and supporters in discussion with men. Younger female employees will frequently play out this role with male employers, making supporting noises and comforting head movements of acknowledgement. Words will be few. Women, by and large, have not been expected to develop an idea but only to expand on ideas pronounced by men.

Feminism, though, as philosophy and means of liberation, has spawned a vocabulary which has taunted and made suspect the male vocabulary imposed on women. A new anger entered women's once placid voices, but also pride and individuality. Female actors, for instance, are every bit as fierce and powerful today as their male colleagues. They train in the same way and reach the same vocal peaks. Equality, of sorts, has been won by women, including the right to use and need words in unblushing ways. Female performers like Madonna do not blush. They frankly speak what is on their mind in spite of who might be listening.

Do men and women need words differently? I'm really not sure about this. I do know that I teach text work to both sexes in precisely the same manner. But one thing I have begun to notice is the way that women are just now beginning to exhibit male voice problems. Powerful women tend to push their voices more nowadays, clamping down on words and hurling them at a listener. Their ability to listen, once a positive characteristic, is showing signs of deteriorating. Even less powerful women are becoming vocally committed to debating but easily become shrill or emotionally unable to make sense. I do know that women are breaking out more with words, firing them in rapid rhythm in ways that only men used to do. But in the process of accelerated change they are quickly acquiring and absorbing male language and all its defects.

Men, on the other hand, who once had trouble hesitating and showing vulnerability in debate, found emotional words hard to speak and disdained feeling when approaching words are suddenly exhibiting all the unbounded passion which was once the domain of women. I shouldn't think it will be too long before we see men more commonly playing Electra and Medea in the way we have seen women playing Hamlet and King Lear! As the barriers between the sexes undergo significant shifts in ground, gender attachment to words is criss-crossing at an even greater velocity. I do see this as a healthy sign of language's dynamism and ability to be non-discriminatory.

Political Correctness

We certainly live in an age where words have lost their innocence. We have reached a stage where 'political correctness', or PC, sends shivers down our spine when a certain kind of language is used openly and publicly.

During the past two decades, as minority groups have assumed their greater share of both rights and power within the mainstream establishment, the way words have been used and abused has become an increasing cause for concern and alarm. Issues of gender, race and sexual affinity are all deeply tagged by the words we say. The meaning of these words may not be so significant if we are 'normal, healthy, white, Anglo-Saxon, Protestant, educated, employed, middle-class, heterosexual males'. Those in power can always afford to use words casually and carelessly; some might say recklessly. But those excluded from this privileged realm can rightly take a very different attitude. They can feel offended.

Words can and do oppress. The whole debate about politically correct speech has admittedly been taken sometimes to comic extremes ('herstory' for 'history', 'the vertically challenged' for someone short), especially in North America where dictionaries of proper usage have appeared. But discussion of words by means of PC has at least exposed a language barrier we have all suffered from in some way. How subliminally powerful words and names can be! The history of oppression is often told by the signification of certain words: 'nigger', 'kike', 'wog', 'queer', 'dyke'. These words not only carry a frightening history of oppression, a legacy of pain, but they are often ugly and deeply unpleasant words to say. They fill the mouth with grim distaste.

If the whole issue of PC words has done anything it has made us stop and think before we speak. It has also unleashed in some quarters, like the world of academia, pent-up rage and fury; a healthy usurpation of power roles typically reserved for certain classes. PC arms the oppressed with a powerful weapon of identification. How that weapon is used becomes a more urgent issue. The concept of PC can normalise and equalise imbalances within the culture of words, but it can also become an inquisitorial tool to root out enemies. It is, after all, correctness with a political slant. One of the great sadnesses about the barriers that words impose is that breaching the wall does not always lead to freedom but to just a different sort of oppression.

I recognise politically correct speech as a potential enhancement and recognition of other people's rights. But that means that our naming and tagging of others must be just and fair.

RP or Not RP

One of the major barriers that many speakers encounter is the choice of accent. Accent correctness is a barrier we often come up against. The professional speaker or actor, for instance, must eventually come to terms with Received Pronunciation (RP) or what is variously termed Standard English.

What is RP? In Great Britain it is a term we give to a standardised pronunciation of British English based on educated speech in southern England. All variants of English (including forms of the language spoken in the United States, Canada, Australia, South Africa and elsewhere round the world) strive for standard, consistent phonetic sounds. So what have evolved as derivatives of RP in each part of the world are such forms as Standard American, Standard Black English, Standard Canadian, even such variants as Standard Caribbean and Standard Intenational English. With so many varieties can there be one 'standard' form of English? It clearly depends on where you come from and how rigidly you interpret phonetic strictures.

One of the great barriers to speaking in public and to speaking the great classical texts is a fear of RP. There are so many misconceptions surrounding this accent, so many competing opinions. Let's explore a few. In actual fact, speaking RP should result in your speaking a neutral accent that reveals neither the class nor background of the speaker except that you have learned RP. A clear, well-defined and energised variant of spoken English is usually the result.

The British royal family and aristocracy do *not* speak RP but versions of high-status, conservative accents which are often unclear, incomprehensible and badly defined. We all imitate this 'snob speak' in jest and frequently mistake it for RP. These are, in fact, habitual modes of speaking, both highly affected and artificial which clutter the basic sound of accent. Speaking RP does not necessarily mean you are trying to sound posh. That is a different subject altogether: one that should fall under the heading of vocal masks.

Only a small percentage of the British population naturally speak RP. Those who do have probably originally learned it for any one of the following reasons: education at a public school where numerous variants of RP are spoken (for 'public' read 'private' in the USA); the speaker has been brought up in a middle- or upper-middle-class, university-educated family based in the south of England; or the speaker's parents are actors! RP's southern English bias revolves round London, the seat of power since the eleventh century.

Like all accents, urban and regional, RP is constantly changing. The sound of it is always on the move. You can classify shifts in the accent just about every decade. So it is possible to detect an RP as spoken during the 1920s that differs from the RP of the 1950s or today. I am not certain what the 1990 version is yet, but certain sounds like 'ju' as in d*u*ke and t*u*ne and 'ua' as in p*oo*r, s*u*re, m*oo*r are disappearing and transforming to pɔ:, ʃɔ:, mɔ:.

This fluid change in accent is important to remember, especially when RP is taught. Some teachers teach the accent too rigidly, chiselling the sound into a student's voice like cuts into granite. Consequently I hear young children, who are very well educated, speaking a 1940 or 1950 version of RP and sounding alarmingly quaint. It is their teacher's accent coming through their voice; frequently a danger when learning RP. It is, after all, passed from mouth to mouth. In North America I have heard actors speaking equally dated versions of British RP that would be laughed off the London stage unless used in a period play. So two of the hazards of RP are that it can sound dated or be taught or transmitted poorly.

It also has to be said that nobody speaks a perfect form of RP, and as we become emotionally engaged or excited our pronunciation of the accent slips radically. And if in such fervent moments it doesn't, then we are not feeling the need to speak naturally and without inhibition. RP can clamp a feeling if adhered to with too much exactness.

We can usually identify a non-English speaker if his or her accent sounds too perfect. A rigidly taught RP can sound unnatural. Quite alien, really. We must allow life experiences to colour and touch our voices. RP can sound like a voice controlled.

An educational debate swirls round the teaching of RP in schools, an effort to create a more widespread, educated accent for the general populace. If RP does carry such power and influence over regional accents, then perhaps we should all learn it to dupe the very system that supports RP.

Amongst many younger British actors today the requirement to speak RP can induce responses of rage and fear. I understand this anger. For many years RP has been taught in British drama schools from entirely the wrong perspective. It has been taught as an elitist accent which a student *must* learn and master as the 'proper' and only way to speak. A lot of our trouble with RP stems from this kind of dictating. This attitude naturally negates and makes other accents seem inferior.

Personally I think it an act of violation of any speaker's right to tell them that their mother accent is not good enough to speak the great texts, especially when common sense tells us that Shakespeare's actors did not speak his texts in RP but in their own mother accents, which were rougher and thicker by today's standards. On this point alone the argument for and against RP rages and rages.

Every day, on whatever side of the Atlantic I happen to be, I come across actors who sound frigid and disconnected from their voices. They have learned to speak RP (sometimes against their will) but sound unnatural. Investigate their voice training and the horror stories emerge. 'I was told my accent was ugly and lower class and that from now on I was only to speak RP.' This is an instance of RP being embraced for all the wrong reasons. Perhaps the speech sounds are clear but not connected to the voice. Here is an instance where the voice is actually rejecting the accent because it creates a barrier.

A sound fastened onto the speaker from the outside can be damaging. At its worst this vocal enslavement can obliterate the speaker's imaginative response to language and words, and encourage an emotional disconnection through the voice. The need for a word is short-circuited by a greater need for an accent. Speech teachers seeking an elitist ideal often fail to recognise the implications of cutting a voice off from its expressive roots. Any voice or speech teacher who thwarts, neutralises or ridicules a student's mother sound plays a very dangerous game. Do any of us have the right to oppress another human being's background, family, class or culture? I think not.

RP Is a Choice

Teach or learn RP as a choice, as an accent that can exist and flourish alongside other native accents. It is a useful accent for any speaker – particularly actors – to have; one of an arsenal of different vocal tools. I, for instance, will lapse into RP if I am speaking before a group because it gives my words clarity. And clarity is, perhaps, the chief reason for using RP. Everyone tends to understand me better. RP is an excellent tool for lecturing.

RP is so clear an accent because it is placed very far forward in the face. Vowel and consonant sounds are not lost. The consonants define the word and the vowels launch the sound into the world. These factors make it an ideal accent to support in space.

British actors need RP for commercial reasons. Its acquirement improves their work opportunities (as does keeping their mother accent!). The major theatre companies and broadcasting outlets in Britain still like to employ actors for classical roles who can speak RP effortlessly. In a large theatre especially it can be heard very easily because it directs communication better. This once rigid attitude is relaxing as more and more TV and broadcasting companies, which have traditionally demanded RP, do more regional programming with films and series set far away from London. (In North America I don't think the demand for RP has ever been as strong as it is here in Britain.) Nowadays I wouldn't be serving my students' best interests for employment if I didn't teach them RP. But that could change.

RP is also an accent understood by all English speakers throughout the world. Many regional accents are not. RP is easier for the listener to decipher. Physically efficient when spoken, RP marries well with the microphone. It is the accent you hear most often on BBC newscasts, though most informal 'chat' shows tend to avoid it. In fact, I think radio and television – more than the stage – have done a great deal to increase the appetite for RP. We prefer to listen to it as a sound for the transmission of complex ideas. We tend to 'trust' a speaker who uses this accent (though there is no reason why we should).

Choice remains the key word in my mind when it comes to

speaking RP. I must always recognise that learning RP can be excruciatingly painful for some speakers. It might mean taking on the sound of their historic oppressors. For instance, Irish- or Welsh-speaking students have centuries of aversion to encounter as they mouth RP. The same is true for non-white speakers. In parts of the world where speech accents are a battleground, speaking RP can raise a red flag. So RP can lead to vocal schizophrenia. Choose to use it when you must.

Bearing all these provisos in mind let me finally link RP to the whole voice and maybe offer a proper perspective on the accent. When the voice is supported, free, resonating with balance and allowed to leave the body – not contained within it – then RP is a minute shift away from any native accent. It ought not to complicate the need for a word but enhance it.

When you carry that free position of natural speech into the world – sustaining and moving the sound always forward, finishing each word out of you (not dropping syllables or clipping sounds but voicing the complete word), maintaining a full vocal energy on the breath and using the consonants to cleanly define the vowels and words – then you will find that 80 to 90 per cent of RP sounds are in place. Some clearing-up might have to be done among vowels, consonants, rhythms, and stresses, but the accent is there in essence. Remember the times you have heard a well-produced voice in a theatre? Well, chances are, even if the actor was not attempting strict RP, the accent was closer to it than to the actor's everyday accent.

RP, well taught and sensitively urged from the speaker, is a dynamic, energised and clear way of speaking. It aids the clear communication of any text or any speaker's thoughts and feelings. As we liberate our sometimes rigid and suspicious views about RP, we can teach and learn a dynamic, energised and *clear* way of speaking that contains all the richness of other accents and dialects. RP can and should always suit the speaker's unique vocal personality. That must be the rule of thumb for its use.

The flavour of all accents can be contained in good clear speech. RP is not the only way. Although there are movements to free the British from RP snobbery, we still have a long way to go. Many educators would like to make the speaking of RP a school requirement. Contemporary Shakespearean productions, spoken in different accents even when the speaking is clear and the verse structure respected, are still derided. Somehow we have to educate RP speakers to listen to other accents without immediately feeling superior as they listen.

RP should be thought of as one tool but not the voice's only accent. If it is natural and comfortable for you (and it is for many) the need to speak RP will be as great as that of the native accent you were born with.

National Boundaries

The attachments each of us has as a nation to words and their rhythms can turn speaking into a territorial issue with very restricted boundaries.

My non-English friends who come from cultures where ideas are exchanged more fiercely are continually bemused by the British habit of 'indirection'. Confrontation is avoided. Debate is diverted. Words are used as delaying tactics. What we do have is politeness, charm and irony – each one a means used to deflect serious issues and drift away from real need. In fact, we have created a whole wealth of literature that breeds these characteristics in abundance. We are so skilled with words, so verbal that communication is often like a well-articulated mist that wafts over us but says nothing. I have often thought that our inability to be direct and blunt, especially when it is too late, has been part of the reason why we tend to fall out with other nations. We will not commit ourselves to words fully. It may also explain why we think other cultures are crude and too straightforward. George Bernard Shaw said, for instance, that England and America were two nations divided by a common language. Witty, wise and true. But also, like we British, a bit stand-offish.

As a child living in an English household forever being visited by waves of Dutch relatives, I would listen with keen curiosity as misunderstandings were aggravated simply by opposing attitudes to words. The Dutch aunts and uncles never seemed to know 'how to behave' according to us. The English side of the family was shocked, for instance, by the blunt and 'rude' replies of the Dutch. English question: 'Did you enjoy your meal?' Dutch answer: 'Nah!' My mother was often at her wit's end when faced with 'no compromise' replies like this. The Dutch just were not interested in politeness for its own sake. As Britain heads into Europe's embrace in the next century you will frequently hear the many ways in which our words and theirs are simply not on the same channel.

It is entirely fair to say that boldness and directness are a regional difference (though I will be accused of making generalisations). Plain-speaking northerners from Yorkshire or Scotland have never been quite trusted in the south of England and vice versa. Celtic races can easily out-talk Anglo-Saxons. Just listen to the level of talk in a Dublin pub as opposed to a London one. In Dublin you are surrounded by words, feasted by them, but in London you can feel isolated and even quite starved. In America quick-talking northerners with their fancy words are still an object of distrust by many southerners and westerners.

The fact that language and words separate according to race and colour goes without saying. You could say, moreover, these north–south/east–west divides are true in every country and part of the world. Dialect means that some variegated countries will always be in some constant state of opposition and tension, as between the parts that make up India. I'm sure that neighbouring nations in the Far East have a distrust of each other's words. Both languages and dialects drive us apart.

Though this subject is far beyond the scope of this book, I

think we would all agree that language and dialect – one culture's association to words battling with that of another – has aided in the kind of tense linguistic 'balkanisation' we are currently witnessing in Northern Ireland, Belgium, Canada, South Africa, reunified Germany, the 'free' states of the former Soviet Union and, sadly, the Balkan countries themselves. Make no mistake about it: language, choice of words and particularly accent can trace contentious lines of battle. Hate and nationalism need words just as much as conciliation and diplomacy do.

The corruption of one nation's language by that of another is always a combative issue. The blending of French with words taken directly from English (e.g. *le drugstore* rather than *la pharmacie*) is a serious issue in France and also French-speaking Canada. It points, in fact, to the real culprit at the root of the problem: the tendency of English to reign as the supreme language round the world. English is, as we know, the language in which most commerce is conducted. It is even the language with which air-traffic controllers guide people from around the globe to their final destinations. English is the new imperial language. Like all imperialistic gestures it is subject to revolts in attitudes.

Overcoming the Speech Barrier

If we are ever to fill our speech with a greater need for words we must consciously recognise that barriers of all sorts do stand in our way. They are part of the inbred traditions of a language and the deep-seated traditions of our culture. It takes, I always say, lots of courage to use words fearlessly, to know them and to trust them. As long as language is in peril we will always feel that speaking is a daunting task. And using words freely is, I think, one of our greatest freedoms.

We simply have to learn how to overcome the speech barrier and start to find a new voice. And once having found it connect it with the word.

Part Two
VOICE AND THE TEXT

Your monument shall be my gentle verse,
Which eyes not yet created shall o'er-read;
And tongues to be your being shall rehearse,
When all the breathers of this world are dead;
You still shall live, – such virtue hath my pen, –
Where breath most breathes, – even in the mouths of men.

Shakespeare
from Sonnet 81

4 Finding a Voice

Releasing Physical Barriers

In order to fully experience the need for words and begin connecting voice and the text, we often have to get past all the physical barriers that constrain the voice as it attempts to make contact with words.

A simple voice preparation is a good place to start. These are exercises that help put you in contact with speaking needs.

You first have to find your voice before you can begin to work with it. By 'find' I mean physically getting in touch with the voice and the sounds it can make. The poet Yeats called poetry 'a mouthful of air'. Any speaking we do is based on the same premise: we breathe the words out of us. The act of speaking is also a breathing act. Confidence with words often begins with experiencing just how much you can do with breath – that mouthful of air which forms words.

Clear connection with words will always remain difficult if any aspect of the body, breath, voice and speech is blocked, barricading sound within us. Sound must escape easily. We might have a burning desire to communicate expressively, but if the physical voice is blocked then our inner voice simply will not be able to fight its way free and release itself.

Getting 'In Voice'

We want to be 'in voice' each time we speak words, especially if we speak them on an extended basis. Many actors, for instance, will say they are 'in the part' when what they are doing, thinking and *saying* as the character all become one connected means of expression. When an actor reaches that point in a performance his or her voice is usually working freely and easily. The needs of a role, together with the compulsion of a motivated action, have freed the voice. The voice now acts in concert with your ideas and intentions as a speaker. This is a classic example of motivation – our inner need – carrying the voice outwards. But this formula doesn't always work. You may feel so right inside and yet the voice comes out sounding all wrong.

So what can we do to find our voice?

As a voice coach I naturally prefer to get the voice warmed and working so that the need for words can be immediately and physically realised in the speaking act after it is first experienced as an impulse. My aim with any actor or speaker is first to free the voice so that it is supported, placed and flexible throughout any speech activity. In other words, your voice must be primed to respond effortlessly. Once that is accomplished, the voice is ready to range anywhere and fully reflect your thoughts and feelings and, in the case of actors and public speakers, the specific demands of an extended text. Essentially, the speaker has to become the vessel for the text.

Focal Points

Let's begin by focusing on the key physical components of good voice work:

- *Body*   Speaking is a physical activity. The breath, voice and speech are generated and powered by the body. If there is unnecessary tension locked in the shoulders, neck, jaw, spine, ribcage, stomach, legs, knees and feet then full vocal release is very difficult to achieve. Correct posture and centring the body are all part of the speaking act. Physically, you should feel a need and readiness to speak; be ready to put actions into words.

- *Breath* Breathing should be free flowing and full at all times when we speak. The breath powers and supports the voice like wind does a sail. Breath is the guiding energy. But breath also connects us to our emotional and intellectual right to speak. Remember that breath has the capacity to either block or release any kind of trauma. Any holds in the breath can cut us off from fully experiencing a word. At all times in the speaking act we need to be able to breathe the word, the thought, the feeling. Connection with the breath is vital.
- *Voice* Once set loose by the breath the voice should be free: neither held in the throat nor locked behind the jaw. By its very nature a voice is open. It must remain relaxed. Any physical constraint in any area that affects the voice needs relaxation, too, so the voice can rise through the chest, throat and mouth to bubble out of us. A word, once connected to, must leave the body effortlessly, not struggle to be free. It should bob off into space as lightly as a mouthful of air gently exhaled.
- *Speech* The muscles we use in the speaking act should clearly, efficiently and economically articulate vowels and consonants, constructing words out of raw sounds. Never confuse this with artificial means of elocution. Speech forms words, kneading them into shape. It is a natural process that we can always improve upon and make more efficient regardless of what accent or dialect we choose to employ in speaking.

Simple Voice Workout

What follows is an abbreviated vocal workout that should help you prepare for speaking in such a way that every word sounds apt and needed. What you are trying to do here is join up body, breath, voice and speech into one efficient chain reaction. One element needs and depends on the others for support.

These exercises address some of our most nagging voice and speech habits. You will find these same exercises in much greater detail in 'The Voice Workout' section of *The Right to Speak: Working with the Voice*. What I shall give you here is a version of that scheme.

Always remember that the emphasis in these warm-up exercises is on relaxation. They are *not* designed to keep you fit but to release tension, the principal barrier to voice and speech. The action in all these exercises should be gentle and massaging.

Never work to the point of discomfort. Never exert too hard.

1. Preparing the Body

- Take a centred position. Stand comfortably, feet slightly apart though not spread too wide. Your feet should be parallel to one another and directly under your hips, efficiently supporting your body weight. Feel rooted to the ground. Feel in touch with it for the purposes of support. Working barefoot is best. Avoid shoes with heels that angle you to the earth or athletic shoes that cushion you from the earth.
- Looking straight ahead, fix your eyes on a distant point just above the horizon. Relax.
- Let your neck and shoulder muscles just drop naturally into place, relaxing any bunched-up or hunched tension. The neck and shoulders are a prime area of tension. Just dropping them should yield instant relaxation. Neither stand rigidly 'at attention' nor allow your spine to slump. You should feel comfortably upright and relaxed.
- Start releasing tension around the shoulders, neck, upper chest and facial muscles. After each of the following exercises it is important to allow the part of the body you have just worked to find its own placing. You'll know when this has happened because excess tension will disappear. The part will feel relaxed. So neither control nor place muscles. It is equally important to breathe easily and calmly throughout these exercises. Never force anything.

  Follow this sequence:

  – Circle the shoulders around. Release.
  – Swing each arm like a water wheel and let it drop back into place at your side.
  – Lift and drop the shoulders until they fall into place naturally.

- Gently allow your head to drop onto the chest and massage the back of your neck.
- With the head still down, gently swing the head back and forth across the chest. Let the weight of the head do the work and not excess force. Be careful not to wrench your neck needlessly.
- Keep the jaw free and unclenched.
- Drop the head onto the chest and then allow its weight to flop the whole torso over from the waist. As you flop over neither lock your knees nor strain your back. Tension will signal if you are pushing too hard.
- Once flopped over, shake the shoulders out and try to release the neck. Spend a few seconds in this flopped over position and then slowly come up through the spine, gently, to standing. The head should be the last thing to find its place.
- Once back to the centred position neither place the shoulders nor heave up the upper chest as though 'at attention'. Keep the chest open and neither tightened nor lifted. Keep the spine flexible, neither rigid nor slumped.
- Gently massage all your facial muscles.
- Bunch up the face then release.
- Stretch the mouth open and then release.
- Gently rotate the jaw.
- Smile, and keeping the smile in place, open the jaw.

A few repetitions of these exercises will help you to poise and centre your body and free the muscles that help the voice transmit speech.

Any time you approach speaking and feel tension in the body, stop and try all or even just some of these exercises. They will help you to prepare for free and invigorating speech. The voice cannot work properly if blocked by useless physical tension. I know I keep saying this like a refrain but it is critical. In fact, you work against free speech if any form of useless tension is present. Useless tension cuts off need. It's amazing how eager the need to speak becomes when the voice learns to work from a relaxed position. This really is one of the secrets of a successful voice. Practically all of us 'tense up' and become rigid when we speak – especially in public or on-stage. Next time, just relax and instantly notice the difference. Breathe in and breathe out in a regular pattern. Never suck in breath and hold it inside yourself. That throws off rhythm. Throughout these exercises, and any others you try to release your voice, remember that relaxation is the first step to finding a voice.

2. Preparing the Breath

The aim here is to drop the breath as low as possible into the body so that it can be as free as possible. A deep natural breath will effortlessly power the voice and propel words into space with greater force and ease. Most of us speak on short sprints of breath, bursts of power. For brief units of speaking this may be satisfactory but not for the longer intervals needed, for instance, to act a stage role or deliver a lecture.

The lower we breathe, as we connect to words, the greater an emotional satisfaction we experience in the spoken words themselves. Breathe deeper and deeper, lowering the breath down into the groin. As you do so intone: *mah, may, me, may*. You'll both hear and experience the sounds becoming richer and more meaningful as deep breathing begins to help voice the sound.

How do we get to the lower breath? Try the following sequence:

- First get the body centred and aligned as you did above ('Preparing the Body'). Remember never to lift the shoulders or the upper chest while breathing. This blocks the free passage of breath. Take all the time you need to breathe. Sense a nice, steady rhythm. Don't rush or snatch breath. Intake and exhalation should be natural and steady, lengthening and becoming stronger with each breath. Concentrate on the breath.
- While standing centred, flop over to one side. Breathe. Feel the ribcage on that side open.
- Repeat on the other side. Return to centre.

- Gently hug yourself across the chest. Keep the arms snug but loose, your hands reaching back towards your shoulder blades. Breathe deeply.
- While in the hug, flop over gently from the waist. Knees unlocked. Breathe. You should begin to feel the back ribcage open. Let your arms drop down towards the ground and come up slowly until the head tops out the spine.
- Standing centred and breathing, try to feel the sensation of the back opening. This is the breath reaching deep into areas we usually block it from touching.
- Get onto your hands and knees. Head down, neck released. Breathe in and out, allowing your stomach muscles to release. When you return to standing centred you should feel that your breath releases lower and deeper into your groin. For extended speaking and a heightened use of words this is the deep source of breath.
- Standing centred, eyes looking to a point on the horizon, breathe in and release on an 's' sound: *sssss*. When you feel the breath is no longer comfortably underneath the sound supporting it (or you are 'out of breath') recover the breath. Repeat this three or four times.
- Press gently on the diaphragm (just around the midriff) without tightening the stomach muscles: repeat the sounds *ha, ha, ha; he, he, he; ho, ho, ho*. You will actually begin to feel the inner breath pressing against your hand. Keep repeating the sounds until the sensation is steady, lasting and confident. Drop your hand and come back to centre.
- Now connect the breath to your voice. Sigh out, feeling the breath muscles working the ribs, diaphragm and stomach underneath the sound. Next count, feeling the same connection: *1* breathe; *1,2* breathe; *1,2,3* breathe, up to a count of *10*.
- Immediately speak any text that comes into your head, no matter how mindless or improvised, feeling the same breath connection and support as above. Speak in short units and then in longer and longer units on a single support of breath.

3. Preparing the Voice

Never push the voice. Never force your voice to do more than it can. You should feel neither strain nor overwork in the throat. Vocalisation should always feel effortless. Your breath should be powering your voice, *not* your throat muscles. This is a crucial fact to remember. Consequently always keep relaxed around the jaw and shoulders: the first place where tension is sure to surface.

Try the following:

- Yawn and while yawning gently begin to speak. The speaking should feel effortless and without tension.
- Lightly hum. Hum any note but keep the feeling of the yawn in your throat as you do this. Your throat will feel more open and relaxed. Do this for a minimum of two sustained minutes at least. If your jaw and shoulders are relaxed you'll notice quite a difference in the length and strength of the sound.
- Fix your eyes on a point straight ahead and just above the horizon. As you hum down through your range 'think' your energy *up* to that point on the horizon. You'll feel the voice being sent out in an arc. Neither slump your body nor let your voice drop.
- Once you feel your voice 'starting' more easily and warming, begin to try and 'place' the voice forward on a hum or an 'oo'. You should feel the sound vibrating on the lips.
- Hum into your head. Then into the nose, face, throat and chest. Move the voice freely around these areas, from one to the other.
- Intone or chant some texts or sounds. From this exercise take yourself into normal speaking.
- 'Hmm' or 'ha' up and down through all your range. Now speak on the various notes.
- Remember, never push or force the voice. Get to notice its strengths in various registers.

4. Preparing the Speech Muscles

Lips, tongue, jaw, soft palette all aid in the articulation of sound. For clear speech these muscles must work effectively.

Here are some routines to practise:

- Move the lips in all sort of ways. Push them forwards, stretch them back. Pucker them. Blow through them.

- Stretch the tongue in and out of your mouth, down over your chin.
- Work the soft palette (the soft fleshy area above the back of your throat). Say the phonetic sounds *k*, *g*, *ng* which will exercise the back of the palette.

Do all these next exercises quickly and lightly.

- Repeat these sounds: *bah, bah, bah; dah, dah, dah; lah, lah, lah; gah, gah, gah.*
- Repeat these sounds: *the, the, the; ra, ra, ra; mah, mah, mah; vah, vah, vah.*
- Exaggerate vowel sounds before coming back to speaking them normally. At this point you should try to feel the sounds as far forward in the face as possible: Phonetically repeat the sounds *OH, OU, OI.*

5 Voice into Text

Connecting to a Text

I believe that as you unlock a great oral text in the act of speaking it, you instantly connect across time to the writer writing the words onto paper. At least that is a sensation I would like you to begin experiencing.

This is not a mystical notion but a way of arousing a practical partnership between you and the writer of the text. I feel, for instance, that you collaborate with Shakespeare when you speak his texts. You complete his job for him and in a new key through your voice and the act of speaking his words aloud. You begin to know and appreciate the written cues he gives you that are there for the voice. You begin to breathe at the same points as the writer, your heart beats with his or her rhythm, you imaginatively move with the writer across time and space. This familiarity between you and the writer makes the speaking of a text a great comfort. Suddenly all trepidation evaporates as you fulfil your part of the compact by needing the text, by making a vital connection with it.

When a speaker needs and connects to a text in a genuine way you continually sense an invisible, harmonious thread stretching between writer and speaker. Time instantly collapses and the word lives again in a timeless zone. It breathes, exists in space. The speaker becomes the writer's vessel just as the writer is a vessel of other unseen creative forces. The greatest writers, the ones who endure over centuries, are like messengers of a huge universal consciousness and the speaker must serve the needs of such texts with particular care. Investing speaking with that kind of importance makes the act more compelling.

Following from this point of union between speaker and writer, there will be another one between speaker and audience: a perfect triangle of communication eventually forms with the word 'need' labelling each apex. When this connection is made, then we have achieved the need for words. All points of the triangle achieve measured satisfaction and harmony.

Experimenting with Language

It is crucial for everyone to experiment with language aloud, in all its myriad forms and structures, as often and in as many ways as possible. We have to feel words on our lips and then see the reactions they can have on others.

To that end it is extremely useful to discover how we use language, to find out what language tools we have at our own disposal, as a step towards speaking other people's words. By understanding how we can use words effectively, how we can be brave with words, we can uncover voice clues in a formal text more easily. These voice cues help our interpretation in ways that are more immediate than intellectual means.

Sounding Real

The job of a professional speaker – actor, lecturer, broadcaster, lawyer, politician, teacher, salesperson – is to make every text they speak sound authentically their own, to make it sound *real*. I often think that sounding 'sincere' is more of a trick device used to fool a listener. Sounding real means sounding genuine. It's a state of speaking we want to achieve again and again without the kind of charades taught by public speaking consultants.

Nothing sounds worse than an artificial attachment to

language or the inappropriate use of words. Whenever we speak a text we must re-discover it anew, speak it as if for the first time. Speaking it as if you, the speaker, were minting and discovering words right there on the spot. Words must have a vivid reality for the listener.

Any professional speaker who has to deliver material not their own should be aiming to captivate the listener and take him or her on a journey of discovery. You can foster any belief, sell any product, enforce any ideology, solicit from your audience any response, if what you speak has the ring of total authenticity. Speaking can, of course, be put to good or ill uses. Jesus Christ was a charismatic speaker but so was Adolf Hitler. I tend to think that much of history has been swayed by great moments of oratory spoken by charismatic speakers. Think of someone like Mahatma Gandhi, for instance. The powerful influence of his message of non-violence was conveyed largely through the power of words. Many peacemakers wield words rather than swords.

Language Exercises

Here are some language exercises I use with actors to help develop an awareness of how words work and can be used most effectively. Feel free to cross-refer the work I demon-strate here and improvise around the ideas and texts. Think of this as playtime for your language muscles. You can't fail if you remain open to experimentation and think of wordplay as games.

1. Simple Storytelling

I tend to believe that if we can tell good stories then we can learn to be good speakers. A great British actor said in a recent newspaper interview that the secret of acting was the ability to tell a good story and make people listen. So telling a story is where both good public speaking and good acting begin.

A story must maintain the listener's interest. Its trajectory is measured by a beginning, a middle and an end. It must have the pace, precision and length of thought to hold us in its grip. Storytelling is at the heart of any traditional narrative. Homer was a storyteller as were Shakespeare, Jane Austen, Dickens, Virginia Woolf, Mark Twain and the thousands upon thousands of writers whose work has endured and still seems most convincing when read aloud. Even good poems are stories. Song lyrics tell stories. We all like stories told to us in narrative form. All of us naturally listen to words constructed in the order of 'what happens next'. The best public speakers promise to impart something – a story – in what they say.

Here are a series of exercises to help you find your voice as a storyteller. As you perform these exercises, aim to incorporate a beginning, a middle and an end. This three-part structure is one of the simplest and most effective ways to get across a point.

- *Sound Story*   First tell a story using no words but only sounds. Try to be as specific as possible and begin to appreciate the power of silence, pause, repetition and climax. Ghost stories are easy as are war scenes because they are all full of clichéd sound effects. Notice how everyday sounds (a clock ticking, a police siren, the wind, the rain) all create specific atmospheres, environments and time zones. They also captivate the listener. This exercise can be done in a group (where it works best) or one on one with a partner.
- *The 'Seven Word Story'*   Choose only *seven* words to tell a story. Any of the words can be repeated as often as desired. In fact, the repetition might unlock a rhythm in the story. Be as specific as possible and communicate as fully as possible. One of the many benefits from this exercise is that by only having seven words you begin to weigh word choice more carefully. You also begin to test the significance of one word

joined to another. For example, try this combination offered by one of my students, Elizabeth Mills:

stamp, stamp
stamp, stamp
rustle, rustle
click
aim
bang, bang
thud
silence
stamp, stamp

Be as abstract, lengthy and playful as you want. It is not necessary to achieve perfect sentences. You are using sound and opposing word values to conjure impressions in the listener's mind. Try to be clear and precise. Use all your voice in this exercise.

- *Everyday Object* Describe an everyday object (a pen, iron, television set, book) accurately, assuming your listener has never seen the object. Only name the object after the description. Describe it without using useless phrases ('you know', 'a thingy', 'sort of'), useless repetition, 'um's and 'ah's, and without using your hands to gesture, shape or illustrate. In fact, keep your hands under control as you describe the object. Not only will this exercise focus you in on an accurate choice of words to aid you but the structure, quality and, above all, accuracy of the description will have to be explored. You will also discover the importance of pace. The speaker will have to sense how quickly the audience is following the information. You will soon realise how much you rely on physical gesturing in communicating once the power is taken from you and how *unspecific* your vocabularly probably is. So work hard at finding the right language, letting your inarticulateness find a need for key and essential words. This exercise is also great for listeners. To be fair to the speaker the listener has to concentrate vigorously.
- *Extraordinary Object* Now do the same description exercise as above but with an extraordinary object; maybe a fantastic invention. Suddenly other forms of language will emerge. Simile, imagery and a rich use of adjectives. Once more search for precision in your description. No gestures, no

useless verbiage. Stick with the simple, essential words that you really need in this instance.

- *First Person Narrative*   Tell a story in the first person, either fiction or non-fiction, concerning, say, an embarrassing or humiliating event. It can be funny or tragic. For some reason most listeners connect best to this kind of story and the exercise soon has a snowballing effect. It encourages others in a group to tell similar stories. This is a particularly good exercise to use when a group are very reticent in speaking to one another or are just beginning to work together. In the course of the exercise you must reveal something about yourself. It is a liberating exercise as long as you don't get too psychological. Try to remain anecdotal and matter-of-fact, *not* confessional. In the course of this exercise you suddenly discover how you can have power over others, how you can make people listen to your words.

- *Myths and Fairy Tales*   Have a session telling homemade myths and fairy tales. This is a favourite exercise for children but works just as well for adults. The more the speaker can dramatise, believe the material and make contact with the audience through the power of narrative the better the connection between speaker and listener. The aim is to tell the story so that we learn from it and are not just diverted by effects. If voice effects help the story, all well and good. But be strict and economic on this point and try to concentrate on words instead. In fact, if you work towards an ending perhaps your tale will contain a moral. You might learn, in the process of this work, how disconnected we are from stortelling; how *undramatic* we make great stories sound. But working from a need to tell will quickly reveal how exciting storytelling can be. Such is the case with ancient bardic traditions. Stories of this kind are powerful and work on many levels of understanding. The child will hear certain things that the adult will miss and vice versa. In other words, we hear different messages in these stories at different times in our lives. It is a thrilling exercise to do with mixed age groups. You will probably find that simple language works best along with short, active sentences. Maybe a hero or heroine is at the centre of the tale. Maybe there is also an antagonist. Also think of ways that you might arrange your audience for greater effect; perhaps in a circle. But always draw your audience into the story; never leave us excluded. Depend on our need to know 'what happens next'.

2. Epic Storytelling

One of the tasks that actors especially must perform when they play the great classical texts is realising epic stories with truth. An actor must tell stories that not only have a universal appeal but are full of high states of emergency that require all the resources of emotion, imagination and intellect to be channelled through words. Frequently these are tales of survival and odyssey. The stories have a cost, the price of speaking them is high.

Unfortunately many of us, as we tell stories, deaden the dramatic effects. We lower the cost of speaking because we speak from a reduced need. We tend to devalue a great story in order to make it immediate and intelligible, only using language and references that are close to us. We make poetic stories sound prosaic, lively tales sound dead.

If we allow stories to take on an 'epic' scale – an urgency and bigness – our language, choice of words and focus become transformed and more pressing. The size of what we say increases. The need swells. Language becomes more poetic, vivid and intense. We begin to need words as we never needed them before. Useless words are generally abandoned and the story is told graphically yet simply.

Look, for instance, at one of the messenger speeches in Greek tragedy to see how a story can take on epic need. This one is from Sophocles' *Oedipus the King*: the report of an Attendant (who could be a man or a woman) of the death of Jocasta (Oedipus' mother and wife) and Oedipus' self-blinding. Try speaking this monologue aloud, needing each word to put across the story:

> ATTENDANT: Her own hand did it. You that have not seen,
> And shall not see, this worst, shall suffer the less.

But I that saw, will remember, and will tell what I
  remember
Of her last agony. (*Pause.*)
You saw her cross the threshold
In desperate passion. Straight to her bridal-bed
She hurried, fastening her fingers in her hair.
There in her chamber, the doors flung sharply to,
She cried aloud to Laius long since dead,
Remembering the son she bore long since, the son
By whom the sire was slain, the son to whom
The mother bore yet other children, fruit
Of luckless misbegetting. There she bewailed
The twice confounded issue of her wifehood –
Husband begotten of husband, child of child.
So much we heard. Her death was hidden from us.
Before we could see out her tragedy,
The King broke in with piercing cries, and all
Had eyes only for him. This way and that
He strode among us. 'A sword, a sword!' he cried;
'Where is that wife, no wife of mine – that soil
Where I was sown, and whence I reaped my harvest!'
While thus he raved, some demon guided him –
For none of us dared speak – to where she was.
As if in answer to some leader's call
With wild hallooing cries he hurled himself
Upon the locked doors, bending by main force
The bolts out of their sockets – and stumbled in.
We saw a knotted pendulum, a noose,
A strangled woman swinging before our eyes.
The King saw too, and with heart-rending groans
Untied the rope, and laid her on the ground.
But worse was yet to see. Her dress was pinned
With golden brooches, which the King snatched out
And thrust, from full arm's length, into his eyes –
Eyes that should see no longer his shame, his guilt,
No longer see those they should never have seen,
Nor see, unseeing, those he had longed to see,
Henceforth seeing nothing but night . . . To this wild tune
He pierced his eyeballs time and time again,
Till bloody tears ran down his beard – not drops
But in full spate a whole cascade descending
In drenching cataracts of scarlet rain.

> Thus two have sinned; and on two heads, not one –
> On man and wife – falls mingled punishment.
> Their old long happiness of former times
> Was happiness earned with justice; but today
> Calamity, death, ruin, tears and shame,
> All ills that there are names for – all are here.

The messenger's task, like all bearers of bad news, is to bring an epic tale of horror onto the stage before a huge audience, filtering it personally through him/herself. She/he was eyewitness to the event. The most important thing here is to communicate the tragic events that have just happened as though freshly experienced. Notice the simplicity in the choice of the words (simple nouns and animated verbs) and how the telling shocks us yet helps us experience what the Attendant has witnessed with her/his eyes and has 'seen'. The story is told in a very soundly structured way: it has the important beginning, middle and end.

If you hold onto the events and speak them in an ordered way, you will make your way through the speech with ease despite the horror of the vision. If you allow emotion to detract from the primary need to tell the story, you will be awash with grief. The story will short-circuit and cut-off. Don't pull off the rawness of the words. Be specific. Trust the telling and the tale.

Here is a simple exercise to encourage the increasing of stakes in storytelling until it becomes more epic. During the exercise the speaker should quite naturally begin to use more simile and metaphor, but the language should also simplify as the telling need grows. You can use the most mundane activities and situations as subject matter. Start with low stakes and lever up the speaking in stages:

- Describe the exact route you take to get from home to work. From this description the listener should get a clear and precise plan of the journey. It will probably sound very dull and prosaic.

- Now describe the same journey but this time imagine an overpowering event occuring along the way – a chaotic traffic jam or a sudden storm. Use the strongest yet simplest words as part of your description.
- Repeat the journey a third time with the overpowering event but this time add some huge, unstoppable consequence that follows from the event: the earth opens to swallow all the traffic; a cyclone carries it away.
- Now on the fourth telling of the journey the overpowering event plus the unstoppable consequence meet up with a new power which saves the day and brings you safely to work.

Notice that in each of these steps you are upping the stakes. Description is growing and growing. The telling of the tale has greater urgency in each instance. The teller and the tale become more connected. You become involved not in everyday events but in epic (life and death) circumstances. The need to tell each sequence grows as well.

You can, of course, extend this exercise on epic storytelling in any direction you choose. The important thing to experience is how rich and varied but precise your words become. The speaker, as the situations intensify, becomes more and more heightened. But your telling of the tale, as it becomes more urgent, may also become clearer and simpler. The more impassioned you become the more control you can exert.

Other ways of doing this exercise are through describing any of the following:

- A meal. This grows from an ordinary into an extraordinary meal. An event happens during the meal to bring it to an unexpected climax.
- A meeting. A parting.
- The revealing of a secret.
- A love affair: a happy one, a sad one.

Build up the pressure on any story and travel in any direction your imagination desires. The results will be fun and the language pay-offs huge.

3. Debating

Debate – discussing or disputing issues – lies at the heart of most drama and most spirited conversation. It can be a fun contest or a deadly confrontation. It forces us to be quick and resourceful with words.

To debate we must be able to listen, cajole, contain our anger and respond to different points of view. Blocking through silence is not allowed. As we listen to another opinion we must try not to dismiss but assimilate. Today discussion is often only the telling of personal anecdotes which rarely advances a debate but only becomes a self-serving monologue. Our own points of view, our own entrenched solipsism, have cut us off from the potential of other people's opinions. This brings us back to an issue I raised in Part One, 'tabloid thinking': we shriek headlines at each other but never advance much beyond slogans. 'Abortion is wrong.' 'Foreigners get out.' 'AIDS is a disease of a sick society.' We live and speak clipped slogans without taking time to look at another point of view or dig further into an issue to discover the roots of complex histories. We tend to look at superficial results as opposed to examining cases systematically through words and discussion.

Without debate we quickly become entrenched in obsessive opinion rather than thoughtful discernment, refusing to allow a discussion to move into unknown, uncharted areas for fear we will be out of our depth. It's as though we don't want ideas to shock or thrill us. Twenty minutes later we are still stuck on the same point. This isn't debate but thinking stuck in place. As you debate you should be aiming to advance an argument cogently through time, to cover, say, at least ten new points in twenty minutes.

In order to speak weighty classical texts convincingly, for instance, we have to be able to debate without prejudice. We must be able to: (1) open up an argument, (2) explore it, (3) arrive at a conclusion. Look at the structure of any Shakes-

pearean sonnet, speech or play and you'll notice that the same
three-part principle applies, as it does in most forms of
classical rhetoric. Look at any scene from a George Bernard
Shaw play. Each of these forms of writing is structured as a
debate. Debating, like thinking, must always move ahead,
and never stay stuck. Ground must be covered; ideas discovered, rejected, modified and assimilated. In a debate it is
absolutely essential that you respect and listen to the other
point of view.

Here are some ways you might get started on generating
debating skill. These exercises must be done with partners or
in a group.

- 'The Balloon Debate' is a light-hearted and quick way to
  start. Imagine your group is travelling in a hot air balloon.
  The balloon is perilously losing height by the minute.
  Members of the group have to be thrown overboard to lighten
  the weight and to save lives. Each individual knows his or her
  fate if they were to survive: perhaps be the inventor of the
  wheel or champagne or become the next Shakespeare. The
  debate begins with each person spelling out their potential
  gift to the world and what he or she will do to improve it.
  The group judges when and if you are to be thrown
  overboard. The group must make an objective judgement.
  The survivor will be the best debater; the one who proves his
  or her position and worth by skill and coherence, not by
  harangue or bullying. You cannot 'buy' or cajole your way
  out of this situation. Everyone must be given equal time to
  speak and be respected while speaking. Allow yourself a good
  fifteen minutes for this exercise. At the end of it try and list
  what was most skilful in the debate and why the best debater
  survives the crash to become what he or she is fated to be.
- Any debating of passionate issues should be accompanied by
  stringent rules of etiquette. You cannot resort to personal
  attacks and slurs. To this end debate a viewpoint opposite to
  your own; particularly a point you find personally abhorrent
  (e.g. if you are anti-feminist take the feminist side).
  Remember that ideas must move forward and constantly
  breed new ideas until an edifice of opinion forms. Avoid
  reiterating the same few points. Seek new aspects in the

argument. Equal time is given to each side to advance a
position. They work to a clock, so timing is essential. The
speakers must be heard by the whole group. That is, no
mumbling or incoherence. Expletives used only if
appropriate! Heckling is not allowed. Listen, assess and
respond. Try to retain calmness and control. Aim to interest,
amuse and inform the audience. Breathe and take your time.
Have the humility to be affected and to change your point of
view. Don't be threatened by new ideas. You are not a failure
if you either change your opinions or learn something new.
Quite the opposite. You've grown. See, too, if you can find a
voice very unlike your own; one that sounds neither
pretentious nor ill-informed but imbued with knowledge and
belief.

4. Forms and Codes of Language

Any great writer will draw on all the organic uses and codes
of language we all readily have at our disposal. It is always a
relief to recognise that Shakespeare's shift from verse to prose
is really the shift we all do every day from formal to informal
codes of discourse in order to suit the tenor of the situation. I
always find it useful for speakers to notice the skill they all have
in speaking coded language drawn from their own experience.

In the 1960s the British sociologist Basil Bernstein grouped
these spoken codes under two useful headings: elaborated and
restricted codes.

Elaborated Codes: If we can speak an 'elaborated' version of the
English language, we use acceptable forms of English that any
educated speaker will be able to understand. This elaborated
code involves a formal rather than a colloquial or vernacular
use of the language. It is a clear, efficient and accurate use of
idiom that allows us to employ a wide range of creative phrases
and grammatical variety like subordinate clauses. Elaborated
codes are generally carried in clear, accurate sentences.

However, it is important to realise that certain activities
could not be fully described in elaborated codes. Try describ-

ing any sport accurately without using jargon or more restricted words. Imagine describing serving a ball in tennis in just an elaborated code. Also remember that many elaborated speakers use the code to blind us with words and say absolutely nothing. I think some politicians have developed this technique to speak for hours sounding plausible without saying anything. We might only use elaborated code formally: with people we don't know well or when we feel we must keep the conversation on a clear, unemotional basis.

We all use elaborated codes, perhaps, when we talk to our bank manager or the principal or dean of our college. We are always at an advantage when we use this coding in a court room. Educationally the most privileged pupils in schools are educated to use elaborated code while others are left to speak more restricted ones. There is no doubt that those speakers with access to elaborated language can communicate with power figures more successfully than those who have only restricted jargon in their repertoire.

Any writer of the Age of Reason – Swift, Pope, Samuel Johnson – and many later Victorian writers explore all their ideas in elaborated verbal codes. When academics deplore the debasement of language, they are making a plea for clear, elaborated speech without the use of restricted words.

- Try doing a speaking exercise in which every word, phrase and sentence of a given address must be understood by each listener in a group. Describe a complex idea like the world economy or conservation by using language that will convey these ideas to a non-specialist audience. The language you use should *not* contain slang, jargon or unrecognisable words. The listener(s) should instantly challenge anything that is not clear. You'll quickly discover that this is a hard assignment because so much discourse is carried out in restricted codes.

Restricted Codes: In restricted codes language is used more informally or there is a higher incidence of specialised or technical jargon and slang.

Many professions (like medicine or computing), social groups (races and nationalities) or people engaged in physical tasks (baking a cake, playing cricket or baseball) can only best communicate by means of restricted codes. For a code to be restricted it means we need some form of initiation into that codified language. We can't talk about nuclear physics or building construction without a restricted learned language. For a doctor it might mean six years of training to speak the language of surgery or for an office worker it might take three or four days to crack the office code. For the initiated, codes then become second nature and are frequently applied to other areas of life. When snooker first appeared on TV it took me, a snooker novice, three weeks of constant watching to crack the language code of the game. People who know the language use it freely. I haven't yet managed to crack American football terminology and I think that many Americans and lots of Britons can't crack the jargon of cricket. Many jobs like laboratory work cannot be performed without a code. To talk the process through in an elaborated code would take hours. Restricted codes often serve as a kind of shorthand.

The restricted code list is infinite and we come up against it daily: legal terminology, the technical process in a theatre, acting terminology, a golfer hitting a ball, waiters calling for an order, mechanics describing an engine fault, dentists speaking to their assistants while examining your teeth, box office staff selling seats, pilots coming in to land, gardeners planning a garden, sailors rigging a mast. Couples have restricted codes. Offices, companies and professions have them along with secret societies and security services. It may be crucially necessary to have a restricted code to perform a task. But it is equally true that many people and groups develop restricted codes to keep others out. Surely doctors often relish the fact that the patient has no idea of what is being talked about: our bodies are being described in language we cannot always understand. Cliques of people develop a code so that others are denied access to the group. Actors smugly talk a restricted film, TV and theatre code indecipherable to the uninitiated.

Sociologists, philosophers, artists, dancers, sales reps each invest in a restricted language that an outsider cannot comprehend. The examples are infinite and ever-changing. A restricted code might only exist in a single London or Los Angeles street or only between two people speaking. There was a case a number of years ago of twin sisters who had manufactured a language completely their own as a means of sealing themselves off from the outside world. They would only speak to one another in this special tongue.

Codes are always on the move, changing and re-forming. Some restricted words eventually appear in dictionaries as standard phrases. One of the reasons we see such a greater preponderance of new dictionaries in bookshops these days is because of the greater instances of code language becoming common parlance. Restricted codes have made English both more dynamic and also less meaningful. Code language can either pinpoint our knowledge instantly or act as a series of passwords that either give or deny us access to other areas of life. Codes apply in high-society cocktail parties and also in high-rise council tenements. They give us a tremendous confidence and sense of belonging when we speak. They may even give us a sense of prestige and separateness.

Many accents and dialects are restricted. The questions to ask as you work on this enormous variety of codes are:

- How long does it take to learn?
- How universal is it? Would a computer operator, for instance, understand this code throughout the world?
- Is the restricted language moving into an elaborated use? There is frequently movement and adaptability between codes. Computer language is entering an elaborated form. Navigational codes became common in the English language around the eighteenth century. Slang words become respectable when usage makes them so.
- You may understand a code but can you speak it without

sounding like a fraud? You may have to shift your whole speaking energy and placing. Try listening to an RP speaker speaking Cockney rhyming slang or a northern text. Equally a Standard American speaker tackling Tennessee Williams. Can you detect flaws in the speaking voice's manipulation of the code?

Bearing the above in mind, try the following exercise in restricted codes:

- Allow each person in a group to speak versions of *three* restricted codes that each has used and knows well. It will be a very rich experience for the whole group to both listen and try to decipher what is said. It might range from professional jargon to street rap or pidgin English. Notice how instantly articulate and animated the speakers become if they are familiar with a restricted code. They become aware of their linguistic power over others. Suddenly someone who is uneasy speaking formal, elaborated language can freely express himself through a restricted code. Physical body language, for instance, is often brought into play, animating the communication.

- Here is an example of how this might sound if we were to speak using only clichés as our code. Speak aloud the following speech written by Paul Brown, one of my students:

> My boy Gordon Bennet, he's a law unto himself. Always wants to run before he can walk. 'Don't count your chickens before they hatch,' I tell him but he don't want to listen. He's as thick as two short planks, a real sheep in wolf's clothing. He's put all his eggs into one basket. A bird in the hand is worth two in the bush, I always tell him. But then it's always him with egg on his face. Hoisted on his own petard, he was. He jumped the gun, landed in the thick of it and, presto, a shot-gun wedding!

- Now move the work into a written text. Most writers explore shifting codes. Look at any dramatists from Shakespeare to Pinter, for instance; Congreve to Bond; Shaw to Beckett; Chekhov to Osborne. Isolate the code any individual writer uses. Here's a very brief exchange from Shakespeare's *Love's*

Labour's Lost, for example, in which two comic characters enamoured with their own intelligence and self-satisfied pedantry attempt to speak the word 'afternoon' in a restricted code:

> ARMADO: Sir, it is the King's most sweet pleasure and affection to congratulate the Princess at her pavilion in the posteriors of this day, which the rude multitude call the afternoon.
> HOLOFERNES: The posterior of the day, most generous sir, is liable, congruent, and measurable for the afternoon. The word is well culled, choice, sweet, and apt, I do assure you, sir, I do assure.

One example of restricted codes that transforms into utter garbled absurdity is Lucky's non-stop mock-philosophical speech in Samuel Beckett's *Waiting for Godot* which begins:

> Given the existence as uttered forth in the public works of Puncher and Wattmann of a personal God quaquaquaqua with white beard quaquaquaqua outside time without extension who from the heights of divine apathia divine athambia divine aphasia loves us dearly with some exceptions for reasons unknown but time will tell . . .

On a daily basis we all probably speak more in restricted codes than elaborated ones. We can effortlessly shift codes perhaps twenty times throughout a day. The richer our lives the more codes we acquire and the more flexible our use of words. This flexibility may mean we can understand a code but not convincingly speak it. The stumbling block usually comes when we have to speak a text. If this shift in everyday speaking is so easy then why do we find it so hard to change and communicate different codes when speaking a text?

5. Imagery

Imagery comes into our spoken vocabulary when the need for words forces us to find and make urgent comparisons. We use a *simile* when we compare one thing to another with the use of 'like' or 'as' ('My love is like a red, red rose') and we use a *metaphor* when the need to compare is so immediate that we replace one thing with the image of another ('My love a blood red rose'). Images can be cogent and condensed flashes or highly extended passages that go on for lines and fill pages. All great poems, for instance, are extended attempts to find images for what we see, know and experience.

> The poet's eye, in a fine frenzy rolling,
> Doth glance from heaven to earth, from earth to heaven
> And, as imagination bodies forth
> The forms of things unknown, the poet's pen
> Turns them to shapes, and gives to airy nothing
> A local habitation and a name.
> Shakespeare, *A Midsummer Night's Dream*

We all resort to imagery, using similes and metaphors, when our world shifts from a lower gear into a higher one, from normality to abnormality, from coolness to heightened passion. Using images can be thrilling and unpredictable because the best images, when spoken, should sound freshly minted and newly discovered. In fact, when an image sounds tired and predictable we know it has wandered into the realm of the cliché. When we speak in images we tend to bulk-up our ordinary use of language with similes and metaphors that enlarge our need for words. I think that a regular use of images makes us bolder, better speakers. Their use need not add artificial ornamentation to the way we naturally speak.

Listen to anyone's language as they describe witnessing an unpleasant accident. They will be using these forms of language. Great feeling draws out of us this kind of language so that we can either compare the event to something momentous or horrific or else portray the event in a shockingly colourful way to capture its indecency.

Great texts do this all the time, for example in Enobarbus' description of Cleopatra in *Antony and Cleopatra*:

The barge she sat in, like a burnished throne
Burned on the water. The poop was beaten gold;
Purple the sails, and so perfumèd that
The winds were love-sick with them. The oars were silver,
Which to the tune of flutes kept stroke. For her own person,
It beggared all description. She did lie
In her pavilion – cloth of gold, of tissue –
O'er picturing that Venus where we see
The fancy outwork nature. On each side her
Stood pretty dimpled boys, like smiling Cupids,
With divers-coloured fans whose wind did seem
To glow the delicate cheeks which they did cool,
And what they undid did.

The full power of the vision best comes to life when spoken aloud.

Actors, I notice, will often be suspicious of imagery in a speech. 'Can we cut this bit?' they will ask. Think rather of the overpowering need that imagery signals. Only through imagery can we capture and fix for a listener certain moments, certain pictures. The use of imagery for most contemporary speakers is, I think, oddly embarrassing. It goes back to an initial observation I made in Part One about our distrust of eloquence.

If a speaker is daring enough to explore imagery in his or her own language the practice will help you to tackle and appreciate the constant use of imagery in a text. It will also help you value what is excellent in great writing.

Here is a simple exercise to make imagery a greater part of your speaking habit:

● Describe a feeling solely through imagery by using simile and/or metaphor. Don't identify the subject of the feeling (e.g. love or hate) but convey it only by means of apt words and phrases. If you get stuck try using phrases such as: 'It's like a . . .'; 'Imagine . . .'; 'I remember . . . .' Try to be as simple as possible rather than wildly extravagant. Can the listener or group name the feeling? First do the exercise describing a negative feeling and then do it again exploring a positive feeling. The negative always seems easier at first to describe. Here is how one student writer, Tim Marchant, describes watching the rain.

> The colours swirl and mix,
> Light turning to khaki,
> Then to blackness.
> Disappearing down the drain.
> Swallowing the day.
>
> The watercolour sky
> With too many washes,
> Now lies limp.
> Pale, soggy-grey paper.
> Utterly lifeless.
>
> The rain spills down.
> Collecting in dark pools.
> Changing from crystal
> To muddy brown,
> There to turn stagnant,
> Like old emotions
> Hoping for better days.

6. Length of Thought

A problem I frequently isolate for professional speakers and actors is that many of us get trapped in speaking uniform, monotonous lengths of thought. Sentences seem to come out of us like regimented, thumping units. Like good writing, good speaking needs variety. Simply by shortening and lengthening the units of our thinking we can enhance our thoughts more fully. You notice this especially in formal sales meetings, for instance, when reports and figures are being read. The listener is invariably falling asleep as one catalogue of figures sounds pretty much like the last.

Here are some exercises to help with the problem:

- The speaker should be able to tell a story in the shortest way possible. So tell a brief story in one minute. Repeat the exercise telling the same story but with the longest thoughts possible. Changing the length of thought will make you think and feel differently. Now take both versions and attempt to tell the story with varying lenghts of thought. What sort of difference do you and the listener(s) notice?

- Tell a long rambling joke which is one thought. Try to make as many diversions as possible and still come back to the main storyline.
- Try to keep the attention of a group while you debate an issue. The group can heckle if they sense you have stopped thinking. Thoughts can end but a new thought must dynamically build on top of another. Try to keep your attention focused on what you are saying.

Next are some contemporary text examples of different thought lengths. As you speak the following extracts aloud, notice how different your internal energy is and how easy it is to become physically dislocated if the thought is too long. Feel how the longer thoughts need a different focus and concentration. Don't stop thinking or sustaining the energy of the argument until you reach a full stop. At that point you can pause and breathe, but never give up and lose the thought's momentum.

I thought I would be nervous but I'm not. Because Jesus is giving me strength to speak. I don't know where to begin because I've been unhappy as long as I can remember. My mother and father were unhappy too. I think my grandparents were unhappy. My father was a violent man. You'd hear my mother, you'd say, 'Are you all right, mum?' But that's a long time ago. I wasn't very lucky in my marriage. So after that I was on my own except I had my little girl. Some of you knew her. But for those of you who didn't, she couldn't see. I thought at first that was why she couldn't learn things but it turned out to be in her head as well. But I taught her to walk, they said she wouldn't but she did. She slept in my bed, she wouldn't let me turn away from her, she'd put her hand on my face. It was after she died I started drinking, which has been my great sin and brought misery to myself and those who love me. I betrayed them again and

again by saying I would give it up, but the drink would have
me hiding a little away. But my loving sisters in Christ stood
by me. I thought if God wants me he'll give me a sign,
because I couldn't believe he really would want someone as
terrible as me. I thought if I hear two words today, one
beginning with M for Margaret, my name, and one with J for
Jesus, close together, then I'll know how close I am to him.
And that very afternoon I was at Mavis's house and her little
boy was having his tea, and he said, 'More jam, mum'. So
that was how close Jesus was to me, right inside my heart.
That was when I decided to be baptised. But I slid back and
had a drink again and next day I was in despair. I thought
God can't want me, nobody can want me. And a thrush got
into my kitchen. I thought if that bird can fly out, I can fly
out of my pain. I stood there and watched, I didn't open
another window, there was just the one window open. The
poor bird beat and beat round the room, the tears were
running down my face. And at last it found the window and
went straight through into the air. I cried tears of
joy because I knew Jesus would save me. So I went to
Malcolm and said baptise me now because I'm ready. I want
to give myself over completely to God so there's nothing else
of me left, and then the pain will be gone and I'll be saved.
Without the love of my sisters I would never have got
through.

Caryl Churchill, Fen

Why has democracy succeeded in America? Of course by
succeeded I mean comparatively, not literally, not in the
present, but what makes for the prospect of some sort of
radical democracy spreading outward and growing up? Why
does the power that was once so carefully preserved at the top
of the pyramid by the original framers of the constitition seem
drawn inexorably downward and outward in spite of the best
effort of the Right to stop this? I mean it's the really hard
thing about being Left in this country, the American Left
can't help but trip over all these petrified little fetishes:
freedom, that's the worst; you know, *Jeane Kirkpatrick* for
God's sake will go on and on about freedom and so what does
that mean, the word freedom, when she talks about it, or
human rights; you have Bush talking about human rights,
and so what are these people talking about, they might as well

be talking about the mating habits of Venusians, these people don't begin to know what, ontologically, freedom is or human rights, like they see these bourgeois property-based Rights-of-Man-type rights but that's not enfranchisement, not democracy, not what's implicit, what's potential within the idea, not the idea with blood in it. That's just liberalism, the worst kind of liberalism, really, bourgeois tolerance, and what I think is that what AIDS shows us is the limits of tolerance, that it's not enough to be tolerated, because when the shit hits the fan you find out how much tolerance is worth. Nothing. And underneath all the tolerance is intense, passionate hatred.

Tony Kushner, *Angels in America*

7. The Stressing Game

I use this game to build up an awareness of stress and inflection.

- Construct a simple sentence of at least six words. (e.g. 'To be or not to be.')
- Speak the sentence as neutrally as possible. The information should be clearly communicated but there will be no nuances or sub-textual meaning in the stress or inflection.
- Now speak the same sentence changing the meaning *three* times. Try to accurately hold each rendition of the different meanings. Even 'score' the sentence in some way by putting marks over the stressed words. Notice how the stress and inflection have changed. If you are doing this exercise in a group, allow the group to analyse where the stresses and inflections are occurring in each reading of the sentence and consequently how the meaning suddenly shifts.
- Now do the same exercise in pairs with a short dialogue. First try some dialogue you have written, then take something from a play or piece of fiction. At this stage you may discover that a stress which goes against the meaning of the language in your chosen scene makes complete nonsense of the text's intentions. But when the stresses are well-placed, the text has greater potency. Try this dialogue between Millamant (a woman) and Mirabell (a man) from William Congreve's play *The Way of the World*:

MILLAMANT: Mirabell, did not you take exceptions last night? Oh, aye, and went away. Now I think on't, I'm angry. No, now I think on't, I'm pleased; for I believe I gave you some pain.

MIRABELL: Does that please you?

MILLAMANT: Infinitely; I love to give pain.

MIRABELL: You would affect a cruelty which is not in your nature; your true vanity is in the power of pleasing.

MILLAMANT: Oh, I ask you pardon for that. One's cruelty is one's power; and when one parts with one's cruelty, one parts with one's power; and when one parts with that, I fancy one's old and ugly.

MIRABELL: Aye, aye, suffer your cruelty to ruin the object of your power, to destroy your lover, and then how vain, how lost a thing you'll be! Nay, 'tis true: you are no longer handsome when you've lost your lover; your beauty dies upon the instant. For beauty is the lover's gift; 'tis he bestows your charms, your glass is all a cheat. The ugly and the old, whom the looking glass mortifies, yet after commendation can be flattered by it, and discover beauty in it; for that reflects our praises, rather than your face.

MILLAMANT: Oh, the vanity of these men! Fainall, d'ye hear him? If they did not commend us, we were not handsome! Now you must know that they could not commend one, if one was not handsome. Beauty the lover's gift! Lord, what is a lover, that it can give? Why, one makes lovers as fast as one pleases, and they live as long as one pleases, and they die as soon as one pleases; and then, if one pleases one makes more.

8. Language that Represses and Offends

I would never enter into this kind of work unless I know a group very well. However, with more and more being said about the subject of 'political correctness', particularly in terms of words, I think that anyone who uses language publicly must have a greater awareness of how words can be socially and politically damaging. It is easy for all of us, especially if we are white, to de-sensitise ourselves to other groups of people by using names, phrases and terms that condescend and mock. We can feel smug and superior to other groups of people and this attitude surfaces in the way we name and talk about others. The words we use frequently expose our views of others, whether conditioned or openly believed. Under this category of work comes the language of racism, sexism, ageism, homophobia, etc. Words can speak the thoughts that alienate a speaker from a listener just as they can equalise and harmonise.

- List a few words and phrases you most abhor and would least like to hear used against you.
- Are there words or phrases you couldn't say about others? Ones you could? Some you hear everyday and let pass by without comment?
- Scout through any tabloid paper and list some of the headlines that express prejudice.
- Everyone should find a piece of writing (explicit or implicit) that illustrates words used in this way. You may have to take time to explain why some of these phrases are offensive. Prejudice can sometimes be deeply subtle.

You will always find that the members of one group think others are too sensitive if they take offence. It is not always easy to change the way someone uses words that damage and hurt. But bringing that language out into the open at least puts it on display for all to hear and then argue over. One of the great crimes committed through this kind of language is the assumption that words don't hurt and that the victim is not experiencing pain.

I have done frightening surveys among my students, asking them to note how many daily experiences they can cite of language that feels oppressive. Some groups came back with totals of over forty instances in a single day. Forty times a day they are carrying the burden of oppression! Naturally, the students who rarely experience this burden – on average once or twice a year perhaps – are generally the ones who believe the rest of us are all being too sensitive on this issue.

But words do carry an offensive power. And no one knows or feels their sting more bitterly than Shakespeare's Shylock, the money-lending Jew in *The Merchant of Venice*:

> Signor Antonio, many a time and oft
> In the Rialto you have rated me   [*rated* = berated]
> About my moneys and my usances. [*usances* = moneylending]
> Still have I borne it with a patient shrug,
> For suff'rance is the badge of all our tribe.
> You call me misbeliever, cut-throat, dog,
> And spit upon my Jewish gaberdine,
> And all for use of that which is mine own.

9. Preparing Your Own Speeches

Speaking a written text is an altogether different experience from publicly speaking in your own words. I know many great actors, for instance, who will freeze on the spot if they have to use their own language. So it is no surprise to me that many people list speaking in public as one of their greatest fears.

What follows are some hints to help you cope in those situations where you have to prepare a speech. I think you can apply these suggestions to many varieties of speeches or presentations: before board meetings, wedding speeches, lectures, introducing a speaker, etc.:

- First structure the speech according to your own thoughts. Think of the model of a well-constructed speech in a play. You open up a story or debate or you gradually reveal an idea. You then explore the box you have opened. The box may have other boxes in it, each one revealing a richer item. You then come to a conclusion. The most common pattern is to have a beginning, a middle and an end. Plus a climax! Try to make and articulate a fully completed journey.
- You may need to make notes as a reminder of the journey –

signposts along the way – but do so on manageable pieces of paper. Card is good and is less likely to shake than paper. Remember that a spoken address is more effective than a read one. Any prepared speech needs the air of spontaneity.

- Ask yourself clear and tough questions as you prepare and make sure you answer the questions thoroughly and clearly. 'What do I want to say?' There is no point in speaking unless you've thought this question through. 'What do I want to achieve?' Are you introducing someone, selling an idea, provoking, persuading, amusing, enlightening? 'Who am I addressing?' A very important but often forgottten question. We have all heard speakers telling jokes that were inappropriate for a certain audience. Know the level of your audience. Sympathise with them. Be in their place before you endeavour to place them on your level.

- Take your speech to the audience. Share it with them. Don't hide behind a lectern or hunch over the prepared text. Look up and out frequently, structuring the speech in such a way that significant pauses will allow both you and your audience to take in what you are saying. Open a direct line of communication.

- Be as concise as possible. Avoid useless phrases, clichés or non-verbal noises: 'uh', 'um', 'you know', etc. Remember that silence is more powerful than grunts or useless language. You need not fill up every bit of space. Avoid repetition of words and phrases unless you can use the repetition for dramatic effect. Directness is more effective than rambling. Unless you can get back easily on the path of the journey – your reason for speaking in the first place – avoid lengthy digressions. Leave an audience wanting more rather than boring them.

- Believe in what you are saying and commit yourself to the need to pass on a message. Any audience will forgive mistakes, hesitations, lapses or mispronunciations if the speaker is committed. An audience will immediately be put off by someone who is tentative, nervous or unenthusiastic. Commit yourself to the need to make this speech.

- There are certain ingredients in speech-making that are always appealing: personal experience, comparisons, facts, timing, revelations, the promise that the speech will arrive somewhere. Above all, good, precise content benefits the

audience most. Never, oh never, go beyond an acceptable
time limit. Remind yourself that boredom has a threshold.

- Use language that both you and your audience comprehend.
  Many speakers make the mistake of trying to use words or
  codes that they don't properly own. They sound false and
  frigid. They try to use words or tell stories that they have
  heard other speakers use effectively, but you must always feel
  at ease with your own material and not clumsily imitate
  someone else's style.

- Try to make eye contact. I know this is difficult for many
  people, but I cannot emphasise how powerful this is. It
  humanises you and brings the audience to you. Conspire with
  the audience. Eye contact also makes it much harder for
  members of the audience to avoid you and not to listen.

- Practise any speech out loud. Practise it in the conditions in
  which you will eventually give it. This will help you avoid
  any discomfort or surprise later on. Is there a lectern, a table,
  somewhere for your notes? Will you be using slides or
  electronic devices? Such things frequently go awry and
  should be prepared and worked with in advance.

- Know what you are going to wear: formal or informal clothes.
  Whether you will be standing or sitting or moving through
  the space. Will the audience have been drinking? If they have
  you will need more focus. Alcohol will not help the throat (it
  dries it), water will lubricate it. Stopping to take a drink can
  be quite a powerful gesture.

- Speak for the audience, not yourself. Embrace them with
  what you have to say.

10. Exercise on Structuring a Speech

Here's a group exercise:

- Each member of the group writes out a sentence on a piece of
  paper. The sentence must, in some way, open up a topic of
  debate. It should pose something.

- The pieces of paper are put into a hat and everyone draws
  one. Give at least ten minutes for preparation. Then each
  person must speak out the sentences and explore the idea
  before coming to a conclusion. At least *seven* points should be
  made. The points should have some connections to the ones

before and, like stepping stones, move the argument forward. The conclusion should tie up all the points neatly.

- Also try to make a point and then take a two-minute diversion related to the point before returning to the original idea.

11. Sounding Words

Here I want to present exercises to release the sensual and physical power of words simply by sounding them.

Working and wrestling with language, painting boldly and vividly with primary verbal colours. All these physical images come to mind as I work to release words. So many of us speak in muted, watered-down colours, delicately dangle a limp foot into the fount of language or pick up words with such fear to keep them at a distance. We often treat words with too much delicacy.

I am asking you to learn to play again with words the way you did as a child, to trust that your intellectual powers are solid enough to risk exploring other areas of needing and knowing the word. The physical, emotional and organic side of language is felt in the sound.

As you experiment with these exercises always return to speaking the text away from the exercise; that is, go back into the text immediately before you have time to think or consider what the exercises may or may not have discovered. You'll instantly notice a big difference in your verbal performance of the text. (Later in the book you will find specific texts where we'll do these exercises again and again.) Always feel free to cross-refer and do not hesitate to use any technique or exercise that will help you free words. Never get precious or try to predict results.

These exercises are useful at all stages of preparation and can be repeated endlessly with new discoveries each time. Even if you have been speaking or singing a text for years, discoveries can be made as you shake the text anew through physicalising the language.

The very act of shifting a text around magically embeds words into your being on a very different level. Releases through the breath and voice reveal hidden sources in the text.

What follows is a sonnet by Shakespeare (Sonnet 94) and then a simple series of exercises to sound the text and get the voice oiled and connected to it:

> They that have power to hurt and will do none,
> That do not do the thing they most do show,
> Who moving others are themselves as stone,
> Unmovèd, cold, and to temptation slow;
> They rightly do inherit heaven's graces,
> And husband nature's riches from expense;
> They are the lords and owners of their faces,
> Others but stewards of their excellence.
> The summer's flower is to the summer sweet
> Though to itself it only live and die,
> But if that flower with base infection meet
> The basest weed outbraves his dignity;
>   For sweetest things turn sourest by their deeds:
>   Lilies that fester smell far worse than weeds.

- *First speak the text aloud on a full voice*
  You cannot prepare to speak by silently reading a text. Speaking is a physical activity. If you do all your preparation in silence then the voice and text have no real chance either to live in you or to inhabit your voice. You must always find a place for the text nearest your voice. Speaking an unfamiliar text lets us make physical or sensual connections more quickly than when the text is an old standby. You must inform all the muscles of the voice of the work you expect them to do and the degree of difficulty that faces them with the words and phrases.
- *Whisper the text*
  This simple exercise helps you to clarify thoughts and reveal the physical and sensual qualities embedded in words. You immediately come in contact, for instance, with all the sibilants; those consonants that elicit a hissing sound (e.g. 'fester').

- *Intone or chant the text*
  This is a curiously clearing exercise. It is calming and vocally very freeing. Length of thought and intensity of emotions are often discovered. Stress and inflection habits are wiped out. This is an especially good exercise for the moments when you feel stuck or stale with the text. Instead of worrying and becoming tense about a text through over-analysing it, take time to intone it. Intoning is especially useful for actors in the middle of a long run. It serves as a refresher, ironing out entrenched rhythms and modes of delivery, freeing stale readings. By making the text sound momentarily unfamiliar it can make it sound new again.
- *Speak the text while moving*
  Do an activity, any repetitive activity like swinging, pacing, sweeping or digging. It not only vocally releases the text but can highlight different subtleties in the language and link words with the physical process of speaking. It also helps to discover pace.
- *Voice first words and last words*
  In verse, especially, sense the journey of a line by speaking the first word in each line right the way down the text (*They, That, Who, Unmoved*, etc.). Then the final word throughout (*none, show, stone, slow*, etc.). Silently think and *breathe* the whole sonnet. But by only vocalising the initial and then final words of each line you will get a sense of how a word instigates and then completes a line or thought. Each line is a separate journey. The first words activate the impulse of the line and the last words complete it.
- *Isolate verbs and nouns*
  Singling out the verbs in a text will sometimes give you insight into the action of the speech. The nouns will tell you its subjects or topics. This shorthand sounding can frequently get you to the root of the text's meaning faster than a silent reading.
- *Voice the vowels*
  Speak only the vowels in a text but make sure you keep connected to the breath of the whole word. This will help you find the depth and emotional intensity in the separate words. For instance:

  > It is the cause, it is the cause, my soul.
  > Let me not name it to you, you chaste stars.
  > It is the cause. Yet I'll not shed her blood,

Nor scar that whiter skin of hers than snow,
And smooth as monumental alabaster.
Yet she must die, else she'll betray more men.
Put out the light, and then put out the light.
> Shakespeare, *Othello*

You will feel Othello's pain in the vowels and also the
containing of the pain when he shortens the vowels at the
start of each line or they are suddenly blocked by sharp
consonants (*It, Let, It, Nor, And, Yet, Put*). The tortured
journey of his soul as he moves on-stage to kill Desdemona is
patterned in that very conflict of sound. It sounds like a
dirge. In order to kill Desdemona, Othello has to harden
himself in the quick vowels sequence (as in *It is*) and not
indulge in the longer vowels (as in *cause* and *soul*). The long
vowels indicate an opening of feeling, shorter vowels contain
or control the feeling. You may also notice that the long
vowels can slow down the pace while the shorter ones throw
you quickly forward. In this line from Sonnet 27 the reverse
is true:

Weary with toil I haste me to my bed

The first set of vowels expresses tiredness and slowness while
the second half of the line speeds you into bed.
   Now do the same with the sonnet.

- Check for imagery by literally looking for 'pictures' in the
  text. If you find imagery then ask why the character needs to
  use that kind of language or suddenly draws us a picture.
  What is happening to him or her? Remember you must
  always see and live the images as you speak them. If you fail
  to do so then the audience can never fully experience them
  either and you will both have missed the opportunity to
  convey an essential item in the text. Spot the images in the
  sonnet (e.g. *Flower* and *weed*).

12. Drawing on Images

It is important to realise that the audience will never see
exactly what you do. Our responses to imagery are always

personal and unique. So give the audience time to have their own experience and form their own impressions of the sound. Words must resonate before the full impression will emerge. This is one of the reasons you cannot pass by an image too quickly. You may also see different pictures every time you speak an image-filled passage. Certainly an actor who plays Hamlet or Queen Gertrude numerous times during a career will encounter new impressions of the text and its images over and over again. Our responses change along with our lives. This is always a crucial fact to remember when working with words.

Here is an exercise to help you feel the richness and imagery in language:

- The speaker speaks a poetic text from a play, poem, or piece of prose to two or more listeners.
- The audience notes the images they either imagine and experience so that there is an immediate response to the speaker. The listeners report what they have actually heard – not just heard aurally but heard and known – and then compare notes. This normally matches the parts of the text the speaker felt, saw or experienced in some way.
- The second time round allow the same speaker to work through the text once again. Any member of the group should spontaneously repeat aloud any words or phrases which especially move him or her. There should be an echo back, a choral effect, from various voices in the group. Sometimes this feedback comes instantly because the speaker is deeply connected to the language's imagery. At other times the exercise will need to be repeated because the image and physical richness are still lacking.
- On the third reading, the speaker is left to speak alone without a response from the listeners. But by this point the process has usually connected the speaker so firmly to the words that he or she will almost anticipate a response back. Suddenly the words are needed more passionately and even feel alive.

13. Antithesis

In rhetoric 'antithesis' means a verbal construction in which words are set in opposition but balanced: e.g. 'brave day sunk in hideous night'. The first part of the statement is the *thesis*, the second the *antithesis*. Both parts are in balanced tension. If you discover that there are opposites or opposition in a line of text, allow the conflict to swing you from one pole to the other.

Here is a group exercise for antithesis. You need at least three people to do this properly:

- First search for a chunk of text rich in antithesis. Something like the following sonnet, 'Description of the Contrarious Passions in a Lover' by Thomas Wyatt:

> I find no peace, and all my war is done;
> I fear and hope, I burn and freeze like ice;
> I fly aloft yet can I not arise;
> And nought I have, and all the world I seize on,
> That locks nor loseth, holdeth me in prison,
> And hold me not, yet can I scape no wise:
> Nor letteth me live, nor die at my devise,
> And yet of death, it giveth me occasion.
> Without eye I see; without tongue I plain:
> I wish to perish yet I ask for health;
> I love another, and I hate myself;
> I feed me in sorrow, and laugh in all my pain.
>   Lo, thus displeaseth me both death and life.
>   And my delight is causer of this strife.

- Notice that straight through the centre of the speech a wall of commas or brief pauses passes. The oppositions in each line lie on either side of these.
- Designate one speaker to speak it out aloud to the group.
- The remaining group is then divided in half, and the two halves move to either side of the room. The speaker remains in the middle and decides on the opposing qualities and conflicts that the antithesis is exploring, e.g. positive/negative, pain/joy, love/hate.

- Each half takes up the cause of one side or the other, physically becoming the personification of that need. As the speaker speaks, each side repeats and reinforces aloud the quality they are supporting. Any word the group hears that reminds them of their purpose can be repeated. Sometimes puns will explode together as all voices join in. The speaker must be free to move between the two groups as a tug of war wages for the speaker's attention. Throughout the exercise the speaker will have been tossed around physically and emotionally depending on the strength of the opposing needs. And if the antithesis is good and remains balanced, the entire group will feel as if they have been riding an emotional and intellectual seesaw.

14. Wit, Puns and Wordplay

Being funny and humorous with words is more of a natural gift than something you can cultivate simply by playing off the words someone else feeds you. When you think of any instance where punning and wordplay is in use, you often discover instances where the listener is taking the speaker's words and turning them about to create new meaning.

The best way of exploring this is to find samples of text where the words are used incisively. Good wordplay is sharp and cunning, not dull or lazy.

Check the text for puns and any sampling of comic wordplay. Speak the words for all their different shades of meaning. Sometimes the shade is an off-colour one. One after the other investigate sentences for new meaning. Experiment with all their potential. What double intention, thought or joke is the word detonating upon the world? Generally the wit within a text grows and explodes in a dynamic way.

- Part of the challenge with puns and wordplay is the ability to maintain speed, agility and meaning. Each aspect must work together. With a partner try this sequence between Viola and Feste from *Twelfth Night*:

Enter Viola, disguised as the page Cesario, and Feste the clown who plays his tabor [drum].

VIOLA: Save thee, friend, and thy music. Dost thou live by thy tabor?

FESTE: No, sir, I live by the church.

VIOLA: Art thou a churchman?

FESTE: No such matter, sir. I do live by the church for I do live at my house and my house doth stand by the church.

VIOLA: So thou mayst say the king lies by a beggar if a beggar dwells near him, or the church stands by thy tabor if thy tabor stands by the church.

FESTE: You have said, sir. To see this age! – A sentence is but a cheveril [smooth leather] glove to a good wit, how quickly the wrong side may be turned outward.

VIOLA: Nay, that's certain. They that dally nicely with words may quickly make them wanton.

FESTE: I would therefore my sister had had no name, sir.

VIOLA: Why, man?

FESTE: Why, sir, her name's a word, and to dally with that word might make my sister wanton. But indeed, words are very rascals since bonds disgraced them.

VIOLA: Thy reason man?

FESTE: Troth, sir, I can yield you none without words, and words are grown so false I am loath to prove reason with them.

VIOLA: I warrant thou are a merry fellow, and carest for nothing.

FESTE: Not so, sir, I do care for something; but in my conscience, sir, I do not care for you. If that be to care for nothing, sir, I would it would make you invisible.

VIOLA: Art not thou the Lady Olivia's fool?

FESTE: No indeed, sir, the Lady Olivia has no folly, she will keep no fool, sir, till she be married, and fools are as like husbands as pilchards are to herrings – the husband's the bigger. I am indeed not her fool, but her corrupter of words.

● This is not an easy sequence of dialogue to get through. You may not know what all the images and allusions refer to. But take a risk and make the words mean what you think they

mean. Make them sound funny. Add physical action. Use
your drum.

- Good wit, puns and wordplay use language anarchically.
  They 'corrupt' words in a frenzied way as in a Marx Brothers
  or Monty Python routine. They juxtapose odd relationships:
  tabor/church; beggar/king; husband/herring. When doing a
  sequence like the above you must allow yourself to enter a
  zany world where words, associations and ideas come
  together with lightning quickness. Forget the intellect when
  playing comedy like this but go, instead, for the collision of
  sounds and images. See if you can find a timing or rhythm
  that suits this exchange.

15. Repetition

When you first pick up a text notice if certain words or
phrases are repeated. When you notice repetitions ask yourself
some crucial questions:

- How often and when? What sort of words?
- Does the repetition show that the thought is hard to move
  on? Maybe the character whose words you are speaking is
  somehow stuck.
- Does the repetition break the thought to expose flashes of
  feeling within the thinking process or join thoughts together?
- Is the repetition a refrain? Repetition often implies that
  rhythm and balance are at work inside a text. Perhaps the
  listener is lulled into a safe haven by the repetition which may
  then change in order to suddenly shock us. Repetition often
  softens the blow of harsh sentiments.

Each of these aspects of repetition can be found in Jaques'
melancholy speech in Act 2, Scene 7 of *As You Like It*. Notice
the wealth and variety of repeated sounds, words and phrases
set within languid, blank verse lines.

> A fool, a fool, I met a fool i'th' forest,
> A motley fool – a miserable world!
> As I do live by food, I met a fool,
> Who laid him down and basked him in the sun,

And railed on Lady Fortune in good terms,
In good set terms, and yet a motley fool.
'Good morrow, fool,' quoth I. 'No, sir,' quoth he,
'Call me not fool till heaven hath sent me fortune.'
And then he drew a dial from his poke,
And looking on it with lack-lustre eye
Says very wisely, 'It is ten o'clock.'
'Thus we may see,' quoth he, 'how the world wags.
'Tis but an hour ago since it was nine,
And after one hour more 'twill be eleven.
And so from hour to hour we ripe and ripe,
And then from hour to hour we rot and rot;
And thereby hangs a tale.' When I did hear
The motley fool thus moral on the time
My lungs began to crow like chanticleer,
That fools should be so deep contemplative,
And I did laugh sans intermission
An hour by his dial. O noble fool,
A worthy fool! Motley's the only wear.

16. Verse

Verse is not something we should fear. It simply puts words
and sentences into different rhythmic structures. It draws the
listener's attention to the manner of what is being said so that
we can hear the matter better. Too much attention is paid to
identifying the form the verse takes. Just be swayed by the
rhythm rather than being too strict about the beat.

When confronted by a piece of verse try doing the
following:

- Beat the lines out, using anything from your finger tips to a
  drum. Remember to allow the stressed syllable or stronger
  beats to take your voice up. Don't allow the beat to pull itself
  vocally or physically inside you. Send it outwards. Do the
  lines scan evenly or is the 'heartbeat' changing, either
  slowing, quickening or becoming erratic? If the text is even
  (regular) then the chances are the situation is under control
  and there is no chaos raging in the speaker. The verse may,
  for instance, be that of a formal court scene. If the rhythm

sounds erratic (irregular) then chaos may be looming or emotions rising. Look at Act I, Scene 1 of *King Lear*. Lear starts speaking evenly and formally until Cordelia's reply of 'Nothing' rocks his steadiness:

> LEAR: [*To Cordelia*] Now our joy,
>   Although our last and least, to whose young love
>   The vines of France and milk of Burgundy
>   Strive to be interested: what can you say to draw
>   A third more opulent than your sisters? Speak.
> CORDELIA: Nothing, my lord.
> LEAR: Nothing?
> CORDELIA: Nothing.
> LEAR: Nothing will come of nothing. Speak again.
> CORDELIA: Unhappy that I am, I cannot heave
>   My heart into my mouth. I love your majesty
>   According to my bond, no more nor less.
> LEAR: How, how Cordelia? Mend your speech a little
>   Lest you may mar your fortunes.

- Are the lines fragmented or frayed? That is, are thoughts stopping or starting mid-line? With a caesura (a pause)? A question? If so the sudden stops may indicate that the process of thinking is not easy. It comes in sudden bursts. Notice how this works in the following passage from *The Winter's Tale* where King Leontes is almost driven mad by the thought that his wife and best friend have cuckolded him. Speak the lines to capture both the fury and chaos of the character's feverish brain:

>   Gone already.
> Inch-thick, knee-deep, o'er head and ears a forked
>   one! –
> Go play, boy, play. Thy mother plays, and I
> Play too; but so disgraced a part, whose issue
> Will hiss me to my grave. Contempt and clamour
> Will be my knell. Go play, boy, play. There have been,
> Or I am much deceived, cuckolds ere now,
> And many a man there is, even at this present,
> Now, while I speak this, holds his wife by th'arm,
> That little thinks she has been sluiced in's absence,

And his pond fished by his next neighbour, by
Sir Smile, his neighbour. Nay, there's comfort in't, . . .

- How long are the thoughts? Are the ideas coming in long arcs
  or are they short and fragmented or a mixture of both? If the
  ideas are tumbling out at length, the intellectual and
  emotional juices are flowing. The shorter thoughts probably
  indicate a grinding of mental and emotional gears. Even
  rhythm and balanced thoughts generally indicate that a
  situation is under control. Here is Leontes under better
  control at the end of the play as his fragmented way of
  speaking has become more balanced:

I am content to look on; what to speak,
I am content to hear; for 'tis as easy
To make her speak as move.

17. Exercises for the Iambic

The iambic is a form of stress which creates a continuous
speaking rhythm. The iamb is a two-part rhythm (usually
made-up of unstressed/stressed beats) of short and long vowel
lengths: e.g. de *dum*. Iambic pentameter verse is simply five
of these sequences put together to form ten beats of alternating
unstressed and stressed beats:

de dum, de dum, de dum, de dum, de dum.
When I do count the clock that tells the time.

Regular iambic pentameter rhythm has a steady tick-tock beat
like that of a clock. It is also, metaphorically speaking, like a
heartbeat or the beat of the pulse: the first rhythm we hear in
the womb, the last we feel before death. The iambic pentameter rhythm is, I think, that primal and consequently that
powerful. It influences the rhythm of our everyday speech
and we often speak in iambic pentameters without being
conscious of it.

Iambic pentameter rhythms can also be quite irregular in the same way that a heart can skip a beat or a pulse quickens:

> My Love is as a fever longing still
> For that which longer nurseth the disease

Like our inner biology the iambic responds to pressure, tension and stimuli, which means the routine stresses may suddenly fall in different places. That is why it is such a natural verse rhythm in which to capture spoken words. It is sensitive to feeling and emotional arousal. You can say the above two lines slowly, using the tick-tock rhythm, but notice what happens if you speed it up and capture its feverish rhythm. Speaking from need often means adjusting the rhythm to suit the need of what's being said or how you are saying it. Iambic rhythm guides speaking but should not rule it.

If you let it, the iambic beat will support your vocal energy, letting you time your breathing to its rhythm. To deny this is a bit like trying to push a rubber ball under the water. It, the iamb, will always force its way to the surface. You cannot suppress the iambic rhythm except through force and pressure. I know many actors who will fight against the rhythm only to end up thrashing themselves. By swallowing the stress beat, denying it is there, the speaker is wilfully clamping the organic nature of the verse, not allowing it to take free flight. The result is unnatural and fraught speech.

Here are some hints to help you navigate passages where iambics are in evidence. Use them in combination with a passage like the following:

> True ease in writing comes from art, not chance
> As those move easiest who have learned to dance.
> 'Tis not enough no harshness gives offence,
> The sound must seem an echo to the sense.
> Soft is the strain when zephyr gently blows.
> And the smooth stream in smoother numbers flows;

And when loud surges lash the sounding shore,
The hoarse, rough verse should like the torrent roar:
When Ajax strives some rock's vast weight to throw.
The line too labours, and the words move slow;
Not so, when swift Camilla scours the plain,
Flies o'er the unbending corn, and skims along the main.
                    Alexander Pope, The Craft of Verse

- Beat out an iambic speech. Speak it aloud. Keep the breath free. Physically feel the rhythm through your body. Let the heavy stesses bring you up out of your body and the lighter stresses ease along the surface.
- Swing your arms up with the upbeat and down with the downbeat of the iambic rhythm. Walk the rhythm. Run and then skip it. After each physical release, stand still and speak the same line(s) of verse feeling the pulse inside you but never dominating the voice. You will feel the iambic lift the energy of speaking and fill you full of compulsive excitement. After you have felt this pulse try experimenting with it, relishing the notion that the iambic creates energy inside you. Never fall beneath or drop off this plateau of energy as you return the speaking to a normal voice. Physicalising the line in order to produce this impact of energy allows you to experience a point of tension that becomes a releasing agent for the speaker and a taut thread between speaker and listener.
- Return again to speaking the lines. Pause with the thought and also against it. Let the energy drop. You will begin to feel the iambic failing to give you energy. You will, in fact, feel both yourself and the verse unravelling through energy loss. Try accompanying this part of the exercise with a physical movement. Slump, for instance, as you pause. As you start to speak again you will have to energise your body doubly. An image I use that you may experience is one of continually falling off a surf-board or skate-board. You keep missing the wave or trip over a rutted surface. Think of the energy you then have to use to get started again.
- Now speak the verse again obeying each natural pause indicated in the lines, but hold the energy at each of these pauses. This will be directly linked to a full active and ready breath that will be in reserve for you when you start to speak again. This way you never lose a state of alertness. You'll

remain like a tiger ready to pounce. This can be done also with movement as well, either walking or moving your arms. This time when you pause correctly and maintain breath, the body remains suspended, it doesn't droop. In essence, the iambic is held on the surface – through any silence. It never loses its energy.

- Now try speaking the same lines in groups of twos or more. You can all use the same speech or a variety of verse lines. First try how it feels when you drop the energy. That is, speak a line and don't pass it on to the next person. Metaphorically speaking you are physically dropping the ball, pulling away, slumping. The person picking up the lines will have no energy to nurture them but must manufacture it out of nowhere. As we know from physics, all energy is transferable and never wasted. Share this rather depressing and draining experience. You are killing the iambic. Everything will seem hard going and sluggish, as when a chorus all stop and start a tune at different points and fail to achieve unity. Every time a new speaker takes over it is like push-starting a car. In a group this works well in a circle.

- Now serve the iambic. Treat its speaking like the running of a well-timed relay. As you hand over the line to the next speaker, keep the energy up. Don't drop off or come up short. This doesn't mean you need push your voice but you stay true to the iambic, pausing just long enough to let it elide and lock with a partner phrase. Physically you give the line over. Think of the gesture as an energised body. You will feel the ease and glory of this shared energy within seconds. The line and the words will become more intense and efficient as the verse travels round the room. In the group exercise the circle will fill with energy and urge itself towards completion. You are now serving the iambic.

- Mouth the text. Silently. Keep breathing and thinking. Really move all the organs of articulation to confront every written sound. Are there pieces of text that are physically difficult to get your mouth round? Are they difficult to say? If so then the idea or emotion could be difficult to face or feel. Anything that is difficult to say, physically, difficult to get your mouth round, is difficult to feel, think or express. After this exercise, the text will be easier to say out loud. It will be clearer and less blocked in many ways.

18. 'Clearing the Thought' Exercise

This exercise can be done in groups of two or more. The group should remain sympathetic and patient throughout this exercise but also tough. I sometimes call this the 'stop the speaker drill'.

- Find a text that is full of complex or long thoughts. The speaker starts the text to try to communicate the thoughts precisely. At any time the audience, if they fail to understand a thought or hear a misplaced stress or emphasis, can stop and ask the speaker a question connected to the text. The speaker can only answer the question by using the text – not paraphrasing an answer – and once having satisfied the questioner the speaker re-speaks the line. For example, this first line of Viola's soliloquy from *Twelfth Night* (2.2.17–41):

    I left no ring with her. What means this lady?

    The sequence of questions might go like this:

    Speaker: 'I left no ring with her.'
    Question: No what?
    Speaker: No 'ring' – I left no *ring* with her.'
    Question: With who?
    Speaker: With 'her' – 'I left no *ring* with *her*. What means this lady?'
    Question: This who?
    Speaker: This *lady* – 'what means this *lady*?'
    And so on through the entire soliloquy.

- This stop and start method can proceed through the whole speech. The questions must be fair, however. If you hear what is being said do not stop the speaker. What normally happens is that the speaker quickly realises that she cannot cheat the meaning or the words and begins to clarify both within a few lines, managing to get through the speech without further interference. I have used this exercise when I know the speaker understands the language of a text but is failing to communicte that understanding fully. Each speaker quickly learns to need the words because the listener needs to hear them.

- This exercise also clarifies stress and inflection. You might also try to stop the speaker if the spoken lines seem off or wobbly. The simple act of having feedback can transform a speaker's needs. The sense of a potential challenge from an audience is enough to make any speaker's communication more muscular. Always remember that when you speak to an audience you assume a leadership or conducting role. They are there to follow the beat you set in motion. And it must be a clear and certain beat.

19. 'I Don't Believe You' Exercise

How many times in the theatre or lecture room have you yearned to shout out to an actor or speaker: *I don't believe you?*

Well, here is an exercise you can do in couples or groups to check on your own authenticity as a speaker. This exercise works well when you feel a speaker has become disconnected from the text. You may sense that either the thought or the feeling is not needed or the words are not 'known' deeply enough by the voice. These forms of disconnection often reveal themselves in the voice as having either too thin or dull a vocal quality or a too rich and sentimental tone. This exercise tackles both problems.

- Quite simply the speaker begins to speak the text. If at any point you do not believe or are not convinced by him or her call out: *I don't believe you.*
- The speaker has to go back and re-speak the text until the rebellious listeners are silenced. That is until they are believers. Be very careful that the speaker keeps breathing and does not resort to pushing vocally but remains steady with the words.

I have often used this exercise with companies of actors who have rehearsed in a very blocked or physical way, when the text has not been fully explored but movement has. The exercise can quickly connect speakers to the need for spoken truth and the by-product will be a clarifying of the story. In this exercise it is better to have an outside judge. That is, someone who can move the exercise when they are satisfied that belief has been met, otherwise members of the audience may get unjustifiably tough or heckle the speaker. This is an exercise that demands toughness from the speaker. But if you look at Mark Antony's long speech to an unruly crowd in the forum in Act 3, Scene 2 of *Julius Caesar*, you'll see him subjected to exactly this same kind of 'I don't believe you' treatment. Try interrupting a speaker as he or she speaks Mark Antony's funeral oration:

> Friends, Romans, countrymen, lend me your ears,
> I come to bury Caesar, not to praise him.
> The evil that men do lives after them;
> The good is oft interrèd with their bones;
> So let it be with Caesar. The noble Brutus
> Hath told you Caesar was ambitious;
> If it were so, it was a grievous fault,
> And grievously hath Caesar answered it.
> Here, under leave of Brutus and the rest –
> For Brutus is an honourable man,
> So are they all, all honourable men –
> Come I speak in Caesar's funeral.
> *Etc.*

- The speaker should use *only* the words that Shakespeare gives you to quell the crowd and make them believe you. Stick with the rhythm. This exercise, in fact, is true to the intention of the text, because in this speech Mark Antony turns the crowd's anger against Brutus and his fellow conspirators. Use the words to get and hold the crowd's attention until they stop interrupting you.

20. The Journey through the Text

Imagine that the first word of any given text is the first step on the road and the final word of the text finishes a journey.

Is the journey straightforward or are there many detours or changes in direction? The more straightforward the easier it will be to speak. But remember that straightforward journeys can be tiring without variety and stops along the way.

- List what has been discovered, how many new ideas and feelings explored (in heightened text you will be amazed at the number of discoveries) and realise that by the end of the speech the character has changed. The act of speaking out loud has changed their inner and outer position in the world.
- As you work through the text note all the rough spots and treacherous corners. See where you will have to slow down as well as where you can speed up. Use the text like a map. There may be descriptive passages where you are just enjoying the scenery and the view. Some points where you may be day-dreaming. Other points where you may have to spring into furious action. Each text journey is different, which is why you must pave the passage carefully in advance.

21. The Story-Line Exercise

This has many of the same principles as the 'I Don't Believe You' exercise above but helps specify the storyline in a speech, scene or play. You can do this by yourself or in couples or groups or more. I have had whole theatre companies do this exercise throughout a full-length play.

- In your own words describe what happens to you in each sequence of action. Clarify what actually happens to you physically. For instance: 'I cross the room, I sit in the chair, the door bell rings, etc.' Don't muddle the action with thoughts or feelings, just deal with the practical facts of what happens next. Phrases like, 'And then I . . .' or 'Now I . . .' will help clarify the moment the text signals.

  As soon as you have done a speech or scene in this way, go straight back and re-speak the text following the path you've laid out. I think you will be amazed how much clearer the storyline has become after doing this diagram of the action the words make you perform. What normally shocks the speaker is how much actually happens in a text. A rich imaginative journey is usually taken.

- Now walk while speaking the text. Allow the different rhythms, phrasing units, changes of thought and emotional mood swings to shift the direction, speed and quality of your walking. In this exercise you will discover many corners, bends and U-turns in the journey of a text. Don't be frightened of permitting the text to throw you forward, slow you down, make great sweeping walks or runs across the room or even stop you cold or mow you down. You are making the intellectual, emotional and *physical* journey of the words actual and real. Imagine that if someone was observing you from above they would see a journey traced out below them, a picture drawn in time and space. When you return to speaking the text standing still, allow your body and voice to be filled with the physical journey you have just experienced. Your listeners ultimately must be taken on an imaginative journey as well.

22. The Discovery Exercise or 'Of Course'

This exercise is used to good effect when a text is exploring many thoughts and feelings simultaneously, each of which is difficult to sort out. When a speaker won't allow himself or herself to experience a discovery or change through discoveries made, he or she will always sound generalised.

- Begin to speak a complex text. In front of each new discovery in the speech insert the words 'of course'. You will be breaking up sentences and perhaps plodding along but this may reveal that one sentence has four or five discoveries contained within it. Weigh the different values of each discovery to see if one is greater than the other.
- As soon as you have laid out the text in this manner, go back immediately and speak it without the 'of courses' and just revel in how many lights are switched on by your voice, head and heart as the discoveries are re-made.
- Try the exercise with this piece from *Macbeth*.

> *Of course* if it were done when 'tis done *of course* then
> 'twere well it were done quickly. *Of course* If

th'assassination could trammel up the consequence, and
of course catch with his surcease, success: *of course*, that
but this blow might be the be all and *of course* the end
all here – *of course*, but here upon this bank and shoal of
time *of course* we'd jump the life to come . . . *etc.*

Now go back and blank out the 'of courses' and experience
how the discoveries live more in your voice. Moment by
moment the words have a more animated expressiveness.

23. The Range Exercise

This is a simple sequence to free up not only your vocal range
but also the emotional intensity of a text.

- Choose an extremely heightened and emotional speech. This
  can be one exploring any feeling you choose. As you do this
  sequence keep breathing as low as possible, making certain
  that the voice stays open and flexible. But don't shout in
  order to achieve this deep intensity. Go in the opposite
  direction, in fact.
- Speak the speech devoid of range. This will make you feel
  dull as well as sounding dull. Your body will probably also
  reflect this dullness by becoming flaccid and diminishing in
  status.
- Next speak the speech in the most extravagant way you can.
  Allow the body to free up and your gestures to be large. You
  will probably sound like an Edwardian actor. At first you may
  feel self-conscious or silly but persevere and you will begin to
  enjoy yourself and feel more and more liberated.
- Now immediately return to speaking 'normally'. You will be
  delighted at how rich your voice suddenly sounds and how
  solid the emotional connections to the text have become.

24. Physical Releases of the Text I

Your body and breath will become more organically connected
to texts if you physically play with and link speaking to
motion. Movement releases what we need to say.

- Walk, run, sit, stand, lie, jump, skip. Throw balls, push carts, swing. All this will help if you do it as you speak. But try to find the movement that best suits the text you are speaking.
- If you throw a ball as you speak, the energy of throwing something away from you will help you to release the words more efficiently. It also makes the process less self-conscious. Then try speaking the same text pulling something into you like a pillow or cushion. A very different kind of speaking energy will be experienced. Emotionally and intellectually you will also feel different. The throw releases the word. The pulling back tends to deny or muffle it.
- Do the same exercise in couples or in a group. The pull-back can also be achieved with a rope held taut between two speakers engaged in a give and take tug of war (see also 'Antithesis' above). The rope must not go slack as either partner or group speaks. You will find that the physical exertion and tension will enter the word and give it a new life and muscularity as energy is expended. You will also notice a greater need for the words because you are suddenly engaged in a contest of strength and will.
- A wonderful exercise for heightened text speaking, particularly verse, is to speak whilst pushing something relatively substantial. As you push you can feel a powerful connection to the breath and body. Push against a wall and speak. Feel how the words enter the wall along with your strength.
- You will gain a similar connection and vitality through a word by holding a chair above your head and speaking. Don't be timid. Hold the chair as though you were about to hurl it at a favourite target. This allows you to experience how much weight certain words carry.
- Working in groups of twos: one partner should try to offer resistance (not too violently) whilst the other speaking partner pushes against him or her with the words. As you begin to feel this pressure coming through the body, breath and voice into the word, you will immediately begin to notice the release when you pull off a word, line or thought. You will vividly experience the denial throughout the body. The person being pushed can also comment on the speaker pulling away from the push. It is fascinating how the energy of the word is so clearly expeienced in this exercise. The need is

actually pressing. The struggle to release words into space has to be active and thus very tangible.

- After all of these exercises repeat the text without the physical activity but retaining the memory of it. There will be wonderful traces of the muscularity of language, line and thought left in even a static speaking position. The voice will also sound richer and more varied and centred. You should be feeling the energy inside as if you have been 'working out' with the words. The exertion will make you feel a greater need to release the inner energy outwardly. You will need the words more and the words will feel absolutely necessary.

25. Physical Releases of the Text II

These are exercises to anchor the text to your physical position. This will immediately affect your thinking, feeling and status as a character.

- Find two different texts. One joyful, one depressed or use the lines (1) 'I am so happy' and (2) 'I feel defeated'. Now slump and speak the joyful text or (1). Stand and open your arms as though you are about to embrace someone you love. Speak the depressed text or (2) with the same embrace. It will feel very odd. Now reverse the physical stances, speaking about joy from the open position. The results will be obvious. The physical attitude will suddenly match or betray the words.
- The same procedure can be used for other emotions. For example, an aggressive stance with a gentle phrase; the pose of a low-status victim delivering a high-status utterance. Reverse and mix stances and utterances.
- By experimenting with appropriate/inappropriate physical stances and texts, you will very quickly realise how important the right physical position is and what body language does to the presence of words. As you adopt the appropriate position, not only will it be easier to speak but it will be easier to feel and think the text together. Body, voice and word spring from the same impulse. They need to work in concert. Of course, there are many times in life when we do say something but mean the opposite. Voice, body and intention

are out of synch. On these occasions our bodies probably reveal the truth that our voices and words disguise.

26. Breath and the Text

Breathing is our most important activity. When we stop breathing we die! Without breath words die as lines falter. Without proper breathing our connection to language flounders.

Breath not only powers the voice but contains our emotions. To feel healthy we must breathe fully. To think clearly we have to take sufficient breath. Just to ascend a flight of stairs without wheezing you have to breathe. If we stint our breath then we often cannot release our thoughts and feelings through words.

A liberating text may sound frustratingly mediocre when spoken by a speaker who cannot breathe in a liberating way or is holding or blocking his or her breath. An emotionally powerful text can sound indifferent and limp if the speaker cannot release his or her lower breath or find the words embedded in the gut. Highly energised thinking in a text may be communicated in a fragmented, nonsensical way if the speaker cannot breathe quickly enough with the thoughts.

These blocks in breathing and in speaking prevent a text's fine intensity, rhythm and pace from being realised.

In an ideal speaking world the breath should be organic to the text and unconscious for the speaker. You should be breathing with the text and for it. For this to happen, the breath system has to be free, flexible and muscular (see 'Workout' on p. 89). If this freedom is achieved, then the speaker can automatically respond to the writer's breath patterns, pace and rhythm. The speaker will pick up the changes of breath in a text and immediately transform his or her own system.

This is the ideal state – breathing with the speaking. However, what normally happens is that a speaker tries to impose his or her own breath habits and patterns onto any text. A text with a different breath pattern cannot be fully released emotionally or intellectually because it is being constrained and strangled.

Here are some exercises to shift breath patterns and unearth other ways of breathing through a text. Again the trick you must play on yourself is to do an exercise and, before you have time to think, go back onto the text and speak it again on full voice. Then you will find you breathe the text differently.

- The basic exercise here is to allow yourself to run out of breath before speaking a speech. When the body needs breath it will breathe of its own accord and by-pass our will.
- After you have run and got slightly breathless, start to speak a speech. Sometimes you will suddenly discover the organic breathing spaces in a text. Your holds on the text will disappear and you will touch a deeper means of feeling the text as well as thinking it. I often think that Messenger speeches in Greek tragedy and Elizabethan drama – where the message must be spoken above and past fatigue – work best for this exercise. Try this portion of the speech of the weary, bloody Captain who reports to King Duncan in the opening moments of *Macbeth*:

> KING DUNCAN: Dismayed not this our captains, Macbeth
> and Banquo?
> CAPTAIN: Yes, as sparrows eagles, or the hare the lion.
> If I say sooth, I must report they were
> As cannons overcharged with double cracks,
> So they doubly redoubled strokes upon the foe.
> Except they meant to bathe in reeking wounds
> Or memorize another Golgotha,
> I cannot tell –
> But I am faint. My gashes cry for help.

- Extend the breath and shift any short breath patterns by breathing in and speaking as far as you can go on one breath. Recover the breath and start again. Go through a whole speech like this. Ignore punctuation and line lengths and just rely on a free, deep breath without any holds or blocks. Be inspired by the message, not the grammar! Breathe in and speak, marking your own pauses naturally. Everything should stay very fluent. This exercise is particularly good for texts that have long thought processes. Contemporary speakers can break up the sense of a very long thought by matching short thought breaths to texts that need long breaths, stacking up and elongating the extended thinking patterns. You will begin to sense a longer arc of thought and, as the breath frees, feel the power of fuller ideas.

- Now deliberately over-breathe a text. That is, break up all those long thoughts by taking too many breaths. The rhythm now becomes choppy and asthmatic. Experience how that interferes with the text's sense. You will probably be taking short shallow breaths and that will also cut you off from the text's emotional power. Your need to breathe suddenly overpowers your need to speak words!

27. Rooting the Word into the Breath

The lower we breathe a word, the deeper its effect on us. If we take a word deep into our own breathing system then its meaning resonates through us in a very different and profound way.

Take an emotional text or several powerful words or 'all or nothing' phrases that encompass love, hate, despair, woe, mourning, joy, fear (e.g. 'I love you'; 'No longer mourn for me'; 'They that have power to hurt'). Pick the kind of phrase that emotionally challenges you and to which you can attach a need.

- Lie on the floor comfortably with your knees up, soles of the feet on the floor. Don't clamp your thighs and keep your shoulders free. Draw in breath, low and deep into the groin. Take your time and don't rush the breath.
- Start to speak the words from that deep position as you exhale the breath. Feel the words that low in the breath. Maybe you have to breathe each word separately at first. You will begin to feel more power as you speak the word.
- Now build up words in a line with the breath. You take a

breath low and speak the first word *I*; then breath *I love*; finally breath *I love you* and so on through the whole of your chosen sentence.

- Rooting words in this manner allows you to build up a whole line or thought. It also gives you confident control over sentences. Many people get emotionally stirred as they do this exercise and discover how connected the word is to the breath and our deepest feelings. So let the emotion join the phrasing because at this point you are linking essential need with words.

- Now just experience how different the feeling is if you do the same exercise from a high rather than low breath. That is, if you breathe high into the chest and then speak the same text. Just try it a few times. The words will not affect or churn you up in the same way. You will probably experience a disconnection from the word rather than the powerful need you get from low breathing.

- Repeat both low and high breath exercises in a standing position.

- Now speak a longer piece of text *without* using much breath or breath support.

- Now do the same piece of text *with* breath and support. There will be no comparison. The second time you will understand and feel the words better. You may also find a new confidence behind the outpouring of the words.

28. Vocal Release of the Text

Here are a few ways of discovering how different vocal qualities inform a text. Each quality will make you feel different and could release new meanings when speaking a text.

After each exercise it will be useful for you to intone the text to 'clean' the words of any prior intentions. Keep breathing and vocally free. Try some of these positions:

- Speak a piece of text while 'thinking' the voice into the head, the nose, the face, the throat, the chest. Each of these positions gives a different vocal quality but also a different

psychology and emphasis to the words. Intone and then speak
the text. New nuances may be discovered.

- Speak off your voice or close to a whisper. Then do the same
  text on full voice. What differences and nuances do you
  sense?
- Speak pulling off the words; i.e. not finishing them. Now
  finish and follow each word and thought through to the end,
  keeping the voice engaged until the end of each word. Does
  that seem more satisfying and controlled?
- Choose a piece of text with high thinking energy like any
  Restoration passage or one from Oscar Wilde. Mumble the
  text first and then speak it clearly. Next speak it *too* clearly;
  over-articulate it. Finally speak it with life but not with so
  much life that the technique of speaking masks the words.
- Take a highly charged emotional text, like one by Marlowe or
  a later Jacobean writer like John Webster. Over-speak the
  vowels; forcibly exaggerate them. Now over-work the
  consonants. Then merge both processes to find the correct
  balance you need.
- Take either kind of text and feel how disconnection occurs,
  intellectually or emotionally, if you push your voice and rant
  or if you embellish the voice and sound too beautiful or
  sentimental. Then intone and speak the text simply, needing
  not only every word but every sound.

Bearing in mind all of these many exercises and their simple
skills, we are ready at last to set the voice free among a whole
group of further text examples.

6 Working Further with Texts

The need for words is born of a pressing need to speak; provided, of course, that we have something to say. In many instances, especially for actors and all other public speakers, that something will be a prepared text.

In the act of speaking we all become actors. So throughout this section I use 'actor' to mean the wide range of speakers who have to do things with words out loud to an assembly of listeners.

How do you learn to need the words of others and then to express them for yourself?

Throughout this book I have been highlighting what I think are some of the marvels of the voice and also many of the barriers which inhibit free vocal expression when we speak words. We've looked at various exercises which I think help a speaker to become more easy and familiar in the realm of words. What I would now like to do is take you on a further journey through a series of familiar and unfamiliar texts so you can begin mating your own voice to the challenge of speaking aloud.

In each of the examples given below you should not just read the highlighted passages but speak them out loud. It is vital that you get the words out into the air and exercise them. Here is your chance not just to work out your voice but to make the crucial connection between the meanings and the sounds of words. I have chosen these texts because of their sound qualities, their specific 'texture'. I also think they challenge you to grapple with them, to rely on your voice to carry you through and to make meaning out of what you speak. I use them to illustrate a number of points over and over again.

The Marriage between Voice and Text

The voice and the text should marry. One is mutually dependent on the other for sound and sense. One ought to partner and support the other in any speaking act. A voice that is lost or uncommitted loses connection with a text. A text that eludes us will never find a voice.

Not only must a marriage take place between the voice and the word in order to release a text, but the great juggling act in speaking a text magnificently is the further marriage between two clear tensions in the text: the overall structure and style of the writing and your very own personal association to words and images.

The first tension could be described as the speaker's respect for the writer's skill, the way a writer marries words and sentences together. All good writing is skilfully wrought. You play the text the way a musician plays a score, adding your own unique expression and emphasis as a crucial ingredient to an imaginative act already in action on the page.

The second tension in this marriage is when the speaker's own experience and creativity must emerge without imposing too heavily on a writer's achievements. Your voice blends with that of the writer. Every individual's connection to a word is unique and this area of work normally satisfies actors more than the first half of the marriage: respect for the writer's words.

In many ways every speaker becomes the new 'author' of a text; your very speaking of it and stress of it will mint an altogether new experience of the words for a listener. So the author's meaning will always be overlaid with your meanings.

Actors who merely – though skilfully – play a text for limited meanings (giving full respect to what they think a writer intends) and obey its rules will give clear, pure readings of the text as far as that is possible. But an audience will quickly detect that the speaker doesn't need the text in a deeply personal way, that he or she has made no intimate investment in what is being said. You can, after all, be too slavish in serving a text. This kind of actor might not care enough about the specific images or be incapable of throwing undiscovered shafts of light onto the words. The audience hears and understands. But are they moved?

At the other extreme, actors and speakers who passionately need and search for more intentions in the words, without strictly obeying the writer's needs, may have a free-spirited time but lose the essential communication. They have personalised a need out of all proportion to either the writer's or the audience's needs. They have overstepped the marriage contract between writer and speaker. To a different extent, not playing the text appropriately will constrict the play's inner power and momentum. The energy locked into a verse line cannot be released or the length of thought carried forward and understood because the actor has so totally gone his or her way.

So two partners – the writer and the actor – must go hand in hand through the process of working on a text. Never be frightened of separating the two halves of the partnership momentarily, letting each go its own way awhile, for the purpose of experimentation before you finally join them together in a lasting bond.

With voice and text work you must constantly explore and experiment, always in search of the right levels and balances. That is, you can break all the rules of verse in order to find and need words and images. Equally you can play the text for all its power in terms of verse structure or iambic line ending, temporarily suspending fine connections to the word, before the two processes come back together. But in the final analysis the writer's text and the speaker's text should sound as equal as can be.

Proper text work is not for lazy or selfish speakers. Balance rarely comes with the first or second try. Like warming the voice you must 'warm' the text. You must be willing to submit the text to its own kind of workout. To marry both forms of speaking the text you will need enormous intellectual and emotional energy: an athletic vocal technique, a spirit willing to experiment and experience sound and sense, a full generosity to share all with an audience by exposing the secrets of the text's form and power. I often think that many actors become selfish where a text is concerned, too quickly imposing a meaning before letting different meanings reverberate for the time being. Actors, I often find, 'set' a text much too quickly, cutting themselves off from the further richness of possibilities.

Every type or style of text requires different points of concentration, different emotional or intellectual tensions. Yet these tensions should not manifest themselves in the voice, but in the word, the length of thought, rhyme, rhythm, stress. The writer's structure will contain the tension and conflict which the speaker must use to release the text's power. Always remember that most great pieces of writing are about struggle of one kind or another. We often write or speak in order to discover meaning by making connections. To do that we often have to list the pros and cons, the positive and negative forces that are in conflict inside a piece of writing. So you have to expect the process of speaking texts to be a tussle. We do have to grapple with words, sometimes working hard to bend them into the shape we desire.

A skilled writer uses a great many techniques which every speaker ought to know about and be able to master. These techniques are not only a map that helps us to enter a text and get our bearings, but crucial signals that actually 'direct' or 'conduct' the voice in the presentation of words. Some of these techniques are implied in the general character of the writer and some are in the specific structure of the words, sentences and paragraphs. All of these techniques – words

we've learned at school and probably forgotten – are worth
recalling before we begin tackling texts in earnest.

Clues from the Great Writers

Every good piece of writing gives vocal clues to the speaker.
Great writers instinctively understand the connection between
the words we say and the intentions behind them. All of the
great dramatic characters, those of Shakespeare for instance,
are revealed through their choice of words. You can do a
useful close analysis of any Shakespearean character just
through his or her speech alone and how a character uses
words and chooses words. In the act of heightened speaking,
characters need and are given words appropriate to themselves
and their dramatic situations. As King Lear's rage is aroused
against his daughter Goneril, for example, he finds it so easy
to summon and release violent, intemperate words. They spit
out of his mouth like flames:

> Detested kite . . .
> . . . Blast and fogs upon thee!
> Th'untended woundings of a father's curse
> Pierce every sense about thee!

But at the close of Lear's terrible and painful journey the
reverse happens as his rage subsides. Suddenly he needs
simple, soothing, uncomplicated words. Words that will heal
his earlier outrages. He has, so to speak, returned to his
senses as in this scene with his good daughter Cordelia. His
words are not divided by rattling anger but come together
harmoniously:

> We two alone will sing like birds i'the cage.
> When thou dost ask me blessing, I'll kneel down . . .

Tempestuous exaggeration has found new simplicity. This is
the language of humility and communion. Lear's kingly,

paternal pride has been humbled. He speaks simple poetry, clear innocent images that heal, not damage. But to reach this simple choice of words Lear has travelled a stormy, tragic route.

The Poetry Barrier

Poetry is a word that sends most speakers into fits of shuddering. Poetry is a barrier because so many of us fear it. What we really fear is some artificial barrier we might call verse structure: the skeleton that holds the shape of a poem together.

Most of us think we would not be caught dead speaking poetry (too artificial, too aesthetic we think) and yet we do it often. We speak it in heightened moments every day, when our language becomes unembellished, direct and to the point. Poetry is often the result. We also come to poetry when everyday, mundane language is not enough to describe an aching need. Poetry is the highest expression through words of our subjective and collective feelings, thoughts and imagination.

Poetry endures and has universal appeal (every culture speaks or writes poetically) because poetry restlessly explores the great feelings and debates that unite and intrigue humankind. We instantly resort to imagery, simile, rhythm and rhyme as we search beyond everyday language to give thoughts a kind of grace. Recall those times when you have spoken from the 'heart' about love, loss, grief, joy, enlightenment. You've searched for the precise word to encapsulate an overpowering sensation. A word that would summarise everything. This effort is the distilling power of poetry at work and yet you are not consciously trying to be 'poetic'. You are trying desperately to express a need through words.

A colleague who is a therapist working with highly disturbed patients, the so-called 'criminally insane', maintains that as a patient begins to talk about his or her life – their deepest troubles and pain – he or she will always do so poetically. I've experienced the same thing whenever I teach in prisons. Whenever our life is in a state of crisis or severe deprivation we find we need poetry. It cuts to the roots of our dilemma more cleanly than wordy prose. As a means of exposure it is instantly naked. Acute images speak for themselves. I think we need poetry always at certain times of our lives. We harbour a secret wish for it and probably resort to it more than we know.

The poet explores and refines the process of emotional articulateness under stress by choosing images, line length, rhythm, rhyme and repetition to create a linguistic scaffolding so that the full intensity of an emotion can be contained, focused and then powerfully released. Poems come in all sizes and shapes. They are limitless in what they can do and the language they can employ.

An American director I know always says that you can tell whether or not Shakespeare trusts a character's humanity because only those with the greatest compassion use poetic images with complete ease. Poetry for them is neither empty nor laboured. Its need is instantly felt.

The Structure of Verse

Verse needs the structure it chooses in order to hold up the words it uses. The scanning patterns we find in verse are really like transmitting frequencies we use to tune in the sound of the poem, making it sensible to the ear. These patterns are signalled in any number of ways: rhythm, line length, rhyme, alliteration, assonance, repetition, etc. Anything that puts words into a conscious pattern on the page may be said to have a verse structure, even though it may not sound poetic in a heightened way. Think of a limerick or doggerel:

> There was a young fellow called Paul
> Who went to a Fancy Dress Ball

He thought he would risk it
And go as a biscuit
But the dog ate him up in the hall.

This is not great poetry, but it does have rhyme at the end of each line which gives it rhythm. Rhyme and rhythm are both features of poetry, but poems need not have any rhyme at all. Blank verse, for instance, is characterised by its lack of end rhyme. The same is true of free verse.

The Way Words Work

When a student or actor learns to work on a text he or she naturally has to learn a new vocabulary for all the tricks of language. Rhetoric, meaning simply the 'craft of speaking', gives us a map of the way words work. Its devices are tools that make us word-conscious. Classical rhetoric fell out of fashion during the 1950s. Yet a pared-down version of rhetoric can be a useful means to finding voice within a text.

What are rhetorical devices? They are simply a means of describing the vocal tricks of the trade, terms that signal what a word or phrase is doing. As long as we uncover the human side of these technical terms we are in no danger of being alienated from their meanings. The experience of language and the universe of words are both an adventure. With the rhetorical device we have a means of searching out the way words work. Here are just some of the many rhetorical devices we use all the time to give our words a special quality:

- *Alliteration*   This term literally means 'putting letters together'. It signifies the repetition of the same sound, more often than not a repeated consonant at the start of each word in a sequence (e.g. the *h* and *b* in 'Hung be the heavens with black'; the *f* in 'Full fathom five thy Father lies'). Alliteration is a common feature of old English verse, continually pops up in Shakespeare, is still used today by headline writers and advertising copywriters and generally captivates the ear with a pleasing repetition of sound. To speak alliteratively and make sense of the wit usually contained in the sounds, one must be attuned to the consonants, as the base-born Edmund is in *King Lear*:

>   Why brand they us
> With base? with baseness? bastardy? base, base? –
>   . . . Well then,
> Legitimate Edgar, I must have your land.
> Our father's love is to the bastard Edmund
> As to th' legitimate. Fine word, 'legitimate!'
> Well, my legitimate, if this letter speed
> And my invention thrive, Edmund the base
> Shall top the legitimate. I grow, I prosper.
> Now, god, stand up for bastards!

- *Anacoluthon*   The technical term for a sudden change in direction in the midst of a speech or line of dialogue, as in Lady Macbeth's:

> That which hath made them drunk hath made me bold.
> What hath quenched them hath given me fire.
> Hark, peace! –
> It was the owl that shrieked, the fatal bellman,
> Which gives the stern'st good-night. . . .

Marked here by a dash, the anacoluthon allows the speaker to perform a 'stop, look and listen' action. The steady resolution of the first two lines is disturbed when Lady Macbeth hears a shrieking owl. Using this device gives the speaking of words instant drama and, in this case, suspense.

- *Antithesis*   A balanced verbal construction in which one part or word (the thesis) is set in opposition to the other (the antithesis) for the purpose of strong contrast or ambiguity, as in these two examples from *Macbeth*:

> So *foul* and *fair* a day I have not seen.

or

> I know this is a *joyful trouble* to you,
> But yet 'tis one.

Antithesis is one of the strongest rhetorical devices we find in
speaking dramatic language because it instantly stresses the
conflict between warring words (*fair* vs. *foul; trouble* modified
by *joyful*). Always search for the antithesis in a passage as you
speak it to capture the seesaw balancing act you are being
asked to perform verbally. Antithetical conflict is quite often
set within strict harmony, as in these lines from two of
Shakespeare's sonnets:

> And see the *brave day* sunk in *hideous night* (Sonnet 12)
> And *loathsome canker* lives in *sweetest bud*. (Sonnet 35)

So you not only have tension between the contrasting words
that are in italics (positive to negative in the first instance;
negative to positive in the second) but you sound a greater
tension in the scheme of an iambic pentameter line as a
whole as potential revolt of opposites threatens to break
the harmony of the entire line. This conflict in opposites
reflects the pendulous swing in the speaker's thought or
feeling.

- *Assonance*   The binding together of words through the
likeness of vowel qualities produces assonance as in *lake* and
fate. More intricate than simple end-line rhyme schemes
(e.g. *lake* and *fake*), assonance captures rhyme through
repeated sounds, as in this wonderfully intricate example
from Gerard Manley Hopkins' poem 'The Windhover':

> I caught this morning morning's minion, king-
> dom of daylight's dauphin, dapple-dawn-drawn
> Falcon, in his riding
> Of the rolling level underneath him steady air, and
> striding
> High there how he rung upon the rein of wimpling wing
> In his ecstasy! then off, off forth on swing,
> As a skates heel swipes smooth on a bow-bend: the
> hurl and gliding
> Rebuffed the big wind. My hear in hiding

Stirred for a bird, – the achieve of, the mastery of the
   thing!

You can see how the vowel sounds overwhelm the poem
when spoken and create an exhilarating vocal effect. The
sounds seem freely mixed though the overall structure is
quite controlled.

- *Circumlocution*   A wordy, roundabout way of saying
something quite simple. Official 'bureaucratese' and
technocratic jargon is afflicted with circumlocutions:

   Aero Digital has challenging opportunities for mid-level
   SAS programmers with solid DATA step and MACRO
   programming abilities to augment its current
   employment base.

Simply put, the speaker from Aero has jobs on offer!

- *Climax*   When we speak heightened language the words
ascend step by step towards a climax or payoff. The Greek
root of the word itself actually means 'ladder'. When we
speak with climax inherent in the lines, we almost feel as
though we are climbing towards a plateau against all odds
pulling us in another direction. That's what words are urging
Hamlet to do in this exchange where the Ghost beckons him
one way and his friends the other:

   HAMLET: It waves me still. (*To the Ghost*) Go on, I'll
      follow thee.
   MARCELLUS: You shall not go, my lord.
   HAMELT: Hold off your hands!
   HORATIO: Be ruled, you shall not go.
   HAMLET: My fate cries out,
      And makes each petty artery in this body
      As hardy as the Nemean lion's nerve.

   The Ghost beckons Hamlet.

   Still am I called. Unhand me, gentlemen.
   By heaven, I'll make a ghost of him that lets me.
   I say, away! (*To the Ghost*) Go on, I'll follow thee.

   Exeunt the Ghost and Hamlet

The words here even look like a stepped pathway setting out the tug-of-war for the need of the voices. You never reach a climax without a struggle.

- *Consonance*   The strong use of consonants and consonant clusters produces a sound sharper and often more severe than vowel-driven *alliteration* or *assonance*. Gerard Manley Hopkins' 'Windhover' once more:

> Brute beauty and valour and act, oh, air, pride, plume,
>   here
>   Buckle! And the fire that breaks from thee then, a
>   billion
> Times told lovelier, more dangerous, O my chevalier!

Here the consonants either cut off or enclose the vowels, buckling them tightly together so they cannot release or escape.

- *Echoism*   This delightful device is used when words consciously 'echo' specific sounds for the listener. Here's an extreme example from Steven Berkoff's play *Agamemnon*:

> . . . smooth bore/cannon/trench/mortar/shrapnel/
> tommy gun/and blow pipe/RAT TAT TAT TAT/
> RAT TAT TAT/KA BOOM/KA BLAST/KA BLAM/
>   SPLAT!
> PHUTT! SMASH! PHAM!!!

This is a modern rendition of the kind of echoism you find in Greek tragedy and the works of Homer.

- *Emphasis*   When we speak we are always placing emphasis on one word over another. Through the manipulation of elements like stress, tone, pitch, rhythm, speed or volume we can signal to the listener how we want them to receive our message. A strong emphasis of nouns and verbs over adjectives and pronouns, for instance, can sometimes be a more emphatic way of speaking. The weight we place on one word over another can change the sound in crucial ways. In this passage Macbeth is going off to kill Duncan. Give particular stress to the words in italics and notice what emerges from the emphasis:

I go, and it is *done*. The *bell* invites me.
Hear it not, *Duncan*; for it is a *knell*
That *summons* thee to heaven or to *hell*.

Like the ding-dong clapping of a bell the sound shifts and
alternates: *done/bell*; *Duncan/knell*; *summons/hell*. But
emphasising different stresses may produce something
altogether different from the passage.
- *Euphony*   This term literally means 'sounding good'.
Harmony is euphonious, for instance. It sounds pleasing
rather than harsh. We make harmony with words when we
stress the long vowels and semi-vowels (as in *pleasing*) and
glides (i.e. sounds like 'j' and 'w' which need to slide in a
vowel like 'January weather') which soften the blow of sharp
consonants (as in *harsh*). Great love poetry uses rich euphony
to captivate the listener, as in the first two lines of Romeo's
famous soliloquy to Juliet on her balcony:

But soft, what light through yonder window breaks?
It is the east, and Juliet is the sun.

Progressively, word by word, Romeo's voice is bursting open
like a ray of sunshine. That's euphony in action.
- *Onomatopoeia*   When this device is in use words are simply
being used most freely. When the sound and pronunciation
of a word traps its meaning we are using onomatopoeia,
literally 'giving a name to sound' (e.g. *hiss, ping, bang,
sizzle, gossip, thud*). Lear, during the storm in Act 3, scene 2
of *King Lear*, literally makes the sound effects of the
tempest:

Blow, winds, and crack your cheeks! Rage, blow,
You cataracts and hurricanoes, spout
Till you have drenched our steeples, drowned the cocks!

Drawing on assonance and consonance, onomatopoeic sound
imagines sense. The device is used widely as here in
Tennyson's poem 'The Eagle':

He clasps the crag with hooked hands;
Close to the sun in lonely lands
Ringed with the azure world, he stands.

The wrinkled sea beneath him crawls;
He watches from his mountain walls
And like a thunderbolt he falls.

In Sonnet 127 by Shakespeare, speak the lines capturing the
flavour of just the sounds as onomatopoeic inventions in the
selected words. Use the skill of mingling sound and sense to
capture the essence of the word. Don't even think of abstract
thoughts here but only of the immediate meaning that the
sound invents through the voice:

In the old age *black* was not counted *fair*,
Or if it were, it bore not *beauty's* name;
But now is *black beauty's* successive *heir*,
And *beauty slandered* with a *bastard shame*:
For since each hand hath put on nature's *power*,
Fairing the *foul* with art's *false* borrowed face,
Sweet beauty hath no name, no holy bower,
But is *profaned*, if not lives in *disgrace*.
Therefore my mistress' eyes are *raven-black*,
Her brow so suited, and they *mourners* seem
At such who, not born *fair*, no *beauty* lack,
Sland'ring creation with a *false* esteem.
Yet so they *mourn*, becoming of their *woe*,
That every *tongue* says *beauty* should look so.

● *Puns*   You can get great value out of the playful interaction
   of words that sound alike (homonyms) and have a joking
   relationship. Puns are fanciful formations out of which
   humour explodes from the energetic combustion of sound
   meeting sense: 'A pun is a pistol let off at the ear; not a
   feather to tickle the intellect' (Charles Lamb).

As you work more and more with words and become fascinated with all the activity and action that happens in language,
these rhetorical devices become dynamic tools with which to
craft and hone the spoken word. My aim here has been to
give you not an exhaustive catalogue of rhetorical devices but
merely a taste of the way words will be working in some of
the passages ahead.

Starting with Shakespeare

Where voice and text are concerned there is simply no better writer than Shakespeare.

One could write a whole volume on just voice and Shakespeare alone. I think, though, that it's important to put Shakespeare in the context of other writers, otherwise I'd leave you with the impression that Shakespeare performs the tricks the other writers miss, which, of course, is not the case. To make Shakespeare one voice among many other poets and playwrights allows you to see technique of more variety percolating throughout the body of written English. But starting with Shakespeare does mean that we can look at some astonishing examples of language that release meaning once spoken from need.

It's a difficult task to choose only a few examples from this master of the spoken word. Yet I think if you begin to notice some of the techniques he uses you'll be equipped to make a more certain journey through his poetry and plays on your own.

Why value Shakespeare? Why is Shakespeare such an important writer, adored by all who take the time to speak his words? Why, in fact, do we *need* Shakespeare?

It is generally agreed that Shakespeare's plays and sonnets explore with enormous compassion and variety all the great dilemmas facing human beings in conflict. Nothing about the human psyche and human action seemed to escape either his interest or understanding. When we speak Shakespeare's words today they sound as fresh and meaningful as the day they were written. These aspects in themselves are amazing. But for our specific concerns there is more. He was a magnificent wordsmith who always perfectly mated the needs of the voice with those of the text.

Shakespeare wrote expressly for the speaker, specifically for the actor of the open-air public theatre. He wrote at a point in history when rich speaking – sermons, proclamations, public debate – was the chief means of disseminating information; his culture made its way largely by word-of-mouth. The majority of choices he makes in terms of the form and structure of his verse and prose are there to help you speak, act, feel and experience his texts fully. The text is literally (and literarily) signposted to help you journey through it. If you allow Shakespeare to help you find your way by joining with the text – not fighting it, competing with it or discarding it – you will begin to feel the mighty voice of Shakespeare compelling you and supporting you at every point. His way with words never lets you falter or go slack. Shakespeare's language is rich, dense, exhilarating and yet always apt and succinct – need is accurately articulated; unless the character over-embellishes. Polonius in *Hamlet* does what most politicians do: speaks too much and uses an elaborated code and twisted syntax to confuse his listener even when he is trying very hard to be succinct. Here an exasperated Queen Gertrude catches him out:

> POLONIUS: My liege and madam, to expostulate
>   What majesty should be, what duty is,
>   Why day is day, night night, and time is time,
>   Were nothing but to waste night, day, and time.
>   Therefore, since brevity is the soul of wit,
>   And tediousness the limbs and outward flourishes,
>   I will be brief. Your noble son is mad –
>   'Mad' call I it, for to define true madness,
>   What is't but to be nothing else but mad?
>   But let that go.
> QUEEN GERTRUDE: More matter with less art.

At the time of Shakespeare's birth the English language was brimming with excitement and novelty, discovery and confidence. Earlier Elizabethan writers – like Christopher Marlowe – had begun to stir things up; forging 'great and thundering speech' that sounded more natural than artificial yet still towered above the common means of expression, as in this sample from the opening six lines of Marlowe's *Tamburlaine the Great*:

> From jigging veins of rhyming mother wits,
> And such conceits as clownage keeps in pay,
> We'll lead you to the stately tent of war,
> Where you shall hear the Scythian Tamburlaine
> Threat'ning the world in high astounding terms,
> And scourging kingdoms with his conquering sword.

In this kind of word world, pen and sword were evenly matched.

Language, verse and form had been freed imaginatively. Vocabulary was exploding and growing. The stage was set for one magnificent writer to emerge from the pack. Shakespeare was dropped into the middle of this well-ploughed and planted verbal field and he tended the plants and reaped a fertile harvest. You could speculate that if he had been born in a different time and place he would have expressed his wisdom and compassion for humanity, his keen social and political awareness, through music or painting. Language, speaking and theatre were the most intriguing and exciting means available to him, more overwhelming than musical instruments or canvases. So he used theatre to examine life close up. Words were his means of magnification, as Shakespeare never lets us forget: 'These are but wild and whirling words, my lord' (*Hamlet*).

Speaking Shakespeare's Text

Now please don't misunderstand what I am about to say about the ease of speaking a Shakespearean text.

To speak Shakespeare does take work and loads of practice. None of it is learned in an afternoon or a weekend of workshops or from a book like this. Work on Shakespeare should be a lifetime's preoccupation. You have to be true to the text and serve its marvels in a variety of circumstances.

That takes some experience, effort and understanding. You have to be prepared to broach very dangerous parts of yourself and your imagination if you are to release the language's power and the ideas it explores. You will always find it hard, for instance, to summon the emotions needed to play Hamlet or Ophelia until you have lived for quite a while with the play, the words, the character and even yourself. Every good writer demands that kind of fusion. You never really marry with a Shakespearean text until you show that you need it. The stakes are always high with a writer like Shakespeare and it is very easy to bluff (rant or push) or deny (mumble, devoice, or pull away from the words) the text simply because you have not given it its due. However, I passionately believe that a fear of Shakespeare's greatness and a false impression of his textual difficulty has kept him the preserve of privileged intellects instead of being a part of common understanding. This is one of those sad ironies that I hope education will someday address with gusto.

So let me dispel some nagging myths and barriers. I do not believe, for instance, that Shakespeare is hard to understand if you speak him aloud. I do grant that his work poses a greater challenge when silently read and then only *discussed* aloud. Often, when spoken, a Shakespeare text has clear immediacy and instant identification.

To really come to grips with Shakespeare we first have to be given the chance to speak his words out loud with full permission to fail and stumble on our way to meaning. If you speak and sound enough of Shakespeare's texts you will soon understand them with greater ease. The rhythms influence you and exert a force. His language works on every level. Often we are so frightened of not understanding his plays and poems intellectually that we close our ears. The modern ear, in its desperate attempts to zero in on meaning, too often misses the sensual and emotional pleasures of Shakespearean language, particularly his lush use of imagery. With Shakespeare sense is always twinned to sound. Delight in the latter, and you'll discover the former.

Ultimately, of course, you do have to come to grips with Shakespeare intellectually. And yes, some of his words and phrasings take time to adjust to. Some may even need looking up. He did after all write some 400 years ago! Many of his words are bound to have gone out fashion. Surprisingly, though, many are still very much in fashion.

But starting to work with Shakespeare from the intellectual end may not be the most useful point from which to start the process of enjoying and demystifying him. Speak him aloud – as centuries of school children used to do – and what a world of difference awaits you. I have seen scores of children speak and understand his work on quite powerful levels long before they could understand the thoughts imparted by the words. They have tasted the full score before investigating the different notes and phrases. After all, like any great writer Shakespeare takes every opportunity to play language games. He likes to tease and tickle us with words, trick us into believing we are in a world somewhere else. The words are there to be relished by the speaker. Just think of Shakespeare's clowns. They understand an intensity in the word and image which as adults we might overlook or deny. A friend's eight-year-old child recently left a production of *Romeo and Juliet* thrilled with the image of Romeo being, as Juliet says, cut out as little stars. The child may not have understood the play's total image but he retained one of its most startling and telling metaphors. He was touched by poetry. Shakespeare's brilliance is that he seems to be able to speak to us all over those hundreds of years and across every cultural bias and barrier. He is a genius because he understands our likenesses as well as our individuality. He touches all who take time to breathe, speak and need him.

I have taught all over the world many different types of speaker, both the educated and the so-called 'ignorant'. I have taught in prisons, in schools, to adults and children of all ages and backgrounds, English and non-English speakers. In all instances I find that people have understood Shakespeare intuitively, and, what's more, have enjoyed speaking him. The pure physicality of the language and verse seems to release everyone.

Sadly Shakespeare has been put on a pedestal. I am sure he doesn't want to be placed there. So knock him off! Shake him around! Kick, stroke, roll him about – most of all speak him! He will survive. He *has* survived. In the process of shaking him, breathing him, speaking him and playing him in many different voices you will discover how accessible he is, how he serves and helps a courageous, fearless speaker. He even survives bad productions. And bad actors!

Initially, you must allow yourself complete freedom with a great poet like Shakespeare. Then you must engender a respect for the techniques that Shakespeare, as a writer, has chosen to use. Understand that such passion as his has to be contained and focused, otherwise the heat and lava spewed from his verbal volcano will smother, burn and destroy both the speaker and the listener. Trust the need and fully speak his words and you will stay in control. Not your version of control but his. Remember always that technique is a liberating force, not something that shackles you. The techniques Shakespeare uses must be respected and married to a liberated voice. It doesn't matter which way round you do it but you must find passion and govern it through Shakespeare's written cues:

- You must encounter and use the verse form; the iambic, for instance.
- You must also feel the rhythm and line lengths of varying sorts.
- You must learn to embrace the length of thought.
- You must need the words and imaginatively respond to them.
- You must see the images; the pictures the words artfully conjure.
- You must speak, feel and think simultaneously.

- You cannot think or feel outside the language but inside and with it.
- You must never paraphrase a word or thought to such a degree that it becomes too generalised. Hone the words and images until they become very specific.

In the final analysis you must learn to trust the words and yourself saying the words. You'll quickly discover that thoughts and feelings are actually compressed into the words. That is enough and will be appropriate. Like notes of music, every syllable of Shakespeare must be spoken; neither deny nor dispense with any sound that can help you. Otherwise there will be gaping holes when the text is performed. Action happens in Shakespeare through and with the language. The language is so active and alive that radio versions of his plays – which we can only listen to – sometimes leave us with a more intense impression of the drama than stage productions which we see.

Some of the key points I stress to help anyone speak a Shakespeare text can and should be repeated with any writer:

- Beat the lines to isolate the heartbeat of the text. Then ask yourself: Is it steady or irregular, fast or slow, solemn or playful?
- Mouth the text to feel all the syllables and to experience how sound and meaning marry. Are you being asked to say very little or a real mouthful? A carefully measured phrase or a torrent of words? What do the words say about your character?
- Speak only the vowels to release the feeling and emotion in the text. Is the character full of or bereft of either? Does he or she use or shun vowels, the sounds that frequently signal an emotional quality?
- Grapple with the consonants to feel the physical wrestling within the text. Maybe you are a character of action rather than indecision? Maybe your internal thoughts are in chaos?
- Whisper the words to clarify the thoughts like an inner voice. Are these the expressions of someone contemplative and private?

- Embrace the long thoughts to recognise the distance you must travel. How much breath does it take to make this journey? How does it differ from other journeys in other parts of the text?
- Start and finish the line without falling off it in order to tick off the distance involved in the speaking. Speaking Shakespeare demands, but then builds vocal stamina.
- Intone the text to free it. All of Shakespeare's characters speak in order to release their thoughts and feelings. Never deny them that right.
- See and experience the images as kinds of word paintings. Shakespeare uses a high proportion of similes and metaphors to make abstract thought precise and concrete. They also give his words a high relief and bright lustre.
- Notice the speech and the urgency to speak gather momentum as the drama intensifies. Shakespeare compresses time as his drama unfolds. As time appears to fly, thoughts fly too.
- Note how single words must signal sudden shifts in thought and feeling. It is always startling to realise that Shakespeare uses more monosyllabic words than polysyllabic ones. They are quicker to speak. But just introduce an extra syllable and notice the instance mood shift as in Claudius' 'My words fly up, my thoughts remain below.'
- If you get stuck within a thought, find something momentarily incomprehensible or difficult, don't panic. Go back to the beginning and start to unlock the thought bit by bit. You won't succeed if you bash your head against only a small part of the thought. You have to embrace the whole thought and use it to surge forwards. Shakespeare often writes in relatively large units. Too many speakers become incapacitated by individual words and phrases rather than seek connections further along the line. But we speak in sentences and think in paragraphs. Remember what I said earlier about length of thought (p. 116). This notion is crucial for speaking a writer like Shakespeare.
- A great tip of learning any text is to learn it thought by thought, *not* line by line. Thought by thought keeps the speaking real and honest. It also leads to a greater need for the words. They become necessary steps to a result or conclusion.
- Take a complete and fascinating journey with the text. To

speak Shakespeare you must be intensely curious about where each word will lead you next.

Follow all these suggestions (they are not rules!) but make sure the speaking is at all times connected to the breath and with a free and placed voice. Don't hesitate. Get into the arena and play!

Remember that there is *no* definitive way of speaking any text. Your own *individual* experience of life will cast a unique light on any great text and give the listener a sudden new insight. Your experience must always marry with the writer's to forge one of even greater intensity. I might have heard a particular speech or sonnet thousands of times before but each time I hear it again from the mouth of a new speaker who needs the words I learn something fresh. Each new speaker informs a text differently.

Sonnets

A sonnet is a compact piece of poetic writing (literally meaning 'little sound' or 'short poem') that intensely explores a theme both intellectually and emotionally. The writing marries head with heart. That is the double challenge when you speak a sonnet. It's such a perfect poetic invention to speak because the union between these two is so compact and potentially explosive. A sonnet is never long enough to bore a listener. It normally has fourteen lines of iambic pentameter blank verse and usually ends with a rhyming couplet. Its intellectual progress follows the basic rules of classical thinking found in most plays written into the twentieth-century – from the Greeks to George Bernard Shaw:

- The first line or pulse of thought opens up a debate.
- The idea is then explored in the next eleven lines.
- A resolution or conclusion is reached in the final two lines, generally signalled by the rhyming couplet.

As the sonnet moves forward, thinking begins to focus itself, frequently becoming more personal, and then gathers momentum towards a conclusion which normally begins around the ninth line, ending with a rhyming couplet that ties up all the previous twelve lines.

The basic argumentative structure you find in the sonnet is followed by any reasoned speech-maker or debater, by every judge, lawyer or business executive selling an idea. You make a proposition, gather the reasons or evidence to make it acceptable, and then cap the argument with a punch that irrefutably rings of truth. You'll find this structure at the heart of many jokes, wedding speeches and formal presentations as well. That's why the sonnet form is such a crucial one to master. It is elegant thinking perfected into a simple vocal format.

In a Shakespearean sonnet a particular rhyming scheme is used.

ABAB CDCD EFEF GG.

Notice that a new scheme is introduced every four lines and as the rhyming scheme changes so does the direction of the thought. It never stays stuck in one place. Usually it intensifies or sharpens in some way; moves from the general to the specific. A gear change happens which is signalled in the voice and the manner of presentation.

Let's see how this works. Try reading this sonnet out loud, using some of the tips I've laid out above:

Sonnet 12
    A When I do count the clock that tells the time,
    B And see the brave day sunk in hideous night;
    A When I behold the violet past prime,
    B And sable curls all silvered o'er with white;
    C When lofty trees I see barren of leaves,
    D Which erst from heat did canopy the herd,
    C And summer's green all girded up in sheaves,

D Borne on the bier with white and bristly heard:
E Then of thy beauty do I question make
F That thou among the wastes of time must go,
E Since sweets and beauties do themselves forsake,
F And die as fast as they see others grow;
G   And nothing 'gainst Time's scythe can make defence
G   Save breed, to brave him when he takes thee hence.

Notice that the fourteen lines are one complete thought. It is without a full stop until the very end. So there is one great chunk of continuous thinking at work here. An idea is unlocked box by box, getting roomier and roomier as the sonnet fills out. The speaker cannot stop thinking until the last syllable of the final line. I don't mean to say that you mustn't pause. You must in order to breathe. But each pause must be filled with the expectation that the thought will continue. Words and lines cannot fall. Falling would indicate the end of an idea. The idea here, however, rises and rises. Your vocal effort should keep the idea afloat and alive with each new wave, each new strand of time. Nor does it mean that you must rush or speak the whole sonnet on one breath.

Each word must be discovered and experienced as a step towards a complete journey. The speaker must know that he or she is making a plea to someone to have a child: to procreate. The plea is explored by looking at how time passes and how time wastes everything. The listener doesn't know it's a plea to procreate until the last line. They have heard only the varying descriptions of how time passes and what it does to all of us. The summary takes us by surprise. Notice how the sonnet becomes personal in the ninth line with 'thy'. The focus intensifies with the 'thou' like a beam of light finding what it must illuminate.

Notice how time passes:

- The first line, time passes in seconds
- The second line, days
- The third line, seasons
- The fourth line, a lifetime with the whitening of 'sable' hair

In four lines you have made a complete journey: from seconds through to a whole lifetime. The next four lines are examples from Nature to support the argument. This person's beauty when placed within the context of time is questioned. It also puts the speaker in direct contact with a listener. The couplet gives the answer to 'braving' or defying 'Time', that is 'breed' and reproduce. Make yourself immortal. This is a long, sustained thought but very carefully discovered.

Now go back to the beginning of the sonnet and try something else this second time. Use a few tests to explore how the language is chosen and used to convey meaning:

- Whisper the first line. If you speak all that is written you will hear a ticking clock marking out and eating up the seconds of our lives. Try it now. You deny yourself and the audience this experience if you mumble the words and do not speak the whole text or mark the rhythm.

- The fourth line is difficult to say. We can all just face the passing of time in seconds, days and seasons, but to see our hair turn white is traumatic and is, consequently, physically harder to say. A general rule we can make is that when words are difficult to speak there is often a good reason. A tension or conflict exists in the head or heart. Maybe the line – like advancing age – slows you down. We do this to ourselves in life. Our passions, when held, are often found unreleased in our mouths.

- Although a listener doesn't know why the speaker is speaking the sonnet until the last line, there is a signal to the meaning in line five: the word 'barren'. This gives us subliminally a notion of impotence and emptiness. This kind of signalling or foreshadowing is common throughout poetic writing. The chosen images awaken the listener's senses to themes important to a writer. The images work to heighten and prepare us for the telling moments later on. It is as though the images help us to 'see' into the state of the writer's being.

- With 'borne on the bier' the pun on 'carry' and 'birth' gathers up the double picture of the harvest, but also one of a cart carrying a body to the grave. Birth and death are married in one image. Neither one nor the other is of greater importance; each is held in antithetical tension. 'Time' carries a scythe in folklore. Time will harvest us unless we yield a crop and renew ourselves by breeding children.

- The repetition of the softened 'When' at the beginning of lines one, three and five lulls the listener into a false sense of security, wonderfully jolted by the harsher sound of 'Then', in line nine as the sonnet focuses itself and becomes intensely personal.
- When you play with the vowels in the sonnet you will discover how open they are as in: 'That thou among the wastes of time must go'. We are being blown and scattered into destruction like so many heads of wheat in an open field.
- As you speak the last line you will feel that if you speak the 'd' of 'breed' followed by the 't' of 'to' then this stops you and naturally emphasises the crucial word 'breed'. The main conclusion of the sonnet is physically and vocally highlighted if you speak all the sounds fully and not just pass by them.

Now speak the whole sonnet a third time. Only do it more physically. Sense the wrestling consonants. Don't skid over sounds. Marry the consonants to the vowels. Use the iambic to return the energy of the words: de *dum*, de *dum*, de *dum*, de *dum*, de *dum*, etc. Sloppy speech or ignorance of the iambic rhythm destroys a whole layer of meaning and experience for speaker and audience. Keep the heartbeat pulsing. Maybe even let it intensify.

Shakespeare's use of precise words heightens our linguistic imagination, preparing us for the moment of 'breed'. It is the kind of word we have to need in order to release correctly. The imaginative juices are encouraged to flow to make us more open to dramatic points like this. If you can speak this sonnet and cover the fourteen lines of one thought then you are well prepared to initiate and speak any long thoughts. If you aren't following the thought through but stumbling along, clogging the rhythm, you will notice how the lines are either falling away or not starting with sufficient energy.

All of your effort must be active in pursuit of the last syllable of the last line. Every word is a step on the road to

'hence'. This last word is also a kind of beginning: hencefor-
ward, from this time on.

Taking some of the above work with you, have a go at this
next sonnet. Once more speak it out loud:

Sonnet 35
No more be grieved at that which thou has done:
Roses have thorns, and silver fountains mud.
Clouds and eclipses stain both moon and sun,
And loathsome canker lives in sweetest bud.
And men make faults, and even I in this,
Authorizing thy trespass with compare,
Myself corrupting, salving thy amiss,
Excusing thy sins more than thy sins are;
For to thy sensual fault I bring in sense –
Thy adverse party is thy advocate –
And 'gainst myself a lawful plea commence.
Such civil war is in my love and hate
   That I an accessory needs must be
   To that sweet thief which sourly robs from me.

This sonnet explores the complex pain involved in loving
someone who has betrayed you. The antithesis, the main
device used, swings the speaker between the offender's beauty
and the unwholesomeness of his or her behaviour. Here's a
rough list of the antitheticals – the positive and negative words
– used about the offender, Shakespeare's loved one:

Positive	Negative
roses	thorns
silver fountains	mud
moon and sun	clouds and eclipses
sweetest bud	loathsome canker
salving	corrupting, amiss
excusing	sins
in sense	sensual fault
advocate	adverse party
love	hate
sweet	thief, sourly robs

If you follow the mood swings and pendulum of the language, you will begin to feel the antithetical conflict locked into the sonnet's scenario and structure. In order to successfully tap into this struggle you must need and mean each image as you speak it. To help with this:

- Experience the 'rose' before discovering the 'thorn'. The 'silver fountain' before the 'mud'. Each antithetical value summons a different kind of connection.
- The last line has 'sweet thief' which binds the whole conflict together. The person addressed is 'sweet' but also a 'thief'. How does that colour your attitude? It's an ironic statement, so how would you say it?
- The pain, desire and betrayal are complex and this complexity is matched by the image that unfolds in the last five lines. A wronged man in a courtroom is defending the accused: 'and 'gainst myself a lawful plea commence'. You have been mugged and bring a court case to try your mugger, but then you defend your assailant in court. Quite a turn of events! The prosecution becomes the defence. The image is a difficult one but so is the realisation that the love and the hate you feel can create an inner civil war that means you become an accessory to your own downfall and take a responsibility for your pain: 'That I an accessory needs must be/To that sweet thief which sourly robs from me'.
- Again the lines are physically difficult to speak aloud. They slow you down in an attempt to embrace the destructive course you, as the speaker, are taking. Take that slowing down as a signal that caution is needed for the bending curves ahead.
- Try speaking the lines quickly. It's very difficult even if you have an adroit mouth. Shakespeare is saying: Slow down. Face these words and their implication. Stress them so the listener has to face them as well.
- Notice the brilliant puns that in one word explore the duplicity of our feelings: 'salving thy amiss'. It could sound like 'solving' – reasoning – or putting balm on – 'salving'. You can only get this effect if you speak the sonnet. Reading alone you might miss the pun. Here's another: 'For to thy sensual fault I bring in sense'. Does it mean I bring in 'reason', I bring in 'anger' (incensed) or bring in the purification of sweet-

smelling incense? All are right, all are possible, in complicated
moments of love's passion. These feelings are not simple.
These puns simply explore the complexity of all our intense
feelings and satisfy different needs simultaneously.

- So what is the sin? There is only the evidence in the text to
  give us the quality of the crime: 'stain', 'loathsome canker',
  'sensual fault'. Something that stains and is vilely ill and
  sensually a fault. Connect to the words and use your
  imagination. Only you can make the link. Your imagination,
  as you connect to the images, will find a solution to the crime.
  Shakespeare is handing power over to you to be author along
  with him just as you must hand the pictures over to the
  listener for a further range of connections. We can only be
  'right' in the moment we speak or hear.

- In this sonnet the first thought ends after the eleventh line.
  You then have a three-line thought. This is not regular or
  normal in a Shakespearean sonnet. This irregularity reflects
  the pain, struggle and chaos of the feelings the speaker is
  undergoing right to the very end – the resolving of the poem.
  The sonnet's lengthy units of thought are as difficult as the
  situation described in the sonnet. The knotted form matches
  the twisted feelings felt.

Here's a third one to try speaking:

Sonnet 116
    Let me not to the marriage of true minds
    Admit impediments. Love is not love
    Which alters when it alteration finds,
    Or bends with the remover to remove.
    O no, it is an ever fixed mark
    That looks on tempests and is never shaken;
    It is the star to every wandering bark,
    Whose worth's unknown, although his height be taken.
    Love's not Time's fool, though rosy lips and cheeks
    Within his bending sickle's compass come;
    Love alters not with his brief hours and weeks,
    But bears it out even to the edge of doom.
      If this be error and upon me proved,
      I never writ, nor no man ever loved.

This famous love sonnet declares that true love is unconditional. This is too often spoken romantically if not sentimen-
tally. That is the easy and safe way of approaching this sonnet.
But it is a more powerful and direct statement than that. A
quick check on the language will reveal protesting words like,
'Let me *not*'; 'love is *not* love'; 'O *no*'. All negative and
protestations. The speech is tougher and less pliant than it is
usually interpreted. But you only discover this in the speaking. You must 'hear' how the negatives refute a sentimental
reading.

Remember that the writer's true intent in a heightened text
is found in his or her choice of words. Words don't lie.

This is a very confident and uncompromising sonnet. It is
also very demanding. When spoken with confidence and
frankess, you sound like a lawyer defending a client. In this
case the client is unconditional love versus conditional love.
Both forms of love are being contested here before the listener.

Each quatrain (four lines) ends emphatically with a strong
stop. The sonnet is so confident as it builds that the final
couplet comes out sounding like a sworn oath: 'If this be error
and upon me proved, I never writ, nor no man ever loved.'
This sworn statement is so definite a close that after speaking
or reading thirteen lines of writing we are told that if I am
wrong you haven't read, spoken or heard any of the preceding
lines. Perhaps Shakespeare was tired of all the swearing of
conditional or courtly love that then disappears with time or
the alteration of circumstances. True love is subject to no
conditions. It is and will ride through tempests and even, in
its loyalty, be willing to suffer doom. A few other points to
consider:

- Notice the regularity of the structure. Every change of rhyme
  scheme matches a change of thought. This reflects a sureness
  and confidence in the writing. The speaker of these words is
  never in doubt but always sure.
- Each set of four lines has a wholeness and a frightening
  power. A thought is completed and the speaker has to serve

each of these bold statements. No vocal compromise holds
sway here. Courage is required in the speaking.

- When you beat the fifth line you will feel that you must speak
'fixed' as a two-beat sound, 'fixèd', emphasising the stability
of 'true minds'; like a nail hammered, fixing a mark in time
and space.

- Navigational images and language are scattered throughout
the sonnet. 'True' can describe the precision of a set course
('true' north). The 'mark', 'star', and 'compass' conjure up
pictures of navigational instruments. Love will direct you to a
safe haven and is not affected by the passing of time or lovers
ageing. You will sail to the edge of doom, perhaps tumbling
off the edge of the world. Love is a voyage and true love is a
perilous voyage you need to take. A genuine lover has to be
an intrepid explorer. Throughout we can smell the sea and
see the stars. The journey of love travels across the scapes of
sea and space.

- 'But bears it out even to the edge of doom'. Notice how the
length of the vowel in 'doom' pulls you up and slows you
down so that you can recover to speak the rather cheeky final
couplet. This long vowel device often helps the speaker make
a difficult emotional or intellectual transition, in this case
from the love taking you to the edge of doom to the rather
frivolous final couplet.

- Notice how light the iambic is in the couplet compared to the
previous twelve lines. There is a mood change that somehow
makes you smile. The rhythm as well as the content lightens.
This lightening device employed after profound statements is
used by many good speakers. It's not that Shakespeare is
putting off the issue, but by making us smile at the end he
sweetens the anticipation that love brings. We might not feel
so inclined to attack his point of view! All of a sudden he
provides us with yet another view of love's many facets.

- As you speak this sonnet feel how solid, strong and
uncompromising the structure and language are. As a speaker
you are not going to budge on this issue or be interrupted and
knocked off your perch. By not giving in to romantic
sentiment you show the steeliness of a tough, genuine lover.

- 'O no!' This needs very clear, secure and defined speaking.
The short burst stops us in our tracks before we get the
wrong idea.

Here's yet another sonnet to try. We travel from love to lust:

> Sonnet 129
> Th'expense of spirit in a waste of shame
> Is lust in action; and till action, lust
> Is perjured murd'rous, bloody, full of blame,
> Savage, extreme, rude, cruel, not to trust,
> Enjoyed no sooner but despisèd straight,
> Past reason hunted, and no sooner had
> Past reason hated as a swallowed bait
> On purpose laid to make the taker mad;
> Mad in pursuit and in possession so,
> Had, having, and in quest to have, extreme;
> A bliss in proof and proved, a very woe;
> Before, a joy proposed; behind, a dream.
>   All this the world well knows; yet none knows well
>   To shun the heaven that leads men to this hell.

This sonnet, reflecting the madness and chaos experienced when our sexual desires swamp our reason, is written very precisely but with a dangerous sense of chaos that could erupt into violence. It lacks harmony in its form and is therefore frightening to speak; especially lines like: 'Mad in pursuit and in possession so'. Twelve lines spurt out of the speaker's mouth. The momentum is unnerving and out of control. The twelfth line ends with 'dream' – a long settling vowel – which will give the required time to change and calm down to give the philosophical remark contained in the couplet. It's as though a nightmare ends and we come back to our senses. The iambics in the couplet suddenly feel safe. We can breathe again evenly after all the fraught, snorting breath in the lines above. The physical quality of the words is no longer violent but held and reasoned. Some other points to consider:

- When whispering the text you will notice how physical and violent the choice of words is – they are almost rapacious and wild.
- 'Th'expense of spirit in a waste of shame'. An ejaculation

starts the sonnet: 'Th'expense' spends an important part of you which just shoots out on the sibilants. No balance or harmony here.

- The pun on 'spirit' is very accurate – spirit and semen – both are spent in lust.
- In order to understand the opening of the debate we have to tumble into the second line, 'Is lust in action'.
- The list starting in line three is violent and yet still very specific. Things are already upside down and out of proportion as we reach 'not to trust'. Would you trust lies, murder, cruelty, savagery?
- Feel the swoop of energy that drives you through

> Past reason hated as a swallowed bait
> On purpose laid to make the taker mad;
> Mad in pursuit and in possession so,

The words in heat keep urging you on.

- At this point you cannot stop and perhaps you are suddenly out of breath – as you would be in the actual situation. Physically you are being asked to imitate the action in the words. Some inner compulsion drives you forward.
- 'Had, having, and in quest to have, extreme'. The time sequence here is back to front, signalling the final couplet. We will reconstitute and do it again.
- 'Bliss' is the first vividly enjoyable word after ten lines of violence. The orgasm is expressed immediately as 'a very woe'. Very appropriate vowel sounds. As you call out in satisfaction you have begun to regret your behaviour.

The skill in speaking this lust-ridden sonnet is to be specific with the language while riding the surge embedded in the verse. Naturally in highly motivated moments we do see and experience specifics yet are thrown forward by the body's extra adrenalin. Remember any incident in life when you have been heightened or driven. You can remember very clearly many details and specific feelings. Shakespeare is asking you to undergo the same process here. Allow the adrenalin through but still permit yourself to communicate the actual details of the event or passion without being lost in its heat.

Again, need, need, need drives the thoughts into the words and marries sound to action.

Shakespeare's Speeches

Imagine as you work on any great text – especially the most familiar ones – that it is an unknown work. Never be thrown or overawed by its familiarity. Your very speaking of it will transform it into something new. Imagine it's the first performance and the audience doesn't know the play or what comes next and you are the first speaker to have ever tackled this text. Look for everything I have talked about in the sonnets and do all the basic text exercises that I have listed at the beginning of this section on each subsequent speech.

Never believe that Shakespeare, or any great writer, can be boring. It's enough for you to deliver the goods. You don't have to make a great work more interesting. Trust it. Your experience of life must be used to enhance, not mask, a text's inherent values.

Well, why not start with one of those towering speeches most of us would be frightened to try first time out. Whether you are a man or woman, have a go at this soliloquy of Hamlet:

> HAMLET: O that this too too solid flesh would melt,
>   Thaw, and resolve itself into a dew;
>   Or that the Everlasting had not fixed
>   His canon 'gainst self-slaughter! O God, O God,
>   How weary, stale, flat, and unprofitable
>   Seem to me all the uses of this world!
>   Fie on't, ah fie! 'Tis an unweeded garden
>   That grows to seed; things rank and gross in nature
>   Possess it merely. That it should come to this –
>   But two months dead – nay, not so much, not two –
>   So excellent a king, that was to this
>   Hyperion to a satyr, so loving to my mother
>   That he might not beteem the winds of heaven
>   Visit her face too roughly. Heaven and earth,

Must I remember? Why, she would hang on him,
As if increase of appetite had grown
By what it fed on, and yet within a month –
Let me not think on't; frailty, thy name is woman –
A little month, or ere those shoes were old
With which she followed my poor father's body,
Like Niobe, all tears, why she, even she –
O God, a beast, that wants discourse of reason,
Would have mourned longer – married with mine uncle,
My father's brother, but no more like my father
Than I to Hercules. Within a month,
Ere yet the salt of most unrighteous tears
Had left the flushing in her gallèd eyes,
She married. O most wicked speed, to post
With such dexterity to incestuous sheets!
It is not, nor it cannot come to good.
But break, my heart, for I must hold my tongue.

Hamlet has not yet seen the ghost of his father when he delivers this, his first soliloquy in the play. Consequently his main motive, revenge, is not yet an issue. He has been left on his own with his thoughts after the exit of his mother and uncle (the new king).

Look at the structure of the speech. The layout of the lines and the flow of the thoughts are continually interrupted by exclamations (plus dashes put in by later editors of the play but interesting cues to work with): 'O God, O God'; 'Fie on't, ah fie!'; 'nay, not so much, not two'; 'Heaven and earth, Must I remember?' The straightforward rhythm seems to falter and buck along the way. It is like when your car engine is out of tune. The motor splutters and the timing is all off. Hamlet is in pain, turmoil and confusion. We all have to speak our pain irrationally and in fits and starts. It might take years in therapy to reach a point of understanding this inner turmoil. Hamlet performs his own self-analysis in front of us. Every word is chosen and needed because of its weight. They are like heavy millstones round his neck: 'O that this too too solid flesh'. An extremely laboured way to begin. He locates the

source of his pain and betrayal right at the end of the speech
as the pace quickens. Up to then he is talking only about the
results of his pain, not its source. He wants to die, fade away.
The world is corrupt. Then he talks about the death of his
father, the love his parents had for each other. The marriage
to his unworthy uncle. Then he says right at the end 'With
such dexterity to incestuous sheets!' The real source of the
pain lies in this provocative image of his mother in bed with
his uncle. 'Incestuous sheets' is difficult to say and always
slows down the speaker if he is to make sense of it. The image
is difficult and hard to see and imagine, but is vivid and
grotesque. It's also tangled like an undergrowth and very hard
to say; almost a tongue-twister.

The out of tune engine, Hamlet's strained consciousness,
comes in the moments when Hamlet tries to stop himself
seeing and understanding his fear. Perhaps he is too frightened to find out what emotional probing will reveal. He's
always in a thicket of thought. It's like knowing that if you
open a box the most dreadful creatures will crawl out. You
keep trying to close it but you can't resist playing with the lid
and the string, taking a peek inside. Here, as he plays with
the box, words and images fall or slide out. Then they teem
out.

As soon as Hamlet has spoken and confronted the monster
thought – incest – he no longer needs to speak. Nothing can
be done about it and his heart will break but he must keep
peace. The turmoil could remain forever private. That could
be the end of the play except Horatio comes in with news of
the ghost! Suddenly we are on a new track and into the main
action of the play. Hamlet will need to move outside himself
if the play is to proceed. The engine that drives him will have
to accelerate smoother.

The hesitation and confusion and headbeating are all
reflected in the structure of the verse. At the first performance
of *Hamlet* the audience would have understood that an
intelligent man was having difficulty in putting his thoughts

together clearly. They, like Hamlet, would discover in this speech fragments of the full story to come: pictures of a funeral, a wedding, an unweeded garden, a great love between Hamlet's father and mother. Him stopping the wind roughening her face, she hanging on to him, addicted to him. Then all the fragments come into shocking perspective. Some other points to consider:

- Because of the stop and start motion felt in the text a speaker cannot possibly speak this speech effortlessly and fluidly without violating the vocal structure of the verse. There is too much irregularity in brief, clotted phrasings. The final two lines are calm after the spectre has been recognised.
- Look how many words are repeated and doubled: 'too, too'; 'fie, fie'; 'O God, O God'; 'Why she, even she'; 'Within a month' – a rarity in Shakespeare. This indicates the struggle of moving forward on the journey. They are also fevered reactions to what Hamlet sees in his well-attuned 'mind's eye'.
- And yet when Hamlet dares to move forward, the verse flows and each word is very specific. 'Weary, stale, flat and unprofitable' are all different, measured descriptions of the world. They all inform us differently and are the product of a selective and well-ordered mind. Hamlet knows words and uses them well.
- How human it is for Hamlet to have noticed his mother's shoes at the funeral and then at the wedding – the small snapshot details that make the whole horror possible to imagine and more personal.
- When you do the exercise of seeing images you will realise how simple and apt they are. They are not hard to connect to, but poignant and clear, neither difficult nor academic:

> – The body melting into dew.
> – An overgrown garden.
> – A face flushed with tears.

   The classical allusions to 'Niobe' and 'Hercules' may need looking up in notes but then you will discover they are appropriate examples. The mind, as we speak, always finds an apt image to explain itself in speech.
- Notice the pun on 'soiled' or 'sullied' when 'solid' is spoken.

- 'a dew' could mean goodbye (adieu) or a moist dew.
- Don't pull off the 'O'. It indicates a release of feeling. Shakespeare hasn't indicated a word, only a sound. Use it. Never underestimate the power of sounds. They are so easy to swallow or ignore. If you swallow them you kill an energy and fail the intention of a line.
- Try walking as you speak the speech, changing direction with each gear change. You will rapidly begin to feel how much energy surges through Hamlet.
- As you whisper the speech you will feel the stops built into the heavy consonants. Also try to experience how the fractured thoughts pull you rapidly through the ends of lines. Appreciate and use the chaos of the iambic. Feel the different energy flow that accompanies the changing length of thought.
- Notice how there is a need in Hamlet to continue speaking. He cannot stop until he reaches the image of the sheets. Once he has spoken that he finds a peace, however painful. That peace is at least spoken. The source of the pain is finally uncovered: a sexual liaison between his mother and his uncle.

You have just tackled and worked on one of the great soliloquies of Shakespeare. It is not hard to understand when you take the time to pick your way through its sounds. It is a human cry that is reflected in the structure and language of the speech. What we have explored is just a particle of all there is to say about this speech from the perspective of speaking and needing to say it. It is, after all, the need for the words that pushes Hamlet on from sentence to sentence.

Let's turn our attention to a more comic speech from *Love's Labour's Lost*:

> BEROWNE: And I, forsooth, in love – I that have been love's whip,
> A very beadle to a humorous sigh,
> A critic, nay, a night-watch constable,
> A domineering pedant o'er the boy,
> Than whom no mortal so magnificent.
> This wimpled, whining, purblind, wayward boy,
> This senior-junior, giant dwarf, Dan Cupid,
> Regent of love-rhymes, lord of folded arms,

The anointed sovereign of sighs and groans,
Liege of all loiterers and malcontents,
Dread prince of plackets, king of codpieces,
Sole imperator and great general
Of trotting paritors – O my little heart!
And I to be a corporal of his field,
And wear his colours like a tumbler's hoop!
What? I love, I sue, I seek a wife? –
A woman, that is like a German clock,
Still a-repairing, ever out of frame,
And never going aright, being a watch,
But being watched that it may still go right.
Nay, to be perjured, which is worst of all,
And among three to love the worst of all –
A whitely wanton with a velvet brow,
With two pitch-balls stuck in her face for eyes –
Ay, and, by heaven, one that will do the deed
Though Argus were her eunuch and her guard.
And I to sigh for her, to watch for her,
To pray for her – go to, it is a plague
That Cupid will impose for my neglect
Of his almighty dreadful little might.
Well, I will love, write, sigh, pray, sue, groan:
Some men must love my lady, and some Joan.

Here a proud man, who has mocked love and lovers, comes
to realise, in front of the listener, that he has finally fallen
victim to love himself. His downfall is pronounced and total.
The text flows unchecked by anything other than commas and
natural pauses. The verse is free, the vowels are open and
generous. The soliloquy is not clotted and knotted like
Hamlet's above.

As an exercise, try just speaking the vowels alone down to
'tumbler's hoop'. As Berowne opens his heart to us he opens
the vowels he uses. It is almost as if the speech is delivered
with arms outstretched and opened wide. This is a character
embracing his fate. Berowne is falling in love – something
physically is happening to him – and the vowels and free-
flowing thoughts help him give free expression to a sudden

discovery. The openness of the sounds and in the verse are things we can instantly feel even before we tackle the intellectual arguments in the text. This is a way to approach any speech on initial contact.

Speech, voice and meaning are working in concert. A generosity of sound harmonises with Berowne's own awakening graciousness as he begins to look unstintingly at himself and his past behaviour. He is relieved that he has taken the plunge with love, he has allowed himself to fall. He lets go of all his brittleness, machismo pride and fear. Suddenly Berowne is liberated by pure, unbridled feeling. The liberation enters his body and his speech. Note the long, sweeping, even thoughts. There is a disruption in the line at 'O my little heart' and 'What? I love, I sue, I seek a wife?' These highlight his vulnerability but they are not jagged interruptions like those of Hamlet. All elements in the speech support Berowne's free fall into love. Mark the lengths of thought and the evenness of the iambic.

Shakespeare gives Berowne a whoosh on one hand and balances it with a clear-sighted view of the realities of himself and the lady he loves. Berowne has fallen for the least conventional of the three eligible girls. Like a German clock never going right, she (Rosaline) has black hair (very unfashionable then), two pitch-balls stuck in her face for eyes and someone who has 'done the deed' (she is not even a virgin). She's a modern woman, not someone on a pedestal. She's also a good match for Berowne's quick wit. She complements hin nicely.

In a play about courtly, conditonal love, it is a relief to see someone openly declare love, warts and all, in a totally unabandoned fashion. Berowne recognises how vile he's been to other lovers, a 'whip', a 'beadle' (a policeman), a 'critic', 'constable', 'a pedant', over this little boy (i.e. Cupid). Here is a very mocking yet fun line-up of consonants – w's, j's, p's, d's. Love leads men to do everything Berowne hates yet he clearly examines himself and love and realises he too will follow that path. He is merely a new recruit in the love brigade. He looks at the woman he has fallen for and as he recognises she is not the ideal woman, he also realises it is his punishment for ignoring love for so long. But he's going to do it. The rhyming couplet wraps up the whole journey with odd emphasis:

> Well, I will love, write, sigh, pray, sue, groan:
> Some men must love my lady, and some Joan.

Berowne metaphorically looks into a mirror and sees an honest portait. He doesn't deceive himself. The specificity of each example, the complete lists, must not be lost in the momentum of the marriage between the verse and vowels. The lists of examples cover all the possibilities. The examples get worse and worse as Berowne dares himself to go forward step by step. To me the long thoughts match the excitement of an awakening to feeling, but a feeling matching a realistic view of the situation and the sheer enjoyment and excitement of it. The speech literally 'tumbles' as Berowne's mind jumps through hoops. To capture that essence you may want to try speaking the speech as you run! Change direction with each change of thought. Note how breathless both you and the speech become.

This next speech is a more tangled and difficult one from *Measure for Measure*:

> ANGELO: What's this? What's this? Is this her fault or mine?
> The tempter or the tempted, who sins most, ha?
> Not she; nor doth she tempt; but it is I
> That, lying by the violet in the sun,
> Do, as the carrion does, not as the flower,
> Corrupt with virtuous season. Can it be
> That modesty may more betray our sense
> Than woman's lightness? Having waste ground enough,
> Shall we desire to raze the sanctuary,
> And pitch our evils there? O, fie, fie fie!
> What dost thou, or what art thou, Angelo?

Dost thou desire her foully for those things
That make her good? O, let her brother live!
Thieves for their robbery have authority,
When judges steal themselves. What do I love her,
That I desire to hear her speak again,
And feast upon her eyes? What is't I dream on?
O cunning enemy, that, to catch a saint,
With saints doth bait thy hook! Most dangerous
Is that temptation that doth goad us on
To sin in loving virtue. Never could the strumpet,
With all her double vigour – art and nature –
Once stir my temper; but this virtuous maid
Subdues me quite. Ever till now
When men were fond, I smiled and wondered how.

Here you find another man falling in love for the first time but very differently. Angelo is a puritan who is known to be cold, intellectual, clever and unemotional. All mind and no body. He is referred to as the 'precise' Angelo who doles out judgements measure for measure.

Angelo is given ultimate power in Vienna by a departing Duke and immediately attempts to clean up the vice and sexual decadence in the city. This includes condemning to death a young man for getting his betrothed pregnant, as a stern example to others. The man's sister, Isabella – a novice nun entering a convent – comes to Angelo to plead for her brother's life. It is with this young nun that Angelo falls in love. She is the subject of this speech.

With Isabella a feeling of passion strikes Angelo for the first time in his life. The sudden need is experienced in the words. Sexually he wants her, and that makes Angelo, he realises, a hypocrite. He is feeling the same emotions as those for which he is executing Isabella's brother. Different factions war within him. The discovery for Angelo is confusing, thrilling, frightening and unstoppable. All these factors are locked into the structure of the text and have to be released by the speaker.

Beat the lines. Notice how jagged some sections are. The

first six lines will give you a clear idea of that. I get a feeling
of a man breaking out of the shell of propriety and restraint.
Angelo twice asks the question, what is happening to him.
'What's this? What's this?' He echoes himself in an effort to
push himself forward or perhaps in an attempt to stop himself
feeling these feelings. Another two questions: 'Is it her fault
or mine? The tempter or the tempted, who sins most, ha?'
For a moment he is prepared to blame a young nun for
turning him on. Then 'ha'. In that one disturbing sound,
more jolting than 'O', Angelo brings himself to discover the
truth however horrifying it is to him. 'Not she; nor doth she
tempt; but it is I'. The final placement of the vowel 'I' is
stabbing and self-damning.

What follows is a journey into Angelo's desires and needs.
The language is violent and deeply sexual in its feeling and its
physicality as well as religious. The quality of the language
reveals Angelo's turmoil. That is, between the church and his
sexual feelings. 'lying', 'corrupt', 'raze the sanctuary', 'pitch
our evils there'. This frightens Angelo with its vividness, he
breaks into 'O fie, fie, fie'. Then the picture of having a hook
baited with a saint to catch the saintly Angelo. Beautiful and
positive words are mated with negative, murky ones. Angelo
is being thrown around by thoughts and images. The words
are like a fitful seizure.

What intrigues me is the fact that Angelo the puritan
suddenly has all those sexual words available to him. Where
did he learn them? He might have blocked them up before
but they're there in his gut and now bursting forth. Somewhere all through his life he has known these words but now
they have meaning and a need to be said. Once released these
words possess and control him like a demon.

When you mouth the text you will immediately feel how
physical the language is – how violently disturbing. The
consonants contain the vowels, always on the edge of opening
up too much as Angelo struggles to comprehend the power of
his heart pounding for the first time in his life. For example,

just notice how many t's are used to hold onto the passion in the first half of the text. He's tried. He's been to strumpets but they've failed to 'stir his temper'. As Angelo thrashes around in a sea of feeling and desires he tries to be his sober, sensible self with moments like: 'Thieves for their robbery have authority, /When judges steal themselves.' Those attempts fail. His thoughts go back to Isabella.

Notice that most of Angelo's thoughts start mid-line, indicating his chaos. This happens in lines 1, 6, 8, 10, 13, 15, 17, 19 and 21 – not typical in Shakespeare's usual structure unless there is a struggle going on inside a character. This also has the effect of throwing the vocal energy forward. Angelo is letting the horse gallop off. He can no longer rein in his feelings. The lid has been blown off. He throws up question after question in an attempt to understand these racing thoughts. His voice is leading him on. The words used make us feel when we speak them aloud that Angelo is eating sounds for the first time in his life. He feasts on the words, having been starved for so long by repression and silence. The extravagance of the language matches the extravagance of his newly awakened feelings.

However brilliant Angelo's legal brain is, he is like a child where emotional entanglements are concerned. The final broken couplet indicates his half-starved sensibility: 'Ever till now/When men were fond, I smiled and wondered how'. The line leaves Angelo and us suspended. It does not really tie up the speech but leaves the character suspended, almost dazed and full of wonder by his sudden transformation through lust.

Next is a well-known speech from *Romeo and Juliet*:

> JULIET: Gallop apace, you fiery-footed steeds,
>   Towards Phoebus' lodging; such a waggoner
>   As Phaeton would whip you to the west,
>   And bring in cloudy night immediately.
>   Spread thy close curtain, love-performing night.
>   That runaways' eyes may wink, and Romeo
>   Leap to these arms, untalk'd of and unseen.

Lovers can see to do their amorous rites
By their own beauties; or if love be blind,
It best agrees with night. Come, civil night,
Thou sober-suited matron, all in black,
And learn me how to lose a winning match,
Play'd for a pair of stainless maidenhoods;
Hood my unmann'd blood, bating in my cheeks,
With thy black mantle, till strange love, grown bold,
Think true love acted simple modesty.
Come, night; come, Romeo; come, thou day in night;
For thou wilt lie upon the wings of night
Whiter than new snow on a raven's back.
Come gentle night, come, loving black-brow'd night,
Give me my Romeo; and, when I shall die,
Take him and cut him out in little stars,
And he will make the face of heaven so fine
That all the world will be in love with night,
And pay no worship to the garish sun.
O, I have bought the mansion of a love,
But not possess'd it; and though I am sold,
Not yet enjoy'd. So tedious is this day
As is the night before some festival
To an impatient child that hath new robes,
And may not wear them. O, here comes my nurse . . .

Juliet is waiting for night and for the return of Romeo. She has married Romeo and now longs for the physical consummation of their marriage. The text pulses with anticipation, excitement and the frustration that time is not passing quickly enough, the night is not winging into view. It is Shakespeare's brilliant conceit in this play that Romeo and Juliet's happiest, most thrilling moment in life – their romantic coupling – is followed by the most tragic – separation, banishment and death. Coming together and pulling apart are two of the play's strongest movements. The quick pace of the play's action flows through the dialogue and is mirrored in Juliet's impetuousness. This soliloquy is a good example of how quickly you, as a speaker, are expected to make emotional transitions in heightened text.

Try the exercise of breathing in and speaking as far as you can before recovering the breath throughout the speech. You will feel the text rolling through you. You will quite naturally run out of breath because Juliet's excitement makes her breathless.

Thoughts sweep you along. The first thought lasts four lines; the second five and a half lines; the third six and a half lines; the fourth three lines; the fifth is six lines long. The ideas and images move easily into each other like scenery shifting into place. You don't experience any difficulty in moving forward either through imagining or through speaking.

Although the thoughts flow along there is an awkwardness in some of the constructions. On one level Juliet is struggling to understand her passion and also naive about it. Notice how many changes occur within each line and thought. This is the girl who twenty-four hours before was respectfully obeying her mother and preparing dutifully to marry Count Paris. Now she is risking all for love of Romeo. You could say that her need to love has heightened the urgency of her need for words. This is generally true of most Shakespearean heroines.

Notice the repetition of the word 'come'. It's like a prayer, an incantation, yet also signals that although Juliet is a virgin she is only too clearly, or subliminally, anticipating the joy of sex with Romeo. But the notion has none of the smuttiness of Angelo's speech above. Juliet's sexual allusion and wordplay are more unconscious and innocent.

Take a look at the vowels. They are very generous and show how open Juliet is. She especially likes the vowels in 'Romeo'. Look at all the images she conjures: horses galloping, pulling the sun; horses with flaming hooves; night as a curtain, a sober suited matron, night that will become day. She personifies and bargains with night to immortalise Romeo when he dies. Romeo is also like a 'knight' in shining armour to a young maiden locked in a tower. She discusses childhood as though she has grown out of it; the gowns waiting to be worn. She now wants to wear Romeo, his body will enfold her. The images are romantic but also very physical.

Many actresses are frightened of playing the youth of Juliet, feeling you have to be older to act this character. I think if you trust and experience the images you will discover how childlike – in the best sense of the word – they are. You will see the world with the eye of innocence. Juliet is richly imaginative. She talks to the sun and the night as though they were persons. She makes them personified entities, real and palpable. She is frightened as well as thrilled. She blushes. Notice how the safe day turns into the enemy and how night is no longer fearful. Juliet's feelings are tumbling around just like her images.

This next speech is from a late romance, *The Winter's Tale*:

PAULINA: Woe the while!
    O cut my lace, lest my heart, cracking it,
    Break too.
A LORD: What fit is this, good lady?
PAULINA: (*To Leontes*)
    What studied torments, tyrant, hast for me?
    What wheels, racks, fires? What flaying, boiling
    In leads or oils? What old or newer torture
    Must I receive, whose every word deserves
    To taste of thy most worst? Thy tyranny,
    Together working with thy jealousies –
    Fancies too weak for boys, too green and idle
    For girls of nine – O think what they have done,
    And then run mad indeed, stark mad, for all
    Thy bygone fooleries were but spices of it.
    That thou betrayd'st Polixenes, 'twas nothing.
    That did but show thee, of a fool, inconstant,
    And damnable ingrateful. Nor was't much
    Thou wouldst have poisoned good Camillo's honour
    To have him kill a king – poor trespasses,
    More monstrous standing by, whereof I reckon
    The casting forth to crows thy baby daughter
    To be or none or little, though a devil

Would have shed water out of fire ere done't.
Nor is't directly laid to thee the death
Of the young prince, whose honourable thoughts –
Thoughts high for one so tender – cleft the heart
That could conceive a gross and foolish sire
Blemished his gracious dam. This is not, no,
Laid to thy answer. But the last – O lords,
when I have said, cry 'woe'! The Queen, the Queen,
The sweetest, dearest creature's dead, and vengeance for't
Not dropp'd down yet.

Leontes, the King of Sicilia, has gone mad with jealousy. He
imagines that his wife, Queen Hermione, has been unfaithful
with his best friend, Polixenes. Leontes' fevered passion is
destroying his court and one monstrous act follows another.
He has just put his Queen on trial. On suddenly hearing about
the death of her son she has collapsed and has been carried
out of the court. Her lady in waiting, Paulina, now returns to
the court and confronts the King with his misdeeds. She
finishes this list by announcing the death of the Queen.

Paulina returns wailing, her heart is breaking. Feel the
release of sound in a phrase like 'Woe the while'. You can
take this very deep and touch the depth of emotion with the
words. When a lord says 'What fit is this, good lady?', Paulina
suddenly pulls herself together. Mouth the next part of the
text and you will feel how the consonants contain the passion
and stop her from crying. Particularly notice this effect as you
get to: 'The Queen, the Queen,/The sweetest, dearest creature's dead, and vengeance for't/Not dropp'd down yet.'
These words are loaded with q's, s's, t's and d's. Paulina
cannot afford to indulge her pain in pure vowels. It is more
important that she get her message across to Leontes. Her
chosen words bottle and block the tears that would flow were
she not barricading them for the purpose of clear speech.

Up to this point in the play Paulina has been listing Leontes'
past stupidities. But as she updates him with news of the
Queen's death the physicality of the language intensifies,

presumably to keep back the tears. The struggle to speak is also heightened by the repetition of 'the Queen' as if that potent image of an innocent woman says it all. She keeps flashing the image for the King and court.

In a previous scene Paulina tried to convince Leontes of his folly and was interrupted and physically manhandled by lords. She has learnt her lesson. Notice how the verse's structure allows little room for interruption. Thoughts start mid-line and many of them, particularly mid-speech, are long and rapidly move forward. Just examine the thought that starts '. . . O think what they have done' through to 'And damnable ingrateful'.

Throughout Paulina structures her argument carefully despite her passion. She opens by questioning Leontes, 'What studied torments, tyrant, hast for me?' The t's almost pin him to the floor like daggers. She can catalogue his wrongs coherently so she still controls her feelings and focuses her passion on him as a target. She even displays wit and irony. She sarcastically belittles Leontes' previous tyrannies – although terrible – by ironic remarks like ''twas nothing', and 'Nor was't much' and 'Nor is't directly laid to thee . . .' She wittily mocks him by calling his jealousies 'Fancies too weak for boys, too green and idle/For girls of nine'. Paulina is such an interesting speaker because in the midst of losing the Queen she can call forth righteous indignation.

Shakespeare knows that even at the height of pain those people with a sense of humour call upon it for support. Precisely at moments when the actress might get out of control and begin to rant, Shakespeare writes a strong plosive sound (sharply released consonants) to put you back in the moment. For example, 'betrayd'st', 'was't', 'done't', 'is't', 'sweetest, dearest creature's dead, and vengeance for't,/Not dropped down yet.' You have to speak these harsh sounds and not pass over them. Shakespeare wants you to voice a woman's struggle in order to be heard but also structures the voicing of the words so that you will keep speaking and not stop till the very end.

At first the language seems undramatic and almost every-day. On closer examination and work on the text through speaking it aloud, you begin to realise that the simplicity of the language makes Paulina's attack more direct, fierce and urgent. No punches are pulled. No idea is too complex. This directness in the language has to be married to the complexity in the structure of the thoughts. I think this helps the speaker feel the emotional struggle Paulina is undergoing. She's clear and direct but she is still feeling and needing each word and sound.

Try walking while speaking this text, changing direction with each change of thought or pulse in the thought. You will sense how much movement there is in the speech and how many vocal changes occur. It is as if Paulina becomes several women, a chorus of women accusing the harsh Leontes. When you speak the text standing still you should still feel the combined movements of the speech.

Now try speaking the text as if fearing an interruption and retaliation. You will sense how the text's structure prevents you from being interrupted. It keeps going forward avoiding any pause or interference that could silence you. Paulina is a courageous woman. No one has ever spoken to the King in this way. On the basis of Leontes' performance to date, Paulina will be expecting some devious death sentence. But she is determined to speak her mind before her demise and defend the innocence of her Queen. This courage is reflected in the writing and you must leap in and speak the lines with the same sense of fearlessness.

You cannot pat or stroke a speech like this. You need to grasp it firmly and push ahead with it before allowing any intellectual subtleties through. It is like an operatic aria; a woman not willingly submitting to silence without one last reprise. Paulina is centre stage throughout this speech and everyone pays her heed because her sudden need to speak is so overwhelming.

Shakespearean Prose

Prose is often spoken by characters in less urgent states of mind and also by less noble and more ordinary figures. It also indicates a shift of code amongst those who can speak verse or is simply the language of uneducated people who've never learned verse in the first place.

Generally the movement between verse and prose indicates a shift from formal to informal modes of speaking. Certain important issues are addressed in verse (e.g. profound love as opposed to lust) and great public scenes are enacted through the medium of verse. Shakespeare breaks his own rules continually just to signal a shift in voice and the speaking act. A quick look at Act 1, Scene 1 of *King Lear* gives an interesting insight into shifts from prose to verse, verse to prose. The play starts in prose with a private, colloquial scene between Kent and Gloucester but shifts into verse with the King's entrance and court scene and only reverts back to prose when the sisters Goneril and Regan are left alone at the end of the scene to discuss their father privately. High formal drama is sandwiched between these more colloquial prose scenes. The code and language shift tells us we are moving from private to public to private. Our ears tell us that different dramatic moves are under way.

Often the switch between verse and prose helps the audience to recover from the verse's intensity and powerful revelations. Prose cools passion. Prose also relates prosaic facts. It returns us to the norm from a heightened state and allows actors and audience the space to breathe and readjust focus. We are filled with relief when the Porter enters speaking his filthy prose after the horror of Macbeth murdering Duncan (even though the prose speech is charged with humour and hellish inventions!).

Have a look at this prose speech by the clown Launce in
Two Gentlemen of Verona:

Enter Launce and his dog Crab

LAUNCE (*to the audience*): When a man's servant shall play the
  cur with him, look you, it goes hard. One that I brought up
  of a puppy, one that I saved from drowning when three or
  four of his blind brothers and sisters went to it. I have
  taught him, even as one would say precisely 'Thus I would
  teach a dog'. I was sent to deliver him as a present to
  Mistress Silvia from my master, and I came no sooner into
  the dining-chamber but he steps me to her trencher and
  steals her capon's leg. O, 'tis a foul thing when a cur cannot
  keep himself in all companies. I would have, as one should
  say, one that takes upon him to be a dog indeed, to be, as it
  were, a dog at all things. If I had not had more wit than he,
  to take a fault upon me that he did, I think verily he had
  been hanged for't. Sure as I live, he had suffered for't. You
  shall judge. He thrusts me himself into the company of
  three or four gentleman-like dogs under the Duke's table.
  He had not been there – bless the mark – a pissing-while
  but all the chamber smelled him. 'Out with the dog,' says
  one. 'What cur is that?' says another. 'Whip him out,' says
  the third. 'Hang him up,' says the Duke. I, having been
  acquainted with the smell before, knew it was Crab, and
  goes me to the fellow that whips the dogs. 'Friend,' quoth
  I, 'you mean to whip the dog.' 'Ay, marry do I,' quoth he.
  'You do him the more wrong,' quoth I, ''twas I did the
  thing you wot of.' He makes me no more ado, but whips
  me out of the chamber. How many masters would do this
  for his servant? Nay, I'll be sworn I have sat in the stocks
  for puddings he hath stolen, otherwise he had been
  executed. I have stood on the pillory for geese he hath
  killed, otherwise he had suffered for't. (*To Crab*) Thou
  think'st not of this now. Nay, I remember the trick you
  served me when I took my leave of Madam Silvia. Did not
  I bid thee still mark me, and do as I do? When didst thou
  see me heave up my leg and make water against a
  gentlewoman's farthingale? Didst thou ever see me do such
  a trick?

Launce's observations are like common homespun advice. If the speech was in verse it would signal urgency and a higher-status character. Yet Launce's dog is as vital to him as Hamlet's 'To be or not to be'. The character is finding words and finding his way through a problem in as structured a way as Hamlet or Angelo would in a verse speech despite differences in intellect or class. Because a speech is not structured in poetry we sometimes fail to see urgent thoughts leap out at us. Yet Launce's speech to his dog is like the metaphysical dialogue of Samuel Beckett; a comic speech imitating a tragic one. The structure of the speech mirrors verse soliloquies: a debate is opened, the issues explored, a problem confronted and then a resolution, of sorts, reached. The story and problems of Crab are vividly explored through the language. So be as clear and concrete here as you would be in verse. Launce is also a speaker who might use a country dialect. And dialect may easily mask the serious intent behind the words.

The traditional advice given to actors about prose is 'get on with it'. That is, speak it quickly. This is not necessarily sound advice! In some ways it is harder to speak prose as you haven't all the benefits of the structure and hidden energy compacted in verse lines. Don't skip through the debate and miss the urgency. You must be careful to follow the thoughts through the maze and not be beguiled into thinking that they are less difficult. It is easy to become too conversational.

The Verse Duet

In verse dialogue, broken lines often indicate that one character interrupts or harmoniously joins another speaker. I always feel you should experiment with and observe the two-part, two-player harmony of this sort of verse structure. Duets in verse are wonderful fun to act because each speaker keeps feeding the other speaker's need for words. You must pass the speech back and forth like a baton in a relay race. Feed each other with the words and connect.

I realise that different editions of a Shakespeare text might vary these broken lines, but observe and play with these breaks when you encounter them. If lines are picked up and finished by another character in a scene then I think a message is being communicated about pace and the manner of reply. When there is no indication of a full line being completed or picked up, then there are beats of silence often indicating a pause; the verse equivalent of the musical rest.

Here's a good example from Act 1, Scene 3 of *Antony and Cleopatra*:

> CLEOPATRA: Or thou, the greatest soldier of the world,
>   Art turned the greatest liar.
> ANTONY: How now, lady!
> CLEOPATRA: I would I had thy inches; thou shouldst know
>   There were a heart in Egypt.
> ANTONY: Hear me, Queen:
>   The strong necessity of time commands
>   Our services awhile, but my full heart
>   Remains in use with you. Our Italy
>   Shines o'er with civil swords; Sextus Pompeius
>   Makes his approaches to the port of Rome;
>   Equality of two domestic powers
>   Breed scrupulous faction. The hated, grown to strength,
>   Are newly grown to love; the condemned Pompey,
>   Rich in his father's honour, creeps apace
>   Into the hearts of such as have not thrived
>   Upon the present state, whose numbers threaten;
>   And quietness, grown sick of rest, would purge
>   By any desperate change. My more particular,
>   And that which most with you should safe my going,
>   Is Fulvia's death. **[note the pause here for silence]**
> CLEOPATRA: Though age from folly could not give me
>   freedom,
>   It does from childishness: – can Fulvia die?
> ANTONY: She's dead, my queen. **[note the silence here]**
>   Look here, and at thy sovereign leisure read
>   The garboils she awaked; at the last, best,
>   See when and where she died.

Notice how Antony and Cleopatra pick up each other's lines and finish the five iambics until 'Is Fulvia's death'. There is a two-beat pause before Cleopatra replies. Perhaps she needs that time to take in the news. And after Antony says 'She's dead, my queen', he gives himself three beats before showing her the proof and starting the next line.

In my experience, obeying the breaks in the line always helps the acting. Shakespeare hears pauses and knows when they will be useful to the actor. He knows the approximate space the voice needs to generate a response. These are those self-directing notes that Shakespeare puts in all his texts.

I want now to try to use the work we've done with Shakespeare and apply it to a host of other writers from ancient to modern.

Medieval Verse

Have a go at speaking this curious language:

> Wanne mine eyhnen misten,
> And mine heren sissen,
> And my nose coldet,
> And my tunge foldet,
> And my rude slaket,
> And mine lippes blaken,
> And my muth grennet,
> And my spotel rennet,
> And mine her riset,
> And mine herte griset,
> And mine honden bivien,
> And mine fet stivien –
> Al to late! al to late!
> Wanne the bere is ate gate.
>
> Thanne I schel flutte
> From bedde to flore,
> From flore to here,
> From here to bere,
> From bere to putte,

And te putt fordut.
Thanne lyd mine hus uppe mine nose.
Of al this world ne give I it a pese!

This is an anonymous thirteenth-century poem (in 'Middle English') describing how death comes. You will notice, as you speak it, how the poem uses onomatopoeia, repetition, and rhyme. As you speak it out loud don't worry about correctness in pronunciation. Relish the words and speak all the sounds you see. The physical vigour of the piece matches the clear, unsentimental approach to death. All death's less wholesome features are reflected in the physical crudity of the words chosen – perhaps some were made up to suit the poet's imagination, like children inventing appropriate-sounding words. The conjunction 'And', used again and again to list all the ways the body begins to fail as death nears, also serves as the heartbeat of the poem pounding, only to shudder and fail on: 'Al to late! al to late!'

An approximate translation – losing all the fun of the speaking – would be:

When my eyes mist
And my ears hiss [how descriptive 'sissen' is]
And my nose cold
And my tongue folds
And my face slackens
And my lips blacken
And my mouth grins
And my spit runs
And my hair rises
And my heart trembles
And my hands shake
And my feet stiffen
All too late! All too late!
When the bier is at the gate.

The next verse takes us through another list. The journey of the body to the grave – 'putt', a place to put the body, – ending up with us having our house resting on our noses and not giving a piss for the world. 'Fordut' is a wonderful word to describe the sound as the grave closes.

> Then I shall pass
> From bed to floor
> From floor to shroud
> From shroud to bier
> From bier to grave
> And the grave shuts.
> Then my house rests on my nose
> Of all this world I don't give a piss.

We still use very physical and onomatopoeic language today as our descriptions become more vivid or cruder. Expletives and curses are obvious examples. Trust the simplicity of the language and the repetition. The short verse lines move you forward quickly and although they might not have the elegance of longer lines, they do match the hard-hitting message of the poem. We are taken quickly up a ladder. 'And, And, And,' 'From, From, From'. The steps are clear, uncomplicated and consequently often frightening. There is no linguistic clutter to help us avoid the truth. The simplicity of rhythm and rhyme are used to heighten and intensify.

This is language from the gut. Our society will often educate children – who love the physicality of language, repetition and rhyme – to soften the words they use. They are not nice! Perhaps we become frightened of the physical clarity of the sound. This can connect too strongly to the meaning and feeling contained in these powerful words. The actual making of the word can be too violent or sensual. Break all barriers and speak this poem with relish.

You can apply all the above to this brief selection from the York Mystery Plays:

> EVE: A worm, Lord, enticed me theretill: [thereto]
> So welaway   [alas]
> That ever I did that deed so dill!   [foolish]

GOD: Ah, wicked worm, woe worth thee ay!
   That then on this manner
   Hast made them such affray,
   My malison have then here   [curse]
   With all the might I may.

The curious quality of the words and the sounds they make give these speeches tremendous freedom when spoken.

Christopher Marlowe

Marlowe is a playwright so overpowering and demanding on the voice that many actors shy away from him. But I do think that speaking and stressing Marlowe's mighty lines prepares us for other writers like Shakespeare and Milton. Try this speech from Act 1, Scene 3 of *Tamburlaine the Great*:

TAMBURLAINE:
   When heaven shall cease to move on both the poles,
   And when the ground whereon my soldiers march
   Shall rise aloft and touch the hornèd moon,
   And not before, my sweet Zenocrate.
   Sit up and rest thee like a lovely queen.
   So, now she sits in pomp and majesty,
   When these my sons, more precious in mine eyes
   Than all the wealthy kingdoms I subdued,
   Plac'd by her side, look on their mother's face.
   But yet methinks their looks are amorous,
   Not martial as the sons of Tamburlaine.
   Water and air, being symboliz'd in one,
   Argue their want of courage and of wit;
   Their hair as white as milk and soft as down,
   Which should be like the quills of porcupines,
   As black as jet and hard as iron or steel,
   Bewrays they are too dainty for the wars;
   Their fingers made to quaver on a lute,
   Their arms to hang about a lady's neck,
   Their legs to dance and caper in the air
   Would make me think them bastards, not my sons,

> But that I know they issued from thy womb
> That never look'd on man but Tamburlaine.

- First connect with Marlowe's 'mighty' line: judge what difficulties lie in wait. They seem endless when you first speak them.
- Beat out the lines.
- Dive in and speak this section aloud. Within a few lines you will begin to realise how seductive the lines feel. There is a glorious, extravagant pulse in the line that is relentless, but therein lies the trap.
- As the energy of the line seduces you, it becomes very tempting just to speak the dynamic of the line and consequently only communicate form and pulse but not the words. The mighty line can too heavily control the speaker so that we lose specificity and meaning.
- Now take your time and unlock the meaning of each thought. You may have to break the line's energy.
- Speak the speech conversationally.
- Then connect to all the imagery. Before speaking each phrase have some experience of the language even if the images seem clichéd (e.g. 'white as milk'). Respect them and don't take anything for granted.
- Lastly speak the whole speech, overarticulating so that you release the words' physicality.

I worked on this play recently and discovered that Tamburlaine's language was very sensual. At first the actor playing this part was most concerned that the power of the lines would dominate his performance. On closer examination of the language, we discovered that this simple shepherd saw images very clearly and in a childlike way spoke directly to the universe and used words as a physical portrait of cosmic reality. With words he brought the sky and stars down to earth. As soon as these hand grips were discovered, the marriage between the word and the line's power could be made.

Go back to speaking the text with the line's power intact but try to retain the notions of clear thoughts, images and physicality with the words. You may now feel the line unifying with the word.

John Milton

If you want to test and improve your vocal support and sustaining powers, speak any of John Milton's magnificent verse. Here is text that is certain to stretch you, from Book I of *Paradise Lost*:

> *Satan opens the debate*
>   'Powers and Dominions, Deities of heav'n,
> For since no deep within her gulf can hold
> Immortal vigour, though oppressed and fall'n,
> I give not heav'n for lost. From this descent
> Celestial Virtues rising will appear
> More glorious and more dread than from no fall,
> And trust themselves to fear no second fate.
> Me though just right and the fixed laws of heav'n
> Did first create your leader, next, free choice,
> With what besides, in council or in fight,
> Hath been achieved of merit, yet this loss,
> Thus far at least recovered, hath much more
> Established in a safe unenvied throne
> Yielded with full consent. The happier state
> In heav'n, which follows dignity, might draw
> Envy from each inferior; but who here
> Will envy whom the highest place exposes
> Foremost to stand against the Thunderer's aim
> Your bulwark, and condemns to greatest share
> Of endless pain? Where there is then no good
> For which to strive, no strife can grow up there
> From faction; for none sure will claim in hell
> Precedence, none whose portion is so small
> Of present pain that with ambitious mind
> Will covet more. With this advantage then
> To union, and firm faith, and firm accord,
> More than can be in heav'n, we now return
> To claim our just inheritance of old,
> Surer to prosper than prosperity

Could have assured us; and by what best way,
Whether of open war or covert guile,
We now debate; who can advise, may speak.'

Like Marlowe's and Shakespeare's verse, Milton's uses
iambic pentameter blank verse; verse with a strong, steady
rhythm but without rhyme. It is powerful and regular.
Milton's epic and lengthy thoughts, mighty verse lines and
extended similes prove to be the speaker's equivalent of
running a marathon. Have a go at this speech. Speak it,
intone it, breathe it. Beat out the lines.

The epic quality of the structure matches the epic nature of
the story: the fall of Satan and, by extension, of humankind.
A very big story. There is nothing mediocre or everyday here.
Each word, image, thought length and line momentum mirrors the vastness of the story and the cinematic scope of the
narrative.

This excerpt contains only six complete thoughts. Six sweeping sentences. Notice how you must sustain the whole journey
of each thought. Any unfilled pause will make nonsense of the
whole scheme and diminish the energy of the verse.

In true epic style, the last word of each sentence will often
place the whole idea into perspective. So don't be dismayed if
sense is not coming through instantly. Sense and sensation
must have room to build. You cannot starve this text of
oxygen. Breath and support must be there or the sense rapidly
dwindles as you wind down. The rhythm is relentless, matching the epic nature of the poem. Technically this means you
cannot fall or pull back on a word or syllable – you have to
ride wave upon wave of the verse, not fall off the surfboard.

The breath and power required to serve this epic verse will
often mean that a speaker rushes, pushes or loses control in a
desperate attempt to reach the very end. Take it in your own
time and don't worry about the end initially. It is more
important that you experience the fullness of the verse even if
you cannot finish a whole section. If you must stop along the

way, try a language exercise of waiting, seeing and needing every image to maintain control and help you to marry the verse structure with the specific language Milton uses.

Milton was already blind by the time he wrote this masterpiece and it seems to me that the language he uses is his attempt, through words, to recapture his sight. Everything is so visual, so cinematic, so replete with images. Speak the text seeing everything the words describe. See your version of 'heaven'. See, breathe and experience each word or phrase before you speak them out loud. See, especially, the whole process of the fall from great heights in long shot and in close-up.

This work on the text may take time but it will very often give you a clear, constant connection to the language, adding another level of freedom to your speaking. You will fracture and lose the verse, but trust that the verse's power will return after the exercise when you speak the text again not trying to see but believing you have found the images – they will be there. Milton is a speaking equivalent to singing the operas of Wagner or Verdi. You must have full breath support throughout, or you will collapse in the midst of speaking.

Jacobean Drama

Next I am going to make a jump back to Jacobean texts and the plays of John Webster. In many ways these texts need more vigorous speaking techniques than do the texts of Shakespeare. The images are more relentless and there are not so many changes of thought to help the speaker easily plot a journey through a speech or scene. The thought doesn't always underpin the image or feelings.

The breath support, as in Milton, not only has to be strong and constant, but, in order to match the sweeping thoughts and momentous images, it has to be very fluid. Otherwise it is easy to confuse a listener with the tangled words. One full breath recovery after another is required following any stop. The speeches are like extended arias. Rather like a singing position in the breath when you have no hesitation or breath holds, you must just breathe and go. This seems an extreme way to describe the approach to these texts but this extremity matches the content of the plays. Each is about an extreme state or emotion. If the breath is low enough and strong enough, speaking this kind of text is not difficult. In fact, the courage of speaking a text like this will release its inherent, wrestling drama. These are not subtle, intimate speeches but big emotional declarations.

In Jacobean drama you enter a decadent, shameless world, almost hallucinatory and nightmarish in what it sees and reports; a world of disease, lust, lost honour, vanity, revenge, spying and pandering. All is covered in a gilded and gloriously embellished veneer like a baroque decoration. A sick society that is richly decked out for its own pleasure and pain. Very little compassion or forgiveness is found in these plays. All the scenarios and events are extreme. So the language is extreme, too. The deaths and the death speeches are extreme as are all the emotions. When you speak these texts you will actually feel revulsion and grime clinging to the words. The densest and dankest imagery, similes and metaphors are invoked.

No one is safe in these plays nor is the language tame. Characters insult each other in the most hideous fashion. You soon realise that no holds are barred when you speak. This is high-risk dialogue. Some of the words and ideas are so violent and horrific that it is too easy to pull off them and deny the image, sacrificing the text's dramatic intensity. Actors frequently try to normalise the extravagance of the words, phrases and experiences you find in these texts. They often mumble rather than sound the words loudly. In fact, they frequently deny the need for the word. You will need to try all the suggestions prescribed for Milton but you will need more courage to confront the full-blooded colour of the Jacobean world. To release these words into the world with strong support, clarity and focus can seem a frightening task – bluff or denial are the easy options.

Here are two speeches by John Webster, one for a woman and one for a man. The first is spoken by Vittoria in *The White Devil*, answering her lover's accusation that she has been unfaithful. The second is by Bosola, a Machiavellian intriguer in *The Duchess of Malfi*.

VITTORIA: What have I gain'd by thee but infamy?
    Thou hast stain'd the spotless honour of my house,
    And frighted thence noble society:
    Like those, which sick o'th' palsy, and retain
    Ill-scenting foxes 'bout them, are still shunn'd
    By those of choicer nostrils.
    What do you call this house?
    Is this your palace? Did not the judge style it
    A house of penitent whores? Who sent me to it?
    Who hath the honour to advance Vittoria
    To this incontinent college? Is't not you?
    Is't not your high preferment? Go, go brag
    How many ladies you have undone, like me.
    Fare you well sir; let me hear no more of you.
    I had a limb corrupted to an ulcer,
    But I have cut it off: and now I'll go
    Weeping to heaven on crutches. For your gifts,
    I will return them all; and I do wish
    That I could make you full executor
    To all my sins. O that I could toss myself
    Into a grave as quickly: for all thou art worth
    I'll not shed one tear more; – I'll burst first.

BOSOLA: One would suspect it for a shop of witchcraft, to find in it the fat of serpents; spawn of snakes, Jews' spittle, and their young children's ordure, and all these for the face. I would sooner eat a dead pigeon, taken from the soles of the feet of one sick of the plague, than kiss one of you fasting. Here are two of you, whose sin of your youth is the very patrimony of the physician, makes him renew his footcloth with the spring, and change his high-priz'd courtesan with the fall of the leaf: I do wonder you do not loathe yourselves. Observe my meditation now:
    What thing is in this outward form of man

To be belov'd? We account it ominous,
If nature do produce a colt, or lamb,
A fawn, or goat, in any limb resembling
A man; and fly from't as a prodigy.
Man stands amaz'd to see his deformity,
In any other creature but himself.
But in our own flesh, though we bear diseases
Which have their true names only tane from beasts,
As the most ulcerous wolf, and swinish measle;
Though we are eaten up of lice, and worms,
And though continually we bear about us
A rotten and dead body, we delight
To hide it in rich tissue: all our fear,
Nay, all our terror, is lest our physician
Should put us in the ground, to be made sweet.
Your wife's gone to Rome: you two couple, and get you
To the wells at Lucca, to recover your aches.
[*Exeunt* CASTRUCHIO *and* OLD LADY.]
I have other work on foot: I observe our Duchess
Is sick a-days, she pukes, her stomach seethes,
The fins of her eyelids look most teeming blue,
She wanes i'th' cheek, and waxes fat i'th' flank;
And, contrary to our Italian fashion,
Wears a loose-bodied gown: there's somewhat in't.
I have a trick, may chance discover it,
A pretty one; I have bought some apricocks,
The first our spring yields.

Speak both texts with full vocal support and strive for
tremendous clarity. You may need to mouth and intone the
speeches first to feel the whole voice working. Sound the
pattern of the vowels and consonants. There is nothing subtle
or delicate about the language in either of these speeches. The
descriptions each gives are almost too vivid. The verse lines
flow freely, motored by the freedom of the language. Bosola's
speech begins with prose and transforms into verse. Vittoria's
goes out of control by the end. Later generations found this
descriptive vividness and unashamed display of feeling taste-
less and crude. It was thought that we needed defending
from this naked emotionalism. Though they are more revived

now than before, the theatre has still not fully rediscovered Jacobean play texts, like Webster's, completely nor given them a more central place in our repertoire. These are wonderful plays to speak because they display the actor so nakedly.

One of the powers of a Webster play is that on close examination all the words and images are appropriate and necessary. You need each and every one. If stark and vivid language is used and thrown around inaccurately then it diffuses itself and becomes a tedious, obscene harangue, not morally shocking. We all know that swear-words cease to shock us if used too often or without accuracy. We may be offended to hear the word 'puke' or 'whore' used as an expletive, but when we hear it used to describe the thing itself and in context, we are engaged with it. Webster uses a word because his character needs it.

As you speak these texts, you are obliged to mean everything you say. Don't cheat the word or yourself out of connecting to the meaning. My feeling with these texts is that you must, at some stage, sound them fully and allow them to be operatic before you can voice them normally. You need to paint a very vivid vocal picture before they can serve you and you them. I am not suggesting you stay with such an exaggerated delivery, but you need the experimentation to plug into their extreme states and discover how far you can go. The extremes of writing and living on the edge must be married.

Speak only the vowels of the text and, as you do this exercise, keep connected to the breath. Don't pull off a sound. Speak the texts with a free flowing breath. Breathe in. Speak as far as you can without losing support. Recover the breath and continue. These exercises will throw the breath around as well as help you to discover the emotional intensity of the text in various words, phrases and lines. Speak with an imaginative sense of being drunk, drawing on all the vocal liberation that intoxication brings. In other words, enjoy your vileness and release the bile instead of swallowing it. Liberate the words. If you become too intellectually overwhelmed about the meaning of the text, you will lose the stimulus of the words. Through the sound and texture of the words meaning will begin to declare itself. Your initial effort here is to set the text free. Many actors, when they speak lines like these, get a nasty taste in their mouths. Indeed, these speeches are distasteful. Yet they are also hypnotic when the need to speak them marries with the words and the character's state of mind.

After trying these exercises to open the text through your voice, you can come back to speaking the texts with more reality – even experimenting with being conversational – but always keeping the intensity, focus, clarity and liberation buzzing in your voice and through the text. Be probing and sober with this material.

Because you are delving in extreme emotional realms, you will need to perk up your vocal range. Try speaking a speech using too much range and then immediately return to a normal position. The range exercises mentioned in *The Right to Speak* will help (pp. 215–218). The stretch you have given the voice in the first part of these exercises will probably have stayed and helped to inform the normal position. It should help you feel a greater emotional connection to the text.

These texts are so large that they always induce a temptation to push the voice, shout or scream. If you sense you are pushing, shouting or screaming then return to intoning the text gently to free up the voice and then speak and trust the intensity of the word. A vocal push will indicate an emotional bluff instead of truth.

A Modern Jacobean Equivalent

I have sat around in theatre rehearsal rooms with seasoned and hardened professional actors, turning red and hesitating through shock as they have spoken aloud the work of Howard Barker. This contemporary British playwright is one of the great language-based writers. The reason his work is so shocking is that he uses words appropriately. The language almost seems sculpted rather than written. The words are physical, sensual, poetic and as in the Jacobean texts, no punches are pulled when it comes to honesty. So you must seek the truth when you speak a Barker text.

The contemporary text speaker, like the classical one, not only has to understand the words intellectually, but a need for words must come from the gut and not be blocked by either physical or mental censors as it travels up the body and escapes from the mouth. Although Barker doesn't employ the same length of thought as does John Webster you will need the same liberation and vocal free flow as you would for any Jacobean text. Try this passage from Barker's *The Bite of the Night*:

> *A beach.* GAY, *with a stick. A* BOY, *seated.*

GAY: Reasons for the fall of Paper Troy. One! (*The* BOY *hesitates.*) Come on, oh, do come on, or I will beat you!

BOY: Erm . . .

GAY: One! The degeneracy of the aristocracy and their flirtation with the arts. Two! The martial ardour of the warriors could find no satisfaction in origami! Three! Are you listening, I don't think you try at all, this is **History** I'm teaching you! And stop fidgetting, or I will beat you! (*Exasperated pause.*) I sometimes think, people are such swine, such inveterate swine. And then I think, no, you can make them better.

BOY: By beating them?

GAY: By beating them, yes! How else? (*She sees a figure, off.*) Oh, no, here comes that horrid old man again! Don't encourage him. Because he's blind we all go silly, he knows that, he uses that to exploit us. (HOMER *enters, blind.*) **You are not to put your hand into my dress again.** (*He stops.*) I think the beach should be a place for children to be children and not poked about by peculiar old men.

HOMER: You are not a child.

GAY: I am a child. I am thirteen. Obviously I am a child.

HOMER: You are not a child, and I am not an old man.

GAY: Conundrum.

BOY: What?

GAY: Conundrum. He says all these things, these conundrums and things, and the next thing you know –

HOMER: Stop –

GAY: Hand up your –

HOMER: **Stop**. (*She concedes.*) I am not an old man because I know nothing. And you are not a child because you know it all. Now give me your hand (*She extends it.* HOMER *draws it quickly to his crutch.*)

GAY: There! I knew that would happen!

HOMER: **A god lives there**.

HELEN (*entering*). The author of the Iliad.

GAY: He is trying to make me insane . . .

HELEN: The author of the Odyssey.

GAY: **He is trying to make me insane!** (*She pulls away, runs off.*)

HOMER: The young . . .! No charity! So cruel, which is their fascination . . .

BOY: She beats me with a twig!

HOMER: Lucky fellow . . .

BOY: Right round the face sometimes, whip! Because I don't know ten reasons for the fall of Paper Troy.

HOMER: There are not ten reasons.

BOY: That's what I say! (*He hurries off.*)

HELEN: I hate your songs. Do you mind this? The ripping livers and the splash of brains. The prosody is marvellous but. I must say this and fuck the consequences. The torrents of intestine and the ravens picking skulls **I also am so violent**, were you always blind? When their attacks were beaten off we maimed the wounded. With kitchen knives, me and the Trojan woman, hacked them in the ditch, trimming the features off their heads like turnips for the market and their cocks we cropped **Don't say you never heard of this** were you born blind or was it horror spread some merciful film across your retina, and what's pity, I do think pity is no substitute for truth –

HOMER: Helen –

HELEN: **I refuse to clap your songs**. (*Pause.*) I loved Troy, because Troy was to sin. Why did you never say that? But

> him who took me there was not a sinner, only an
> exhibitionist, and not my equal. **Don't you know the hell it
> is to find no man your equal?** Say that, in your next book.
> That was the agony of Troy, not slippery swords or old
> men massacred, but Helen's awful loneliness in dream . . .
>
> HOMER: Helen . . .
>
> HELEN: Do what you like with my daughter – when history
> gets to a child no mother can be of the least relief.

As with Jacobean texts the ideas and words contained here are
hard to relate to initially. Taboos are being confronted and
assaulted, but until you speak the words directly and without
either comment or shame the text cannot work vocally. Barker
uses repetition brilliantly but each repetition is apt and
precise. When the language is obscene it is terrifyingly
graphic. All barriers to vocal modesty must be dropped. The
language must tumble forth uncensored and the speaking
must match this quality. You cannot apologise or hide behind
banal and generalised notions. But, unlike the Jacobean texts,
the journey you make in one short thought of Barker text is
profound and succinct. The language is more stark and less
adorned with baroque touches. The language is modern.
Excess has been stripped away. This starkness makes the need
to connect to a word or image even greater because there are
fewer linguistic gestures to work with. Barker moves the
thought and action rapidly forwards. The speaker needs to
conform with this movement. This keeping up will not require
the breath support needed in Jacobean work, but it will
require not only speech definition but an easy and rapid flow
from one idea to another.

The Age of Pope

Now let's swiftly change both speaking pace and direction.
After the passion of Shakespeare, Marlowe, Milton, Webster
and a modern writer like Barker, with their powerful and
momentous verse lines, vivid images and open vowel sounds,

we arrive at words of a different sort. Alexander Pope signals the Age of Reason when passion was suspect and wild natural feelings were to be contained and controlled. All these attitudes are reflected in Pope's verse style, form and choice of words.

The verse is neither chaotic nor irregular but effortless. It is clipped and trimmed like a perfect ornamental hedgerow. The speaking must match this and be equally effortless. You must communicate confidence and assurance. There are no palpitations in the verse. You will need highly tuned muscles of articulation and a vocal lightness and balance. The iambic is buoyant and musical like Mozart and should never pound in our ears, just tickle them. The words play in our mouths and in our ears. The whole voice is in operation, but you don't need grand vocal explosiveness, rather a voice that is crystal-clear and defined. Yet do not make the mistake of confusing this with some form of artificial refinement. That is not what I mean at all. Being clear and articulate in your own accent is what you should strive for when speaking verse like Pope's. Because these texts become more idea-centred in content, their vocal quality resonates more in the head. The voice moves away from the loins, the gut and the heart and now percolates into the head.

Try this passage from Pope's 'Chloe':

> 'Yet Chloe sure was formed without a spot' –
> Nature in her then erred not, but forgot.
> 'With every pleasing, every prudent part,
> Say, what can Chloe want?' – She wants a heart.
> She speaks, behaves, and acts just as she ought;
> But never, never, reached one generous thought.
> Virtue she finds too painful an endeavour,
> Content to dwell in decencies forever.
> So very reasonable, so unmoved,
> As never yet to love, or to be loved.
> She, while her lover pants upon her breast,
> Can mark the figures on an Indian chest;
> And when she sees her friend in deep despair,

Observes how much a chintz exceeds mohair.
Forbid it Heaven, a favour or a debt
She e'er should cancel – but she may forget.
Safe is your secret still in Chloe's ear;
But none of Chloe's shall you ever hear.
Of all her Dears she never slandered one,
But cares not if a thousand are undone.
Would Chloe know if you're alive or dead?
She bids her footman put it in her head.
Chloe is prudent – would you too be wise?
Then never break your heart when Chloe dies.

Beat out the lines. The lightness and ease expressed in the
lines' regularity and balance and the masterful use of rhyme
should astound you, and yet, though the form is extremely
regular, you will find it so well patterned that it will also
appear conversational despite the conscious crafting in each
line. Notice the brilliant rhyming couplets. I don't think any
other British writer has ever matched Pope's effortless potency
and easy wit in this regard. Generally each end couplet
embraces one thought. So the voice steps from one idea to
another as in a board game. The first part of the couplet sets
up the positive or socially acceptable side of Chloe, the second
part slips the knife in and punctures the image. Pope's
couplets often work in this way: set-up followed by put-down.
The pay-off in the second line must be sounded so that the
voice rises to the discovery the line shares with the listener.
Always remember that you are speaking 'satirical' verse. So
the observations and jokes must be timed and shared.

If you sustain the couplet, the first part naturally flowing
into the second like a sparkling tributary, the rhyme will
neither get in the way nor sound contrived. On the contrary
it will thrill a listener and help to communicate each thought
like a bright burst. Our expectations are aroused as we hear
each new rhyme scheme and that anticipation sets a pattern in
motion which the voice must deliver.

The listener wonders, how will Pope do it with the next

line, and then he does it with wit, skill and even cruelty. The passion that leads to a need for imagery in language is absent. Instead we revel in exact physical and social detail so finely wrought that the speaker knows the poet has thought out the line in detail.

Notice that the language explores and inhabits a real and concrete world. A world of footmen, 'Indian chests', 'chintz and mohair', objects and props replaces or contains feelings. The verse is well-furnished like an elegant drawing room. The voice takes us on a tour. We very quickly get a picture of the rooms, the setting and the social importance of objects. The use of language here displays all too clearly how the Age of Reason will want to contain, understand and control the world, not allow it to be the infinite mystery that is unlocked by explosive imagery or too vulgar metaphor. This kind of language is very controlled. The speaking of it must exude confidence. The world is viewed through the head, not the heart or the gut, like a voice-over to a modern travelogue.

I am not suggesting that there is no feeling either in this piece or in Pope at large. I should think, in fact, that Pope loathed this lady, Chloe, and her pretensions. But through a tricky sleight-of-hand with language and form he harnesses and reins in passions, not allowing them to roam about but forcing them into strict focus so that they can be understood. The energy and precision of the verse requires clear articulation and unindulged vowels. One is not being too lavish here with language. Get on with it and get to the point. Allow it its clarity because the speaker is dissecting his or her subject and analysing a condition in a scientific manner. The precision creates its own form of lavishness.

Enjoy the bounce and wickedness in the verse's frivolity. Notice how energised yet balanced the line is and how enjoyable the rhyme can be if you speak the couplet with a wicked bravado. But recognise, too, that if you slur a word or drop a syllable then you mar Pope's frightening ease not only in verse writing but in the verbal caricature and destruction of his victims. Each word, phrase and couplet must be delivered like a dart that unfailingly strikes its target.

Restoration Dialogue

Many of the qualities discovered in Pope's poetry are similar to the speaking challenges experienced in Restoration plays. You will need tremendous skills in articulation and an all-round effortlessness in speaking Restoration speeches.

In these plays we are planted in a society where speaking, witty repartee, wordplay and competing one-on-one through linguistic skills are the rules of the game. In this world you have to speak-up and never be silent. Those who remain silent are immediately shunned. In plays like these the speaker must be able to turn on a language switch. You are what you speak. I suspect anyone living in this age, the early eighteenth century, who was not successful with words rapidly dwindled from the scene and out of all the important social circles for lack of a voice. The need for words must have been crucial.

Characters duelled with words as much as with swords; wit was rapier-like and razor-sharp. It hurt. You either knew how to lunge and parry with words or others cut you to pieces. The facility with speech was born of thinking and listening skills. You survived through your ability to take in words and turn them back at your opponent. Anyone struggling for a word or stumbling would be interrupted and conquered. Words got you attention and put you in the limelight until you relinquished centre stage to someone of greater skill.

In order to survive the treacherous shoals in this linguistically brutal current you had to put interesting ideas into elegant language which would provoke and intrigue the cream of a reasoning society. Long thoughts (clauses within clauses, boxes within boxes) that require a strong and controlled support system, pace, drive, clarity and a high speaking energy (if you drop a syllable or miscalculate a word someone else will immediately snap it up) are the basic foundation stones needed before you release or can begin to enjoy speaking these texts. The voice is at the front of the mouth for clear, efficient direction of sound.

Take a look at this interchange between Sir John Brute and his wife Lady Brute in the opening scene from Sir John Vanbrugh's *The Provoked Wife*:

> SIR JOHN: What cloying meat is love – when matrimony's the sauce to it! Two years' marriage has debauched my five senses. Everything I see, everything I hear, everything I feel, everything I smell, and everything I taste – methinks has wife in't. No boy was ever so weary of his tutor, no girl of her bib, no nun of doing penance, nor old maid of being chaste, as I am of being married. Sure there's a secret curse entailed upon the very name of wife. My lady is a young lady, a fine lady, a witty lady, a virtuous lady – and yet I hate her. There is but one thing on earth I loathe beyond her; that's fighting. Would my courage come up but to a fourth part of my ill nature, I'd stand buff to her relations, and thrust her out of doors. But marriage has sunk me down to such an ebb of resolution. I dare not draw my sword, though even to get rid of my wife. But here she comes.

> *Enter* LADY BRUTE.

> LADY BRUTE: Do you dine at home today, Sir John?
> SIR JOHN: Why, do you expect I should tell you what I don't know myself?
> LADY BRUTE: I thought there was no harm in asking you.
> SIR JOHN: If thinking wrong were an excuse for impertinence, women might be justified in most things they say or do.
> LADY BRUTE: I'm sorry I have said anything to displease you.
> SIR JOHN: Sorrow for things past is of as little importance to me as my dining at home or abroad ought to be to you.
> LADY BRUTE: My inquiry was only that I might have provided what you liked.
> SIR JOHN: Six to four you had been in the wrong there again,

for what I liked yesterday I don't like today, and what I
like today 'tis odds I mayn't like tomorrow.

LADY BRUTE: But if I had asked you what you liked?

SIR JOHN: Why, then there would have been more asking
about it than the thing was worth.

LADY BRUTE: I wish I did but know how I might please you.

SIR JOHN: Ay, but that sort of knowledge is not a wife's talent.

LADY BRUTE: Whate'er my talent is, I'm sure my will has ever
been to make you easy.

SIR JOHN: If women were to have their wills, the world would
be finely governed.

LADY BRUTE: What reason have I given you to use me as you
do of late? It once was otherwise: you married me for love.

SIR JOHN: And you me for money: so you have your reward,
and I have mine.

LADY BRUTE: What is it that disturbs you?

SIR JOHN: A parson.

LADY BRUTE: Why, what has he done to you?

SIR JOHN: He has married me.

First of all, notice the pace. The ideas and words come
lightning quick. In order to speak quickly you must also be
thinking quickly and the speech muscles must be ready to
respond accordingly. The scene begins as a whirlwind and
gradually funnels down to a few concluding words in the final
lines. This is the very opening of the play, and the audience
are being hurled directly into a torrent of words that express
anger. You must take them along with you.

Notice the long arc of thoughts. You have to reach the last
word in many thoughts before the whole unit becomes clear.
Sir John speaks in complex aphorisms. Lady Brute sets them
up with her simple questions or statements. As an exercise it
can be useful to try speaking each of the sentences here on
one breath. This is only an exercise so don't feel that it is the
way to tackle these elegant thoughts once up and speaking
them. But the exercise will give you a sense of the complete
scope and shape of the thoughts, and where to place stress
and emphasis. The thoughts must knit and lock together.

In Restoration texts lists are always in evidence. Notice Sir

John Brute's opening catalogue. All his senses encounter the obstacle 'wife'. Then he lists how weary he is of her and marriage, it outdoes a boy with his tutor, a girl and her bib, a nun of penance, an 'old maid of being chaste'. Then he lists his wife's virtues but he still loathes her. The list encompasses all possibilities so the litany becomes an oral device. If you speak a list with that in mind the text cannot be boring. Discover all the options. Like Pope, the language does not encompass richly ornamented imagery. The speaker's passion lies in thinking out a nagging feeling in prose, not experiencing it directly in heightened poetry. Yet the intentions are just as visceral.

Sir John provokes and Lady Brute defends herself. Rather than spew vile language (as the Jacobeans – Webster's Bosola and Vittoria – do above) they quarrel with well-constructed sentences, niceties and scorn. It is as though all feelings are channelled through their heads and diverted away from the heart.

You should also sense, when you speak any dialogue like this out loud, that there is a shared energy between the two speakers. One voice feeds into and needs the other. Conversations are never allowed to sag or wane – energy is built up, not diminished. In fact the speaking energy is kept aloft and taken further. It is like kicking a ball into the air and then never allowing it to touch the ground. The dialogue, in fact, is like a game of volleyball in which each speaker tries to get a point over the net. That is a good way to approach this kind of text. Try to keep the words in the air not just with power but as delicately and deftly as possible. They must never be allowed to drop and fall to the ground. A point goes to your opponent if they do.

Apply all the same principles immediately above to a scene from *The Way of the World* by William Congreve. This is a love scene and marriage proposal. Here again are lists, long sustained arcs of thinking, clear, elegant reasoned language, energy and intense listening. We met this same play earlier (p. 120) when 1 talked about stressing words.

MILLAMANT: It may be in things of common application; but never sure in love. Oh, I hate a lover that can dare to think he draws a moment's air independent on the bounty of his mistress. There is not so impudent a thing in nature as the saucy look of an assured man, confident of success. The pedantic arrogance of a very husband has not so pragmatical an air. Ah! I'll never marry, unless I am first made sure of my will and pleasure.

MIRABELL: Would you have 'em both before marriage? Or will you be contented with the first now, and stay for the other till after grace?

MILLAMANT: Ah! don't be impertinent. – My dear liberty, shall I leave thee? My faithful solitude, my darling contemplation, must I bid you then adieu? Ay-h adieu – my morning thoughts, agreeable wakings, indolent slumbers, all ye *douceurs*, ye *sommeils du matin*, adieu? – I can't do't, 'tis more than impossible. Postively, Mirabell, I'll lie abed in a morning as long as I please.

MIRABELL: Then I'll get up in a morning as early as I please.

MILLAMANT: Ah! Idle creature, get up when you will. – And d'ye hear. I won't be called names after I'm married; positively I won't be called names.

MIRABELL: Names!

MILLAMANT: Aye, as wife, spouse, my dear, joy, jewel, love, sweetheart, and the rest of that nauseous cant, in which men and their wives are so fulsomely familiar – I shall never bear that. – Good Mirabell, don't let us be familiar or fond, nor kiss before folks, like my Lady Fadler and Sir Francis; nor go to Hyde Park together the first Sunday in a new chariot, to provoke eyes and whispers; and then never to be seen there together again; as if we were proud of one another the first week, and ashamed of one another ever after. Let us be very strange and well-bred; let us be as strange as if we had been married a great while, and as well-bred as if we were not married at all.

MIRABELL: Have you any more conditions to offer? Hitherto your demands are pretty reasonable.

MILLAMANT: Trifles! – As liberty to pay and receive visits to and from whom I please; to write and receive letters,

without interrogatories or wry faces on your part; to wear
what I please; and choose conversation with regard only to
my own taste; to have no obligation upon me to converse
with wits that I don't like, because they are your
acquaintance; or to be intimate with fools, because they
may be your relations. Come to dinner when I please; dine
in my dressing room when I'm out of humour, without
giving a reason. To have my closet inviolate; to be sole
empress of my tea table, which you must never presume to
approach without first asking leave. And lastly, wherever I
am, you shall always knock at the door before you come in.
These articles subscribed, if I continue to endure you a
little longer, I may by degrees dwindle into a wife.
MIRABELL: Your bill of fare is something advanced in this
latter account. Well, have I liberty to offer conditions –
that when you are dwindled into a wife, I may not be
beyond measure enlarged into a husband?
MILLAMANT: You have free leave. Propose your utmost; speak
and spare not.

This is an excerpt from what has been called a 'proviso scene'.
Millamant and Mirabell, initially a combative couple like
Beatrice and Benedick in *Much Ado About Nothing*, will marry
if their provisos (terms) are acceptable to one another. In their
masked and insincere world, they are amazingly direct with
each other. They are also on equal terms and very well
matched as a couple and as speakers. Perhaps this marriage
will be happy. The speech is a catalogue of will's and won't's.
Through the lists we get a very clear picture of how this
society placed values on an individual, particularly a woman.
The level of listening and concentration Mirabell offers to
Millamant displays his respect and love for her. He allows her
the room to speak. He never interrupts, he never slanders
her. He has rather a healthy respect for her. Mirabell's verbal
parries are not defences but actually help Millamant to
continue. They are not there to undermine her case but to
support it. Although they are enjoying this scene – and it can
be performed like a dance to capture the essence of 'fancy
footwork' in the sentences – you can still sense that it takes a

lot of energy to speak it. Notice how Millamant bursts into each of her sections with an exclamation that sets off her monologues. And this is but one small part of a very involved play. The drama is made up of many such journeys strung together.

I think that nowadays many young people only connect verbal energy with aggression. They fail to see how it can be as joyous, graceful and scintillating as it is here. This is a scene in which speaking together is a genuine pleasure. The two voices have to partner each other as in a duet, guiding one another through the mounting key changes of the word music. In fact, as through dancing it, one way to enter this dialogue is to sing it to each other. The musicality of the long line first has to be experienced before it becomes second nature in the speaking. By the end of the interchange the couple have become, ironically, husband and wife. Suddenly you realise you have both been dancing and singing a courtship.

Oscar Wilde

I am now making a gigantic leap to the end of the nineteenth century, to Oscar Wilde. All the voice and speech skills needed in Restoration and eighteenth-century texts are required to speak Wilde. Of course the wit and subject matter differ but the love of a rapier-like attack through words is the same. You need the same speech clarity, energy and vocal lightness you have been using above. Wilde does not work by vocal bluntness, so, as with Vanbrugh and Congreve, any observable effort in speech would mar the marvellous ease and elegance in the writing. An Irishman, Wilde – not a wealthy man but someone who came from a good social background – was accepted in a very exclusive English society because he could entertain and hold forth brilliantly at any dinner table. This passage is from *A Woman of No Importance*.

LADY STUTFIELD: The world says that Lord Illingworth is very, very wicked.

LORD ILLINGWORTH: But what world says that, Lady Stutfield? It must be the next world. This world and I are on excellent terms. (*Sits down beside* MRS ALLONBY.)

LADY STUTFIELD: Everyone *I* know says you are very, very wicked.

LORD ILLINGWORTH: It is perfectly monstrous the way people go about, nowadays, saying things against one behind one's back that are absolutely and entirely true.

LADY HUNSTANTON: Dear Lord Illingworth is quite hopeless, Lady Stutfield. I have given up trying to reform him. It would take a Public Company with a Board of Directors and a paid Secretary to do that. But you have the secretary already, Lord Illingworth, haven't you? Gerald Arbuthnot has told us of his good fortune; it is really most kind of you.

LORD ILLINGWORTH: Oh, don't say that, Lady Hunstanton. Kind is a dreadful word. I took a great fancy to young Arbuthnot the moment I met him, and he'll be of considerable use to me in something I am foolish enough to think of doing.

LADY HUNSTANTON: He is an admirable young man. And his mother is one of my dearest friends. He has just gone for a walk with our pretty American. She is very pretty, is she not?

LADY CAROLINE: Far too pretty. These American girls carry off all the good matches. Why can't they stay in their own country? They are always telling us it is the Paradise of women.

LORD ILLINGWORTH: It is, Lady Caroline. That is why, like Eve, they are so extremely anxious to get out of it.

LADY CAROLINE: Who are Miss Worsley's parents?

LORD ILLINGWORTH: American women are wonderfully clever in concealing their parents.

LADY HUNSTANTON: My dear Lord Illingworth, what do you mean? Miss Worsley, Caroline, is an orphan. Her father was a very wealthy millionaire or philanthropist, or both, I believe, who entertained my son quite hospitably, when he visited Boston. I don't know how he made his money, originally.

KELVIL: I fancy in American dry goods.

LADY HUNSTANTON: What are American dry goods?

LORD ILLINGWORTH: American novels.

LADY HUNSTANTON: How very singular! . . . Well, from whatever source her large fortune came, I have a great esteem for Miss Worsley. She dresses exceedingly well. All Americans do dress well. They get their clothes in Paris.

MRS ALLONBY: They say, Lady Hunstanton, that when good Americans die they go to Paris.

LADY HUNSTANTON: Indeed? and when bad Americans die, where do they go to?

LORD ILLINGWORTH: Oh, they go to America.

All Wilde's natural speaking abilities and energies have found their way into his writing. Any speaker here has to imagine a 'Wildean' persona. To release his wit and speaking joy you should try all the exercises for Pope, Vanbrugh and Congreve. You will find that the wit has a more schematic format, like a comedy routine. But do avoid the kind of smug acting that suggests 'I am being witty'. Some of the characters are there in the scene to set up the laugh lines that Lord Illingworth gets to say. The key to speaking this kind of dialogue is to let the humour strike with surprise and without comment. It should sound spontaneous and unforced, as though it were the most natural thing in the world to be this clever and skilful with words (as Wilde himself was). True ease is called for in the delivery. Imagine you are speaking these lines from the comfort of a well-padded and elegant armchair. Illingworth speaks from a position of authority. The voice just casts off the words without hesitation or even notice. The wit is such a habit that the jokes about America are easily manufactured. No holds in the breath, voice or speech should be in the slightest evidence. The high class of the characters breeds confidence in every word they say. They never believe for an instant that they could possibly be boring. Each of these thoughts must organically inform the clarity of the voice as you go through this dialogue.

George Bernard Shaw

The action of Shaw's plays is centred round lengthy, passionate debates. In Shaw's Introductions you will find an account of the characters so detailed that it even includes indications of what they are wearing. Stage directions are precise and generally work very well. Lots of the author's interjections come in the midst of dialogue. One of my descriptions of a good playwright is that you don't need any stage directions, the text reveals all. Shaw is one of the exceptions to the rule. He wants to push a speaker into feeling the full substance and weight of one of his characters. He also wants to push you as the character into the whirl of the on-stage debate. A successful production of a Shaw play will have the audience swinging from one point of view to another as though we were at a furious tennis match. As each character speaks we should be won over and then change allegiance when a new speaker states his or her position. Eventually we leave the theatre intellectually invigorated because we've encountered so many sides to an argument which the writer always leaves open. Shaw wanted to sting us with new and sometimes outrageous ideas. His aim was to get us to think. All the characters have enough grace to listen to each other and give space to another viewpoint, knowing that they will be given time to respond. The debate is opened and then explored with wit, intelligence and grace. The ideas have to be clearly conveyed by very confident voices, depending solely on words to frame the terms of debate.

When you speak these lines you are an advocate for your own character's position. The ideas and how those ideas transform characters are what creates the drama. Shaw is very hard to edit because each idea is linked to the last one and grows and develops from it. The build is gradual and inevitable. The thoughts are crucially linked together. So he doesn't work in cut versions. The whole is better than a part. And the voice must become accustomed to this accumulation of cause and effect. It must remain dynamic in order to hold the audience's ear. Speaking in a Shaw play is like being part of a party conference or a platform committee. Part of the speaking job is to frame arguments and counter arguments. You can't be frightened of passionate debate or bored by words when you come to Shaw. He will catch you out if you are either. The language must constantly thrill you. Think of the carefully graduated speeches as a series of light bulbs that flash on as you discover a new stage of a progressive idea.

Vocally I place Shaw in a line after Pope, the Restoration writers and Wilde. Of course he is more overtly political than many of these writers. He was a socialist trying to rock a sedentary society. But the techniques required to speak Wilde, Congreve and Vanbrugh are very much the same here. Language is a tool of reason and fine debating skills are essential. Apply all the exercises to Shaw's texts that have to do with clarity, sustained support, lightness and ease of speech, a listening energy, a thinking energy that is reflected in the pace and intellectual passion and a clear development of thought and argument.

Read and experiment with the following excerpt from *Major Barbara*. Undershaft – a millionaire arms dealer – is debating with his daughter Barbara, a Major in the Salvation Army. Despite yourself, as long as Undershaft's speech is invested with a true passion, I think you'll find you can be swept away by the brilliance of his argument and his means of expressing it.

> BARBARA . . . [*sudden vehemence*]: Justify yourself: shew me some light through the darkness of this dreadful place, with its beautifully clean workshops, and respectable workmen, and model homes.
> UNDERSHAFT: Cleanliness and respectability do not need justification, Barbara: they justify themselves. I see no darkness here, no dreadfulness. In your Salvation shelter I saw poverty, misery, cold and hunger. You gave them bread and treacle and dreams of heaven. I give from thirty shillings a week to twelve thousand a year. They find their own dreams; but I look after the drainage.
> BARBARA: And their souls?

UNDERSHAFT: I save their souls just as I saved yours.

BARBARA [*revolted*]: You saved my soul! What do you mean?

UNDERSHAFT: I fed you and clothed you and housed you. I took care that you should have money enough to live handsomely – more than enough; so that you could be wasteful, careless, generous. That saved your soul from the seven deadly sins.

BARBARA [*bewildered*]: The seven deadly sins!

UNDERSHAFT: Yes, the deadly seven. [*Counting on his fingers*] Food, clothing, firing, rent, taxes, respectability and children. Nothing can lift those seven millstones from Man's neck but money; and the spirit cannot soar until the mill stones are lifted. I lifted them from your spirit. I enabled Barbara to become Major Barbara; and I saved her from the crime of poverty.

CUSINS: Do you call poverty a crime?

UNDERSHAFT: The worst of crimes. All the other crimes are virtues beside it: all the other dishonors are chivalry itself by comparison. Poverty blights whole cities; spreads horrible pestilences; strikes dead the very souls of all who come within sight, sound, or smell of it. What you call crime is nothing: a murder here and a theft there, a blow now and a curse then: what do they matter? they are only the accidents and illnesses of life: there are not fifty genuine professional criminals in London. But there are millions of poor people, abject people, dirty people, ill fed, ill clothed people. They poison us morally and physically: they kill the happiness of society: they force us to do away with our own liberties and to organize unnatural cruelties for fear they should rise against us and drag us down into their abyss. Only fools fear crime: we all fear poverty. Pah! [*turning on Barbara*] you talk of your half-saved ruffian in West Ham: you accuse me of dragging his soul back to perdition. Well, bring him to me here; and I will drag his soul back again to salvation for you. Not by words and dreams; but by thirty-eight shillings a week, a sound house in a handsome street, and a permanent job. In three weeks he will have a fancy waistcoat; in three months a tall hat and a chapel sitting; before the end of the year he will shake hands with a duchess at a Primrose League meeting, and join the Conservative Party.

Notice that Shaw's writing is precise. Not only trust the language but trust the punctuation – something you can't do in Shakespeare, because it was added by later editors. The passion goes through the head into the word and is then placed in a finely constructed sentence. The heart is in the reason. Emotion and intellect are finely married and balanced. The ideas follow a clear plan to build a well-constructed edifice. Respect the construction's blueprint and the dramatic construct will build itself. Compromise or pull away and the text will crumble. Overwhelm reason with passion and the words will be out of synch.

Styles in Speaking Texts

All the texts in this section, from the Restoration through Shaw, are generally meant to be spoken in Received Pronunciation or Standard English. Not to comply with this can send an audience storming out of the theatre in horror. You may want to revolt and introduce a new revisionary style, but take caution. I look at it this way. All these plays are examining and confronting the higher echelons of a class system. All the characters speak with confidence because of their education and background. They have the right to speak and need each word they say. These characters not only wanted to speak, but they wanted to sound fashionable – their version of a right way to speak. Above all they want to *impress* us, make us listen. That right and freedom would organically produce a free forward and effortless sound arguably close to RP.

The characters demand to be heard and make their ideas extremely clear. Notice, too, that they speak in fully articulated sentences. It was fashionable to be clear. Word and thought marry in terms of energy. Each of these characters speaks formally. This would lead to a careful, precise choice of words. It would be unnatural either to mumble or distrust words. In fact, each speaker can't wait to speak, to get involved in a linguistic sparring match. Each wants to grab the baton and take up the next leg of the relay before passing it on to someone else. You must guard against improvising on these texts. Every word here is needed and cemented in place by the writer for stressing. Make no additions or emendations when you work with these texts.

Put these organic forces into the voice and you will come up with a sound very close to RP or Standard English; although regional colours can still live in the voice and accent. What often kills these remarkable plays is an actor speaking RP as a plastered-on, artificial effect. This deadens and mutes otherwise great language. By all means try working outside-in. That is, start with an accent you think sounds right. But at some point the work must be directed inside-out. The need to speak must match the way you speak. Never adopt an accent without knowing and exploring where the accent comes from and how you can make it sound natural.

The basic questions you always ask yourself are:

- Why does this character speak like this?
- What social and class influences are in operation?
- Is the accent marring and blocking the content?
- What are you wearing and how does that affect your need for words?
- Who are you talking to and why?

I have sat through too many productions of these plays on both sides of the Atlantic with actors who think a Standard voice is all that is necessary to make them work. It isn't! You have to live through the language and make it second nature to you, which means that the accent must also be natural to the character.

Greek Tragedy

In speaking Greek tragedy we face some of the most harrowing political, social and personal actions that humanity can experience or inflict on one another. After more than two thousand years the plays of Aeschylus, Sophocles and Euripides are still strikingly relevant. Each dramatic age seems to re-invent them for audiences. For me the language, even in modern English translations, is raw and brutal; all blood and bone and little flesh, the words so direct and unsentimental, the emotions unbridled. This can make them seem like terrifying tasks when spoken, and speakers are often unable to relate to their rough power.

When you speak these passages it is easy to understand a key belief of the Greeks: that when you utter words and sounds – 'fury' and 'vengeance', for instance – you release the thing itself into the world. When you hear the vibrant, clear and astounding simplicity of sound contained in spoken Ancient Greek (or what we believe it sounded like from reconstruction) you do feel that words have magically taken on three-dimensional shape.

Unfortunately today the simplicity of word and image, and the horror in the stories, have led actors either to bluff their way through a text – vocally pushing or ranting – or, in the quest for simplicity, to deny the power of the word and merely recite the language as though it came from a naturalistic play. When the language is so raw and potentially dangerous to speak, it is easy to 'comment' on the word and avoid its power rather than confront and experience it head-on; sentimental-ising the feeling rather than connecting to it.

This is an excerpt from the Royal Shakespeare Company's version of Euripides' *The Trojan Women* by John Barton and Kenneth Cavander, directed by John Barton, in 1980. This translation is very sparse and perhaps not as academically pure as some others in print. In many translations you will find a longer, more complex verse line which I think has tamed the brutality of the original. But in this instance I do think all the main challenges I have highlighted in speaking the Greek tragedies can be examined.

This particular bit of text fully explores a most horrific situation. It must be experienced through simple language without bluff or comment and with truth. The Trojan queen Andromache has just been told by the conquering Greeks that her young son, Astyanax, is to be hurled from the walls of Troy and bashed to death. His fate is inexorable. This is her farewell speech to him. She holds on to him as she speaks.

ANDROMACHE: O my son, my love,
　　　　Your father has murdered you
　　　　By being so brave and strong.
　　　　I remember our marriage bed:
　　　　On our wedding night I thought
　　　　That my son would rule the world.
　　　　O Hector . . . Hector . . . Hector . . .
　　　　I wish I had never married him!
　　　　I wish I had never seen him.
　　　　Are you crying, little one?
　　　　Do you understand what is happening?
　　　　You clutch at my dress, you nestle
　　　　Like a bird under its mother's wing
　　　　But there isn't any Hector
　　　　To come and rescue you
　　　　With a spear flashing in his hand.
　　　　Nothing can save you now.

ANDROMACHE *embraces him.*

　　　　My dear baby, my dear baby,
　　　　O you smell so sweet.
　　　　When you were born I wrapped you up
　　　　And gave you my breast to suck.
　　　　O how I worked for you.
　　　　The labour pains, the watching,
　　　　I wasted it all, wasted it!
　　　　Say goodbye to me now.
　　　　It's the last time: do you love me?
　　　　Hold your mother tight.
　　　　Kiss me, let me feel your arms.
　　　　You savages, you murderers!
　　　　What has he done to you?
　　　　He's a little child.
　　　　Take him then, out of my sight,

> Dash out his brains if you want to!
> Zeus does this, Zeus crushes me.
> I have lost my child.
> Now I can go to my new man
> With a light, happy heart!

Speak the text on your full voice, focusing through to the end of every word before reaching the full stop. Avoid the temptation to devoice or pull off any word. Avoid the temptation of pushing or embellishing the words, making them sound artificially poetic.

The temptation to devoice is a denial, to push is a bluff.

You must find a way of being heightened but real, otherwise this great text will not make the passage over time and speak to us today. You may need to intone or chant the text to discover its elemental power. This exercise will cleanse the language of any bluffs or denials you may be imposing on it. It also will keep you focused on the sound. You will definitely need to contact, experience and commit to every word. You will need to feel that you are speaking to a child, to Hector, to the Greeks, to us.

> O my son, my love . . .
>
> O Hector . . . Hector . . Hector . . .
>
> You savages, you murderers.

Unstructured emotion must emerge from the words. You do not speak to make sense but to grieve. The whole history of the Trojan War and final defeat must be captured in this speech. The mother and son connection about to be severed must be felt.

Because the text is so simple yet unrelenting it is easy to forget it has a clear structure which will help you plot Andromache's journey through this appalling moment in her life. She addresses her son; she talks about how his father, Hector, has unwittingly murdered him; she remembers her marriage bed, her wedding night, etc. The history of a life is contained here. If you can stay on the pathway and deal with each thing as it occurs to Andromache then you can't comment or sentimentalise or embellish what is naturally here. So much is happening in such a short time but with such sparse language. Deal with the events just as we deal with the skid on the motorway. We don't have time to show our fear or worry about our fate. We just act: steer the car, brake, watch the mirror. We are surviving, we are heightened and if we had language at that moment I suggest it would be as raw and economic as it is here. The language of most Greek texts is focused and controlled in the midst of stupendous passions.

Andromache has no time for sentimental indulgence. On the other hand, don't become so naturalistic that you can't face the need for the words. You must confront them and then connect to them. Don't swallow 'O' or any of the sounds. Fully release them to create a launch pad into the next word. Andromache is in too much pain and the stakes are too high for her to show any shame in speaking or risk not being clear. The words must come out. Compare this character's vocal bravery with that of Paulina in the excerpt from *The Winter's Tale* (p. 200).

Allow the pulse of the line to find its beat:

> O Hector . . . Hector . . . Hector . . .
> I wish I had never married him!
> I wish I had never seen him.

There is a powerful, poignant pulse under this section that is like someone beating her heart with a stone.

Follow the length of each thought through to the end. Don't allow yourself to become trapped or fragmented with the words. 'You clutch at my dress, you nestle.' If you follow the length of thought down to 'Nothing can save you now' and keep the ideas flowing you won't have time to become sentimental. In dealing with the boy your feelings are kept at bay. But, more importantly, stay with the words and trust their simplicity and power: 'murdered', 'brave', 'crying', 'nothing', 'savages', 'goodbye', 'dash'. Just the sounds alone are emblematic of grief. One hardly has to act them. The sounds clarify their meaning. The union between sound and meaning is so precise and appropriate.

Edward Bond

I want to offer a modern equivalent to mirror the power of Greek tragedy. Edward Bond is a great writer much too underrated and too little performed nowadays. Perhaps because his uncompromising vision reminds us of Euripides' unsentimental view and language. Bond writes about and uncovers the same enormous, elemental issues that are found in Greek tragedy. I also believe he uses similar techniques, especially in the direct simplicity and rawness of his language. This means there are the same traps when it comes to giving voice to his texts. It is too easy to ignore the power of the word and sentimentalise the situations around the political truths by either bluff or denial. In Bond's *Lear* I have chosen a small excerpt where a wounded soldier is dying while the other guerilla soldiers get on with the war.

CARPENTER: Where?
PETE: Stomach.
WOUNDED SOLDIER: It's all right, don't whisper. I won't be a
   nuisance. We said we'd die quietly, if we could. Don't
   scream or ask for anything. It upsets the others and holds
   them up . . .
CORDELIA: You must rest before we –
WOUNDED SOLDIER: Yes, yes. Don't treat me like a child
   because I'm dying. Let me drink some water.
PETE: No.
WOUNDED SOLDIER: It doesn't matter about my stomach. It'll

help my throat. (CARPENTER *gives him some water.*) Yes.
Now go and get ready.

They leave him and get ready to move.

CORDELIA (*to the* LOOK-OUT). Tell them to start moving. Keep
off the road.

The LOOK-OUT *goes out.*

WOUNDED SOLDIER: When it's dark I'll pretend my wife's
come to meet me and they're coming up the road. I put our
girl on my shoulder and she pulls my hair and I say ah . . .
PETE: More tea?
CARPENTER: No.

PETE *empties the tea can and packs it.*

WOUNDED SOLDIER: She sees a bird and asks me what it is and
I say it's a wader but I don't know . . . Who'll tell my wife
I'm dead?

Off, a single shot. No one reacts.

It's dark, there are the stars . . . look . . .

LEWIS *and the* CROUCHING SOLDIER *come back. They pick up
their things.*

CORDELIA: When we have power these things won't be
necessary.

Everyone goes off except the WOUNDED SOLDIER.

WOUNDED SOLDIER: The stars . . . Look . . . One . . . Two
. . . Three . . .

Silence.

You have to decide who the soldier is talking to, but the main
speaking objective here is to trust the clarity of the story. To
unlock the political power of the play there must be no added
commenting on the text, no indications of melodrama or
excessive tragedy. A nameless soldier is dying. He is pragmatic. He needs water but won't upset the others. Very
simply he imagines a meeting with his wife and child. He is
worried about who will inform his wife of his death. He then

counts the stars. These are the facts of the narrative. The speaker's job is how to reproduce the facts with the given words. If Bond wanted sentimental interference to colour the voice he would have added it.

At first we can look at the excerpt and not realise how much is happening. It is only when we trust the words and need them as last gasps of dying breath that the vividness of the description comes into focus. Every word is appropriate and provides exact information. On closer inspection this nameless soldier has been given sparse language, but the words are enough to give him a history and a family.

We end up knowing a great deal about him. Connect to the words, not commenting on or embellishing them, let the words be connected to the deepest breath and a detailed picture and story emerges. These words (like 'stomach') come from a very deep breath position.

It is often the case that the simpler the text the more the actor thinks he should do something with it, should be 'interesting'. But remember simplicity is not boring but profound. Bond's writing, his word choice, is stoical yet passionate and poetic. You notice this best when you speak the words. The sparer the language the more essential it becomes, the more intense the feeling. 'Need' itself is a simple word with a tremendous impact. Embellished language, useless words or phrases are just evasion. I believe that as language is honed down to its simplest form then it is an indication that the situation is equally intense and raw. There is no nonsense involved when a text has reduced itself to simple choices of words; frivolity, wit and language games have no place whatsoever when the stakes are so high that the words have to be so stoic.

With the Greeks and now with Bond we have travelled a good distance from the world of Pope, Congreve and Wilde where language is like a display of fireworks that distracts us from the need for essential, elemental feelings.

Connect and trust the word. Here the word is all you have

to explore unknown and limitless pain. Let it through you without blocking, finish the word off outside you. The word should leave you, no longer be yours. Don't pull back or swallow it. You could argue that this is easier to do with seemingly simple text, but in many ways it seems to me much harder. There is no place to hide. With such texts the need and the language are more naked. The commitment called for here can be frightening but do try to be that free and focused.

Try building a sentence up word by word on breath support until you are vocally free: 'Who'll' [breath] 'Who'll tell' [breath] 'Who'll tell my' [breath], etc., until you find the whole power of 'Who'll tell my wife I'm dead'. Word by needed word you will start to encapsulate the importance of this critical phrase. An idea will form and an image will emerge. As it speaks the voice is dying.

William Blake

At first it may seem very strange for me to include William Blake with the Greeks and Edward Bond. But simplicity of language on top of a mammoth experience connects Blake with them, the word being the tip of the iceberg and yet totally sufficient. Again to speak Blake you have to trust that the marriage of word and form – although simple – is infinitely powerful.

The simple language of Euripides and Bond encompasses huge political and personal tragedies. Blake's words are political and personal as well but also mystical. His poems work on many levels but each level seemingly gives us a vision, a key to a door into the Universe. Read his poem, 'The Tyger':

> Tyger! Tyger! burning bright
> In the forests of the night,
> What immortal hand or eye
> Could frame thy fearful symmetry?

In what distant deeps or skies
Burnt the fire of thine eyes?
On what wings dare he aspire?
What the hand dare seize the fire?

And what shoulder, and what art,
Could twist the sinews of thy heart?
And when thy heart began to beat,
What dread hand? and what dread feet?

What the hammer? what the chain?
In what furnace was thy brain?
What the anvil? what dread grasp
Dare its deadly terrors clasp?

When the stars threw down their spears,
And water'd heaven with their tears,
Did he smile his work to see?
Did he who made the Lamb make thee?

Tyger! Tyger! burning bright
In the forests of the night,
What immortal hand or eye,
Dare frame thy fearful symmetry?

The poem is very satisfying just to read aloud. The rhythm and rhyme bounce you along. But then begin to examine the words. Each one conjures up a deeper, richer experience. The repetition of 'Tyger' is comforting on one hand and terrifying on the other. 'Burning bright' is simple and almost childlike but at the same time each experience of speaking those two words will produce a different sort of burning tyger.

The poem is structured as a series of questions that are never answered, throwing us into an unanswerable universe of meaning compromised by ambiguity. All the words are solid and understandable on their own. Yet they are linked in such a way that we cease to understand their whole significance. No clear picture emerges other than an abstract portrait like one of those primitive paintings by Henri Rousseau. You have to make an imaginative leap of faith in order to make sense of lines like:

forests of the night

distant deeps or skies

When the stars threw down their spears,
And water'd heaven with their tears

All the lines spin us off into the unknown, yet all we are speaking about is a tiger. It is as though the simplicity of the structure and language gives us a secure harness to wander off into eternity.

This is a technique Blake employs constantly. And do try speaking some of his other poems in the *Songs of Innocence* and *Songs of Experience* to discover more examples of this astounding technique. The secure form and sense of individual words give us a feeling of security which is not in the total web of the material. A child will enjoy speaking Blake and will experience the language on a different level to an adult. The poem is like a nursery rhyme.

Anybody who likes complex verse or language might not know what the fuss is about until they dare speak the words with asbolute simplicity and then try to make sense to a listener. Beat the lines, intone the words. Don't deny the structure but let it hold you as you see, feel, smell and hear the words.

Samuel Beckett

Next try speaking this excerpt from Samuel Beckett's *Not I*. This speech is from the beginning of the play. All we encounter on the stage is a lighted mouth. The only character is a speaking voice:

> MOUTH: . . . out . . . into this world . . . this world . . . tiny little thing . . . before its time . . . in a godfor- . . . what? . . . girl? . . . yes . . . tiny little girl . . . into this . . . out into this . . . before her time . . . godforsaken hole called . . . called . . . no matter . . . parents unknown . . .

unheard of . . . he having vanished . . . thin air . . . no
sooner buttoned up his breeches . . . she similarly . . .
eight months later . . . almost to the tick . . . so no love
. . . spared that . . . no love such as normally vented on the
. . . speechless infant . . . in the home . . . no . . . nor
indeed for that matter any of any kind . . . no love of any
kind . . . at any subsequent stage . . . so typical affair . . .
nothing of any note till coming up to sixty when – . . .
what? . . . seventy? . . . good God! . . . coming up to
seventy . . . wandering in a field . . . looking aimlessly for
cowslips . . . to make a ball . . . a few steps then stop . . .
stare into space . . . then on . . . a few more . . . stop and
stare again . . . so on . . . drifting around . . . when
suddenly . . . gradually . . . all went out . . . all that early
April morning light . . . and she found herself in the – . . .
what? . . . who? . . . no! . . . she! . . . (*pause and movement
1*) . . . found herself in the dark . . . and if not exactly . . .
insentient . . . insentient . . . for she could still hear the
buzzing . . . so-called . . . in the ears . . . and a ray of light
came and went . . . came and went . . . such as the moon
might cast . . . drifting . . . in and out of cloud . . . but so
dulled . . . feeling . . . feeling so dulled . . . she did not
know . . . what position she was in . . . imagine! . . . what
position she was in! . . . whether standing . . . or sitting
. . . but the brain – . . . what? . . . kneeling? . . . yes . . .
whether standing . . . or sitting . . . or kneeling . . . but
the brain – . . . what? . . . lying? . . . yes . . . whether
standing . . . or sitting . . . or kneeling . . . or lying . . .
but the brain still . . . still . . . in a way . . . for her first
thought was . . . oh long after . . . sudden flash . . .
brought up as she had been to believe . . . with the other
waifs . . . in a merciful . . . (*brief laugh*) . . . God

Hidden beneath these simple words is the courageous attempt
– like Blake's – to understand the totality of experience! You
must thread each thought through the elliptical pauses with
needle-point accuracy, and again trust the meaning of each
word to understand how it resonates in context with the
others. As sound and words accumulate in a Beckett text we
begin to find the need for it all. Notice how the speaker is
putting words together like pieces from a jigsaw puzzle. He

or she is puzzling out, piecing out a full thought. It is tortuous and slow but progress is being made step by step.

Beckett writes what has been called stream of consciousness. The structure seems not to be a logical progression of ideas, but that doesn't mean it cannot be understood. Each phrase is like a fragment of glass from a stained glass window. The whole is a collage of colours. All are important to the understanding of the whole but they are in disarray, scattered. Talk to anyone in a state of shock – who has been knocked senseless – it might sound like they are speaking nonsense to us but it makes absolute sense to them.

First make a personal connection to everything you say. Just because something is not logical doesn't make it less real. Obey the punctuation. Beckett formulated a very strong structure in his writing. He laboured over it in order to get the correct effect and rhythm. Pauses and punctuation must be obeyed. His groups of ellipses (three dots) are like stepping stones.

Like Blake, Beckett gives the speakers a strong, structural safety net to help us feel secure as we roam across the frontiers of time and logic on a quest for deeper and more metaphysical truths. In this realm all things are possible. Strange meetings, dialogues and memories are encountered and recounted, yet the language is simple and must be explored with a clear intensity. You make of it what you will.

The vision comes in fragments. These fragments not only punctuate the piece but give the listener an unbearable sense of time returning on itself. The voice must actually stop and start time. Trust that every fragment is needed and will take you on further even though the path seems clotted and confused. Each word is like a clear shaft of light trying to illuminate a mystery. Beckett knows that in the end words are all we have as a means of making sense. Speak them with that confidence and clarity. Even though you may not understand them, remember that the structure and quality of words will produce an effect not necessarily in the bounds of reason but on other perhaps more emotive levels, rather like the effect of music. We may not be able to understand all those dots and dashes but we do experience movement through them – the music – and understand something.

Harold Pinter

Much of the exploration I have been doing is through texts that use language to actively explore, confront and probe ideas, feelings and great philosophical issues.

Since Anton Chekhov there has been a strategy among playwrights to *hide* behind words and not use them for exposure. This process has been loosely termed communicating 'sub-text'. Something is going on underneath the text which is not necessarily explicit in the surface language which can seem either nonsensical or prosaic. What you speak isn't always what you mean or what you are feeling. I feel very strongly that the strong accent modern actors place on sub-text has led many either not to trust the word enough or to become hesitant in vocal power and delivery. There is a misconception that if the word is in some way inappropriate then it must be mumbled. Sub-text sometimes hinders our commitment to words and phrases.

I contend that you use as much vocal energy to deny or keep any discomfort at bay as you would if the words were addressing a situation openly and fully. It takes, perhaps, even more energy for denial. At least the appropriate word releases the pain and energy rather than bottling it up. We don't in theatre explore situations of pure stasis. Something is always happening and the words we use describe action. The shift from Shakespeare to Pinter requires a shift not in the energy of playing but in gearing the power of the language quite differently.

Many playwrights I have worked with passionately deny the notion of naturalistic text if that means the actor speaks it without tension or need. Like most people, I have spent family meals when the topics of conversation were seemingly trivial yet the energy with which we talked about food, the newly decorated bathroom, the dog, the latest shopping expedition was hiding a passionate need to keep a family disagreement at bay. The same use of energy applies to sub-text in plays.

Harold Pinter's early plays used prosaic, ordinary conversation to keep fear and violence in check. By talking about 'cornflakes' and 'fried bread' in a play like *The Birthday Party* it is almost as though characters can keep their deepest fears and anxieties – the sub-text of their lives – hidden beneath banal conversation. Many of us use the technique of talking 'normally' in the face of a potentially violent scene in a desperate attempt to prevent violence from happening. But maintaining the 'normal' in order to stave off a disagreeable confrontation takes incredible energy and clarity. Words may not be the tools, levers, weapons that Shakespeare employs: instead they are shields and deflectors. They blunt any suggested or overt attack. The famous Pinter pause allows the truth or fear to resonate in the silence. In this passage from *A Night Out* this kind of commonplace language, full of sub-textual riches, can be seen in action:

> ALBERT *is coming down the stairs. He is wearing his jacket. He goes towards the door. His mother calls from the kitchen and goes into the hall.*

MOTHER: Albert! Where are you going?
ALBERT: Out.
MOTHER: Your dinner's ready.
ALBERT: I'm sorry. I haven't got time to have it.
MOTHER: Look at your suit. You're not going out with your suit in that state, are you?
ALBERT: What's the matter with it?
MOTHER: It needs a good brush, that's what's the matter with it. You can't go out like that. Come on, come in here and I'll give it a brush.
ALBERT: It's all right . . .
MOTHER: Come on.

They go into the kitchen. She gets the brush.

Turn round. No, stand still. You can't go out and disgrace me, Albert. If you've got to go out you've got to look nice. There, that's better.

She dusts his jacket with her hands and straightens his tie.

I didn't tell you what I made for you, did I? I made it specially. I made Shepherd's Pie tonight.
ALBERT [*taking her hand from his tie*]: The tie's all right.

He goes to the door.

Well, ta-ta.
MOTHER: Albert! Wait a minute. Where's your handkerchief?
ALBERT: What handkerchief?
MOTHER: You haven't got a handkerchief in your breast pocket.
ALBERT: That doesn't matter, does it?
MOTHER: Doesn't matter? I should say it does matter. Just a minute. [*She takes a handkerchief from a drawer*]. Here you are. A nice clean one. [*She arranges it in his pocket.*] You mustn't let me down, you know. You've got to be properly dressed. Your father was always properly dressed. You'd never see him out without a handkerchief in his breast pocket. He always looked like a gentleman.

In this small scene of a 'normal' mother and son routine, you can feel the tension, conflict and loathing just beneath the surface of the words. Tension and clarity must be hurled into the speaking otherwise the real feelings would surface and the violence explode. The prosaic words are keeping a tight lid on a pressure cooker. Pinter is superby precise in his choice of words. He chooses them as accurately as Shakespeare, so you mustn't be beguiled by their simplicity. You must speak them with need and commitment. The words represent the plate glass window that will keep you safe. Notice a few things:

• The wounding done to a child when a mother says: 'You're not going out with your suit in that state, are you?' A loaded statement with much history behind it. And then to be fussed over with a brush.

- The 'Shepherd's Pie' probably took the mother extra time to make and she believes it is his favourite food. He probably hates it.
- Then the handkerchief, and the comparison to the father as a 'gentleman'.

The mother, in the simplest language, is weaving a deadly web round her son. Every phrase she uses has lethal, emotional blackmail stamped on it. Albert's only defence is to try and not answer her question and to shield himself with defensive questions.

> MOTHER: Where are you going?
> ALBERT: Out.
> ALBERT: 'What's the matter with it?'
>   'What handkerchief?'
>   'That doesn't matter, does it?'

Neither mother nor son appear to be listening to the other or picking up the signals and bad feelings running just under the text. The words are being used to stop each other from telling the truth. The mother wants to own Albert and keep him at home for ever. Albert wants to scream out his hatred and release himself but is too busy fending off his mother's picking. An atmosphere of smothering antagonism is the result. Each hurts the other by indirection.

Pinter's commitment to language is succinctly and brilliantly explored in *Mountain Language*. The theme is simple and historically correct. If you want to destroy a group of people politically you take their language away from them. No 'great' nation is innocent of this act. By not allowing people their mother tongue you disarm them. You repress their culture, their imaginations, their ability to think and of course to effectively communicate.

Working with Song Lyrics

Any good song lyric can be divorced from the music and stand alone as a poem and/or a wonderful story. But with any song you sing you must at some point commit to the words, tell a story or an experience, trust the repetition, the chorus and communicate the words as strongly and clearly as the music. Here are some useful way to work on the lyrics of any song:

- Divorce the words from the music and work on the text in the same way as an actor works on his or her part.
- The music will naturally heighten the language, but find out what is there to be heightened in the first place.
- Many song writers start with the words, a poem or a story. The language inspires the music. Others work in the opposite way but at some point the music needs a word.
- Speak the lyrics of a song – make them make sense.
- Mouth the words so that you can sing the whole word, not leave off syllables and consonants.
- Choose each word. Discover why that word is better than another.
- Sense the journey through a song either as an actual series of events or a more abstract stream of consciousness. There is bound to be a structure and format, a refrain of key words or images. Discover it and trust that the form will help you through the song just as you learn to trust the form of a sonnet by Shakespeare.
- Don't comment on the words, merely experience them on an intellectual and emotional level. The more you can trust them, the more they will mould into the music.
- Find the rhythm and stress in the words, matching this to the music.
- Speak the words so that they reach out – don't rely solely on the music for this – let the words leave you.
- Be focused and specific. If there is a dialogue between two voices in the song then use it for effect.
- If there is a break in the format, use it to shock us.
- Follow and sustain the length of every line and word. Don't let them drop. Use the same technique as you use for good verse speaking.

- At the end of the lyrics know that you have said enough. You have finished, like any speech. I stop when the story finishes or I am satisfied.

Here are two lyrics to experiment with:

The Erl-King by Franz Schubert

Who rides so late through the night and the wind?
It is the father with his child.
He holds the boy in his arm,
grasps him securely, keeps him warm.

'My son, why do you hide your face so anxiously?'
'Father, do you not see the Erl-King?
The Erl-King with his crown and tail?'
'My son, it is only a streak of mist.'

'Darling child, come away with me!
I will play fine games with you.
Many gay flowers grow by the shore;
my mother has many golden robes.'

'Father, father, do you not hear
what the Erl-King softly promises me?'
'Be calm, dear child, be calm –
the wind is rustling in the dry leaves.'

'You beautiful boy, will you come with me?
My daughters will wait upon you.
My daughters lead the nightly round,
they will rock you, dance to you, sing you to sleep!'

'Father, father, do you not see
the Erl-King's daughters there, in that dark place?'
'My son, my son, I see it clearly:
it is the grey gleam of the old willow-trees.'

'I love you, your beauty allures me,
and if you do not come willingly, I shall use force.'
'Father, father, now he is seizing me!
The Erl-King has hurt me!'

Fear grips the father, he rides swiftly,
holding the moaning child in his arms;

with effort and toil he reaches the house –
the child in his arms was dead.

I get along without you very well by Hoagy Carmichael

I get along without you very well,
Of course I do,
Except when soft rains fall and drip from leaves,
Then I recall the thrill of being sheltered in your arms,
Of course I do,
But I get along without you very well.
I've forgotten you, just like I should,
Of course I have,
Except to hear your name or someone's laugh that is the same
But I've forgotten you just like I should
What a guy!
What a fool am I
To think my breaking heart could kid the moon;
What's in store?
Should I 'phone once more?
No, it's best that I stick to my tune.
I get along without you very well,
Of course I do,
Except perhaps in spring but I should never think of spring
For that would surely break my heart in two.

The Schubert is a wonderful piece of dramatic storytelling. The popular song is more abstract but magnificently powerful in the simplicity of words and images. All the words must be connected to, felt and trusted. The form of the song is in understatement but that understatement must hide the seething pain which explodes out in the section which breaks form.

What a guy! What a fool am I
To think my breaking heart could kid the moon! . . . stick to
  my tune.

The end is left hanging in the air like the pain hanging round the heart.

Bad Texts

I can't resist putting in this poem by William McGonagall, a rough and naive Irish versifier of the nineteenth century who has the reputation of being one of the world's worst poets! The lesson here is how much easier it is to speak good text than bad. I have always thought that young actors should go through the experience of doing terrible texts. They spend too much of their time on the great texts and must undergo a genuine shock when they meet a real stinker of a play.

Anyway, have a go at this:

Attempted Assassination of the Queen

GOD prosper long our noble Queen,
    And long may she reign!
Maclean he tried to shoot her,
    But it was all in vain.

For God He turned the ball aside
    Maclean aimed at her head;
And he felt very angry
    Because he didn't shoot her dead.

There's a divinity that hedgeth a king,
    And so it does seem,
And my opinion is, it has hedged
    Our most gracious Queen.

Maclean must be a madman,
    Which is obvious to be seen,
Or else he wouldn't have tried to shoot
    Our most beloved Queen.

Victoria is a good Queen,
    Which all her subjects know,
And for that God has protected her
    From all her deadly foes.

She is noble and generous,
    Her subjects must confess;
There hasn't been her equal
    Since the days of good Queen Bess.

Long may she be spared to roam
   Among the bonnie Highland floral,
And spend many a happy day
   In the palace of Balmoral.

Because she is very kind
   To the old women there,
And allows them bread, tea, and sugar,
   And each one to get a share.

And when they know of her coming,
   Their hearts feel overjoy'd,
Because, in general, she finds work
   For men that's unemploy'd.

And she also gives the gipsies money
   While at Balmoral, I've been told,
And, mind ye, seldom silver,
   But very often gold.

I hope God will protect her
   By night and by day,
At home and abroad
   When she's far away.

May He be as a hedge around her,
   As He's been all along,
And let her live and die in peace
   Is the end of my song.

I am very fond of McGonagall. The verse is so thumping bad that it becomes almost enchanting. I think this is due to the fact that he believed he was a great writer. There is nothing the least bit self-conscious about his writing. If he was trying to parody bad poetry it wouldn't be nearly so funny.

Now try any of the verse or poetry exercises we have been doing on the text. Nothing will work to release this poem. It is stuck in its own world. Rhythm, rhyme, images are all unshiftable. There is no aid for the speaker, no way you can heighten this poem!

Shakespeare does the same in some of his plays. The mechanicals in *A Midsummer Night's Dream* believe they have a great play on their hands and as they treat the text with respect, the audience will laugh. Again, nothing works in the language except the rather endearing confidence of a bad writer in full flood!

Prologues and Epilogues

Here is a way of both beginning and ending with words. In both cases you have to make a special effort to make sense.

First, the Prologue from *Romeo and Juliet*:

> Two households, both alike in dignity
>   In fair Verona, where we lay our scene,
> From ancient grudge break to new mutiny,
>   Where civil blood makes civil hands unclean.
> From forth the fatal loins of these two foes
>   A pair of star-crossed lovers take their life;
> Whose misadventured piteous overthrows
>   Do with their death bury their parents' strife.
> The fearful passage of their death-marked love
>   And the continuance of their parents' rage,
> Which, but their children's end, naught could remove,
>   Is now the two hours' traffic of our stage;
> The which if you with patient ears attend,
>   What here shall miss, our toil shall strive to mend.

This is a simple prologue, but it fulfils all the needs of a good introduction to a theatrical evening. The first moments of a play will communicate the atmosphere of the play, maybe even creating visual images to create a picture of the world. This speech sets the scene, giving us all the ingredients needed for our full enjoyment and enlightenment: who, what, when and where. The atmosphere and any relevant information is all done through words.

The other great purpose of a prologue is to tune our ears to the language of the play. It's rather like the overture in an opera or musical. We hear all the themes in the music, we get a taste now so that we can respond sooner when elaborations on the theme tunes hit our ears again.

Shakespeare prepares us not only for the language of the play – the regular iambic and the rhyme schemes that occur in the play – but the plot is revealed: two warring families in Verona; two lovers who die for love; two sides to everything. The balance is appropriate and like a verbal scales of justice. Obviously Shakespeare wants us to experience more than just a good tale. He wants us to go deeper into the issues, and the language provides us with a back-and-forth rhythm.

I love the phrase 'if you with patient ears attend'. Shakespeare is asking from his audience what every actor hopes for from any audience: attendance with patient ears!

As Duke Theseus tells Bottom in *A Midsummer Night's Dream*, when he offers an epilogue at the end of the mechanicals' play, 'no epilogue, I pray you: for your play needs no excuse'. An epilogue often asks for either an excuse or a good reception for the play. However, there is another reason for an epilogue. It often serves to tell the audience what they have learnt. In Restoration plays, a moral is often given.

Aphra Behn makes a strong plea for women writers and the form of the epilogue to *Sir Patient Fancy* is full of flashy, bravado writing. This must be spoken with relish, ease and a courageous challenge to the audience. In fact, it is a good place to both end what I have to say and give you the speaker one final challenge of matching your voice with a text.

MRS GWYNN (*looking about*):
I here and there o'erheard a coxcomb cry,
'Ah, rot it, 'tis a woman's comedy,
One, who because she lately chanced to please us,
With her damned stuff will never cease to tease us.'
What has poor woman done that she must be
Debarred from sense and sacred poetry?
Why in this age has Heaven allowed you more,
And woman less of wit than heretofore?

We once were famed in story, and could write
Equal to men; could govern, nay, could fight.
We still have passive valour, and can show,
Would custom give us leave, the active too,
Since we no provocations want from you.

For who but we could your dull fopperies bear,
Your saucy love and your brisk nonsense hear;
Endure your worse than womanish affectation,
Which renders you the nuisance of the nation;
Scorned even by all the misses of the town,
A jest to vizard mask and pit-buffoon;
A glass by which the admiring country fool
May learn to dress himself *en ridicule*,
Both striving who shall most ingenious grow
In lewdness, foppery, nonsense, noise and show.

And yet to these fine things we must submit
Our reason, arms, our laurels and our wit.
Because we do not laugh at you when lewd,
And scorn and cudgel ye when you are rude,
That we have nobler souls than you we prove,
By how much more we're sensible of love;
Quickest in finding all the subtlest ways
To make your joys, why not to make you plays?
We best can find your foibles, know our own,
And jilts and cuckolds now best please the town;
Your way of writing's out of fashion grown.
Method and rule you only understand –
Pursue that way of fooling and be damned.
Your learned cant of action, time and place
Must all give way to the unlaboured farce.
To all the men of wit we will subscribe
But for your half-wits, you unthinking tribe,
We'll let you see, whate'er besides we do,
How artfully we copy some of you:
And if you're drawn to th' life, pray tell me then,
Why women should not write as well as men?

Acknowledgements

The author and publishers gratefully acknowledge permission to reproduce copyright materials in this book:

Howard Barker: from *The Bite of the Night*. Copyright ©1988 by Howard Barker. Published by John Calder (Publishers) Ltd, London and Riverrun Press Inc, New York. Reproduced by permission of the Calder Educational Trust, London.

Samuel Beckett: from *Not I*. Published in *The Complete Dramatic Works* by Faber and Faber. Reprinted by permission of Faber & Faber Ltd.

Edward Bond: from *Lear*. Copyright © 1972, 1978 by Edward Bond. Reprinted by permission of Methuen London.

Caryl Churchill: from *Fen*. Copyright © 1983 by Caryl Churchill. Reprinted by permission of Methuen London.

D J Enright: from *Blue Umbrellas*. Published in *Collected Poems* (1987) by Oxford University Press. Reprinted by permission of Watson, Little Ltd licensing agents.

Euripides: from *The Trojan women*, translated by John Barton and Kenneth Cavander. Reprinted by permission of The Royal Shakespeare Company.

Tony Kushner: from *Angels in America*, Copyright © 1992 by Tony Kushner. Reprinted by permission of Random House UK Ltd.

David Mamet: from *Speed-the-Plow*. Copyright © 1985, 1986, 1987 by David Mamet. Reprinted by permission of Methuen London.

Harold Pinter: from *A Night Out*, published in *Plays One* by Faber & Faber. Reprinted by permission of Faber & Faber Ltd.

Dylan Thomas: from *Words*. Published in *The Poems*. Reprinted by permission of David Higham Associates Ltd, 5–8 Lower John Street, London WlR 4HA.

Bernard Shaw: from *Major Barbara*. Reprinted by permission of The Society of Authors on behalf of the Bernard Shaw Estate.

The author and publishers have taken all possible care to secure permissions for extracts used in this volume, and to make the correct aknowledgements. If any errors have occurred, they will be corrected in subsequent editions, provided notification is sent to the publisher.

Patsy Rodenburg is Head of the Voice Departments at Great Britain's Royal National Theatre and the Guildhall School of Music and Drama. She trained at the Central School of Speech and Drama.

Internationally she has taught and presented her voice workshops in North America, Australia, Japan, India and throughout Europe. She has worked with the Royal Shakespeare Company, English Shakespeare Company, Cheek-by-Jowl, Théâtre de Complicité, Shared Experience Theatre, the National Theatre of Greece and Tokyo's Grand Kabuki Company. She has been a Distinguished Visiting Professor in the Theatre Division at the Meadows School of the Arts, Southern Methodist University in Dallas, Texas, and organized the voice programme at the Stratford Festival Theatre in Stratford, Canada.

Through her own London organization, The Voice and Speech Centre, Patsy Rodenburg offers voice and speech consultation and seminars to performing artists, film companies, advertising and media specialists, business executives, education groups and therapists. Her work has also taken her into inner city schools, prisons and various rehabilitation institutions.